The World Economy
after the
Global Crisis

A New Economic Order
for the 21st Century

T0301889

World Scientific Studies in International Economics
(ISSN: 1793-3641)

Published*

19 World Scientific
Studies in
International
Economics

THE
World Economy
after the
Global Crisis

A New Economic Order
for the 21st Century

Editors

Barry Eichengreen
University of California, Berkeley, USA

Bokyeong Park
Korea Institute for International Economic Policy, Korea

KIEP Korea Institute for International
Economic Policy

World Scientific

Published by

World Scientific Publishing Co. Pte. Ltd.

5 Toh Tuck Link, Singapore 596224

USA office: 27 Warren Street, Suite 401-402, Hackensack, NJ 07601

UK office: 57 Shelton Street, Covent Garden, London WC2H 9HE

Library of Congress Cataloging-in-Publication Data
The world economy after the global crisis : a new economic order for the
    21st century / edited by Barry Eichengreen & Bokyeong Park.
        p. cm. -- (World scientific studies in international economics, ISSN 1793-3641 ; v. 19)
    Includes bibliographical references and index.
    ISBN-13: 978-9814383035
    ISBN-10: 9814383031
    1. Global Financial Crisis, 2008–2009. 2. Economic history--21st century.
    I. Eichengreen, Barry J. II. Pak, Pog-yong.
    HB3722.W673 2012
    330.9--dc23
                                                                2012005344

British Library Cataloguing-in-Publication Data
A catalogue record for this book is available from the British Library.

In-house Editor: Alisha Nguyen

Typeset by Stallion Press
Email: enquiries@stallionpress.com

Printed in Singapore.

Acknowledgments

This book has its origins in a research project initiated by the Korea Institute for International Economic Policy (KIEP), Korea's leading think tank. It was organized with the goal of analyzing changes in the world economy since the global financial crisis from a variety of economic, functional and analytical perspectives. The editors would like to thank KIEP for its financial support, which was essential to completion of the project and publication of this book.

The Korea Institute for International Economic Policy (KIEP) was founded in 1989 as a government-funded independent economic research institute. KIEP carries out research on the East Asian economies various aspects of world economy, such as international finance, open macroeconomics, trade and investment. KIEP advises the government on all major international economic policy issues.

Contents

Contributors

Ignazio Angeloni is Advisor to the Executive Board of the ECB and Visiting Fellow of Bruegel, the Brussels think tank. Previously he was Director for International Financial Affairs at the Ministry of Economy and Finance of Italy, in which position he was also a member of the G20 Deputies. Before that, he was Deputy Director General of Research at the European Central Bank and Director of Monetary and Financial Research in the Bank of Italy. He holds a PhD from the University of Pennsylvania and a Bachelor's degree from Bocconi University.

His research focuses on monetary policy issues, the links between financial stability and monetary policy and European monetary and financial integration. He is the author of books and of articles that have appeared in top US and European academic journals.

Barry Eichengreen is George C. Pardee and Helen N. Pardee Professor of Economics and Political Science at the University of California Berkeley. He is Research Associate of the National Bureau of Economic Research and Research Fellow of the Centre for Economic Policy Research.

His most recent books are *Exorbitant Privilege: The Rise and Fall of the Dollar and the Future of the International Monetary System* (2011), *Emerging Giants: China and India in the World Economy*, co-edited with Poonam Gupta and Ranjiv Kumar (2010), *Labor in the Era of Globalization*, co-edited with Clair Brown and Michael Reich (2009), *Institutions for Regionalism: Enhancing Asia's Economic Cooperation and Integration*, co-edited with Jong-Wha Lee (2009), and *Fostering Monetary & Financial Cooperation in East Asia*, co-edited with Duck-Koo Chung (2009). Other books include *Globalizing Capital: A History of the International Monetary System*, Second Edition (2008), *The European Economy Since 1945: Coordinated Capitalism and Beyond* (updated paperback edition, 2008), *Bond*

Markets in Latin America: On the Verge of a Big Bang?, co-edited with Eduardo Borensztein, Kevin Cowan, and Ugo Panizza (2008), and *China, Asia, and the New World Economy*, co-edited with Charles Wyplosz and Yung Chul Park (2008).

Simon J. Evenett is Academic Director of MBA programmes at the University of St. Gallen, Switzerland, where he is Professor of International Trade and Economic Development in the Department of Economics. He is also Programme Director of the International Trade and Regional Economics Programme of the Centre of Economic Policy Research. Professor Evenett is an expert in the commercial policies and strategies of the US, EU, and rising economic powers such as China. He has published over 125 journal articles, book chapters, and books and is a frequent public lecturer, including speaking to corporate executives about international business strategy. Professor Evenett also coordinates the worldwide protectionist monitoring service, Global Trade Alert.

Joseph E. Gagnon is Senior Fellow of the Peterson Institute for International Economics since September 2009. He was Visiting Associate Director, Division of Monetary Affairs (2008–2009) at the US Federal Reserve Board. Previously he served at the US Federal Reserve Board as Associate Director, Division of International Finance (1999–2008), and senior economist (1987–1990 and 1991–1997). He has also served at the US Treasury Department (1994–1995 and 1997–1999) and has taught at the University of California's Haas School of Business (1990–1991). He is author of *Flexible Exchange Rates for a Stable World Economy* (2011) and *The Global Outlook for Government Debt Over the Next 25 Years: Implications for the Economy and Public Policy* (2011). He has published numerous articles in economics journals, including *Journal of International Economics*, *Journal of Monetary Economics*, *Review of International Economics*, and *Journal of International Money and Finance*, and has contributed to several edited volumes.

Marc Hinterschweiger has been a Research Analyst with the Peterson Institute since 2008. He is also PhD candidate in economics at Ludwig-Maximilians University (LMU) in Munich, Germany. His research focuses on the transmission mechanism of monetary policy, asset prices, and financial crises. He previously worked at the Rhenish-Westfalian Institute for Economic Research (RWI) in Essen, Germany. He assisted

Joseph E. Gagnon with *Flexible Exchange Rates for a Stable World Economy* and *The Global Outlook for Government Debt over the Next 25 Years: Implications for the Economy and Public Policy* (2011).

Jinill Kim is Professor of Economics at Korea University, where he has taught since 2010. Dr. Kim received his B.A. in Economics from Seoul National University in 1989 and his Ph.D. in Economics from Yale University in 1996. After working as Economist in the Division of Research and Statistics at the Federal Reserve Board for two years, he became an Assistant Professor at the University of Virginia in 1998. He returned to the Federal Reserve Board in 2003 and served as Economist and Senior Economist in the Monetary Affairs Division until 2011.

Bokyeong Park is Director of the International Economy Department at the Korea Institute for International Economic Policy (KIEP). He has conducted research on international finance and development cooperation at KIEP since 2002. He was a visiting scholar at UC Berkeley and Johns Hopkins University. While working at KIEP, he has also served as a member of advisory committees for the Presidential Office and the Ministry of Foreign Affairs and Trade of Korea. He received his B.A. and Ph.D. in Economics from Seoul National University.

Eswar S. Prasad is Tolani Senior Professor of Trade Policy and Professor of Economics at Cornell University. He is also Senior Fellow at the Brookings Institution, where he holds the New Century Chair in International Economics, and Research Associate at the National Bureau of Economic Research. He was previously chief of the Financial Studies Division at the IMF and before that head of the IMF's China Division. He is a member of an Advisory Committee to India's Finance Minister and Lead Academic for the International Growth Center's India Growth Research Program. He has testified before various US Congressional Committees at hearings on China. He is the creator of the Brookings–Financial Times Global Economy Index (Tracking Indicators for the Global Economy; www.ft.com/tiger). He is also Research Fellow at IZA (Institute for the Study of Labor, Bonn) and Research Associate of the National Asia Research Program.

Nicolas Véron is Senior Fellow at Bruegel, the Brussels-based international economy think tank, and Visiting Fellow at the Peterson Institute for International Economics in Washington DC. His research focuses on financial systems and regulation, including current developments in the European Union. He has been involved in the creation and development of Bruegel since 2002 and has divided his time since 2009 between Washington DC and Europe. A graduate of France's Ecole Polytechnique and Ecole des Mines, his earlier experience combines policy work as a senior French civil servant, and corporate finance as a junior investment banker, CFO of a small listed company, and independent strategy consultant. In 2006, he co-authored *Smoke & Mirrors, Inc.: Accounting for Capitalism*, and is also the author of several books in French. He writes a monthly column on European finance that is published by leading newspapers and online media in most G20 countries.

CHAPTER 1

Introduction

Barry Eichengreen and Bokyeong Park

The global credit crisis of 2008–2009 was the most serious shock to the world economy in 80 years. It was for the world what the Asian crisis of 1997–1998 had been for emerging markets: a profoundly alarming wake-up call. By laying bare the fragility of global markets, it raised troubling questions about the operation of the 21st century world economy. It cast doubt on the efficacy of light-touch financial regulation and, more generally, on the prevailing commitment to economic and financial liberalization. It challenged the managerial capacity of institutions of global governance. It augured a changing of the guard, pointing to the possibility that the economies that had been leaders in the global growth stakes in the past would no longer be leaders in the future.

Given that the 2008–2009 crisis was first and foremost a *financial* crisis, it is appropriate that analysis should start in Chapter 2 with Nicolas Véron's assessment of the causes of recent financial problems and the successes and failures of post-crisis financial reform. The mainstream narrative emphasizes impetuous deregulation in advance of the crisis and a swing back to re-regulation in its wake. Véron offers a more nuanced view: he argues that the traditional separation of macroeconomic and financial policies — the "Tinbergen principle" of assigning monetary policy to the maintenance of price stability and regulatory policy to financial stability — is part of what caused the crisis, and that the development of a synthesis, which flies under the flag of "macroprudential" or "macrofinancial" policy, points the way to a solution.

But the devil is in the details. How exactly macroeconomic and financial policies should be harmonized to ensure financial stability without undermining the efforts of the monetary-policy authorities to hit their price-stability target remains to be determined. The question of how to regulate and, in the worst case, resolve large cross-border financial firms has barely been touched. The international coordination of financial reform has been inadequate; with different countries and regions adopting different approaches, there is the danger of conflicts leading to fragmentation of the global financial space — in other words, there is a risk that the fruits of financial globalization, such as they are, will be lost. Finally, and most importantly, the implications of new regulations and procedures for economic growth remain imperfectly understood.

Another striking aspect of the crisis was the abrupt collapse of international trade, which declined even more than the production of goods and services. Why the impact on trade was so dramatic continues to be debated. There was the collapse of the demand for consumer durables, which bulk large in international transactions. There were disruptions to the supply of trade credit. There was the growing importance, by the standards of the past, of far-reaching and often fragile international supply chains.

Then there was the protectionist response, described by Simon Evenett in Chapter 3. A few governments responded to the crisis and recession with overtly protectionist policies, but more important, Evenett's data suggest, was "murky protectionism" defined to include not simply import tariffs, quotas and export taxes but also subsidies, bailouts, preferential public procurement practices, and other policy supports only indirectly related to trade. The good news, such as it is, is that only 11 nations implemented discriminatory measures covering more than a quarter of the possible product categories. This is in contrast to the Great Depression, when many countries imposed barriers on imports across the board.

Multilateral disciplines, notably those to which governments commit when becoming members of the World Trade Organization (WTO), are widely cited as preventing countries from resorting to a protectionist response. Evenett questions this contention. While no country violated its tariff bindings at the WTO, governments in fact resorted to a variety of other discriminatory measures that were not, in practice, covered by WTO disciplines. Evenett suggests that other factors, such as the opposition of multinational firms to measures that augured disruptions to trade, were a more important source of restraint in practice. Still, if WTO disciplines are not as effective as typically assumed, then the multilateral trading system may not be as robust as the conventional wisdom would have it. Evenett concludes by warning that prudent policy makers should prepare for this possibility.

The global crisis also deepened disenchantment with the structure and operation of the international monetary system. It was already a commonplace that a system in which the US dollar enjoyed the "exorbitant privilege" of providing the vast majority of global foreign exchange reserves was dangerously prone to imbalances. The crisis then highlighted these risks. Official foreign purchases of US treasury and agency securities, by central banks and governments seeking to accumulate reserves, rendered US treasury rates lower than they would have been otherwise and thereby contributed to Federal Reserve Chairman Greenspan's famous bond-market "conundrum." Low treasury rates encouraged investors, stretching for yield, to move into riskier instruments. This fueled the housing boom and the securitization market, permitting the US to crawl further out on an unstable financial limb. Then, in the ultimate injustice, the dollar actually strengthened when the crisis struck, as foreign central banks and governments desperate for liquidity scrambled into dollar-denominated assets.

While this much is clear, less obvious is how to remake the system to avoid such problems in the future. In Chapter 4, Barry Eichengreen sketches likely future trajectories for international monetary arrangements. He is dismissive of far-reaching reforms ranging from a regime based on Special Drawing Rights on the one hand to restoration of a gold-based system on the other. But he is equally skeptical about the viability of a dollar-centric monetary system like that of the recent past. The remaining option being a system organized around several national currencies — not just the dollar but also the euro and the Chinese renminbi — the question then becomes how to ease the transition to such a system and to smooth its operation when it arrives. Eichengreen concludes that reforms of national policies, of multinational institutions like the International Monetary Fund (IMF) and of regional arrangements all will be needed in order to achieve this.

Among the notable long-term consequences of the crisis has been the emergence of the Group of Twenty (G20) as the de facto steering committee for the world economy, displacing earlier advanced-country-centered groupings, notably the Group of Seven/Eight (G7/8). When with the collapse of private demand it became necessary to organize a coordinated fiscal response, it was clear that a group in which emerging markets like China were not represented would not do. The emergence of the G20, which better reflects the composition of the 21st century world economy, was one concrete consequence of the crisis. In a structural sense, it was also perhaps policy makers' most important achievement.

But, institutionally, the G20 remains a work in progress. As Ignazio Angeloni explains in Chapter 5, it has no permanent staff or written constitution. It has no global mandate; why it includes the countries it does reflects the particular historical process out of which it emerged. The details of how the G20 will work with multilateral organizations such as the IMF and Financial Stability Board when additional problems arise remain to be determined.

Angeloni argues that the G20 would be strengthened by measures to enhance its legitimacy; its membership could be harmonized, for example, with that of the Executive Board of the IMF. More could be done to ensure continuity as the chairmanship rotates from one country to another, by inter alia establishing a multi-year work program and a permanent steering committee and secretariat. Most of all, the G20 requires a shared vision of what needs to be done to stabilize and strengthen the functioning of the world economy. At the time of writing, consensus on the important issues of substance — such as reform of the international monetary system, of which Eichengreen writes in Chapter 4 and which putatively dominated the work program of the G20 in 2011 — is notable by its absence.

As the growing prominence of the G20 reveals, another consequence of the crisis has been to enhance the weight of emerging markets in the global economy. Their economies held up best in the face of the shock, and they continue to grow robustly. Eswar Prasad in Chapter 6 marshals a number of indicators showing just how fast the emerging markets of East Asia, South Asia, Latin America and Africa have grown and how importantly they now figure in the world economy.

At the same time, as Prasad explains, these countries face serious challenges in the post-crisis environment. Stagnation in the advanced countries is a challenge for their traditional strategy of export-led growth. Very different economic conditions in emerging and advanced-country regions imply different monetary and financial policies, in turn producing large and disruptive capital flows. As emerging markets as a group become large relative to the world economy, their policies become even more important determinants of global economic outcomes. Hence, the governments of what are still relatively poor economies will have to acknowledge and act on the fact that they have effectively become stewards of the world economy.

Where Prasad considers emerging markets, broadly defined, Bokyeong Park and Junill Kim in Chapter 7 focus more closely on the challenges facing the emerging markets of East Asia in particular. The global crisis of 2008–2009 and, more recently, financial turmoil in Europe had relatively little impact on East Asia's fast-growing economies. To be sure, the region saw an abrupt decline in exports in 2009, but the substitution of domestic demand in the form of government spending and, in the Chinese case, bank lending to the construction sector helped keep growth going in the face of this external-sector weakness. Asian countries had limited exposure to the subprime market in the US, and they had accumulated ample reserves which they could now deploy to keep imports flowing. Aside from a few cases like South Korea, where banks had substantial offshore foreign currency exposures, the temporary shortage of dollar liquidity had little impact on their financial markets. The emerging markets of East Asia, it was increasingly asserted, had successfully decoupled from the advanced-country world.

Park and Kim ask in their chapter whether this will remain the case going forward. As global liquidity strains rose again in the latter part of 2011, a number of East Asian currencies weakened substantially, highlighting the region's continuing dependence on external financial conditions. International reserves, having risen steadily, reversed direction as central banks intervened to support their exchange rates. China, having ramped up bank lending in 2009 and encouraged local governments to borrow, now has less capacity to respond to additional shocks, given heavier debts and the prospect of nonperforming loans going forward. The inflation associated with previous policies of stimulus is, increasingly, a problem. All this heightens the urgency of rebalancing from foreign to domestic demand as a way of reducing the vulnerability of East Asia's emerging markets to external shocks. This in turn makes it disturbing that most of the region's economies, and above all China, have not moved faster to develop their financial markets, strengthen the domestic safety net, and permit the exchange rate to strengthen faster and fluctuate more freely.

But if the challenges that emerging markets will face in the new post-crisis environment will be formidable, they pale in comparison with those that will confront the advanced economies. The advanced economies as a group emerged from the crisis with large budget deficits and heavy debts. Winding down those deficits without derailing recovery and damaging the prospects for growth will not be easy. Deleveraging by households raises doubts about whether consumer demand will be able to substitute for public demand as fiscal consolidation proceeds. All this takes place against a gloomy demographic backdrop that implies rising old-age dependency ratios, heavy pension obligations and health-care costs, and a declining share of the population participating in the labor force.

Joseph Gagnon and Marc Hinterschweiger take up these issues in Chapter 8. They frame their analysis around a number of distinctions. In the short run, there is the distinction between the countries of Southern Europe that face severe immediate fiscal challenges and other advanced countries that still enjoy low interest rates. In the medium term, there is the distinction between countries with more and less favorable demographic outlooks, which in turn point to different prospects for the growth of health-care and pension costs. But, notwithstanding these differences, medium-term fiscal challenges are daunting across the advanced-country world. Under any plausible projection of the evolution of macroeconomic variables, current policies are not sustainable. Difficult decisions are unavoidable.

Gagnon and Hinterschweiger acknowledge the existence of major uncertainties clouding the forecast. Prominent among them are the likely future cost of health-care technology and the scope for delivering health services more efficiently. Also uncertain are the appetite of investors for government bonds and the future path of interest rates. Finally, there is uncertainty about the pace of growth in the advanced economies — about whether that capacity has been permanently impaired by the financial crisis and about whether technical change has been slowed by a "Great Stagnation." But even under optimistic assumptions, current policies, if maintained will result in the explosive growth of public debt and, sooner or later, fiscal crises.

The authors chart a number of paths along which debt-to-GDP ratios stabilize at sustainable levels and crises are averted. The requisite adjustments are straightforward in economic terms: they involve a combination of reduced discretionary spending, increases in current revenues, and reductions in the growth of health-care and pension costs. But timing is everything; Gagnon and Hinterschweiger show that adjustment costs are substantially lower when that adjustment is initiated early than if it is delayed. And the politics, unquestionably, are fraught.

The global financial crisis has cast a long shadow. It has profoundly affected advanced economies, emerging markets and the balance between them. The implications for international trade, the monetary and financial system, and global governance are far reaching. Drawing out those implications and beginning to comprehend what they mean for the future is the task we take up, collectively, in this volume.

CHAPTER 2

Financial Reform after the Crisis

Nicolas Véron

1 Introduction

Financial reform has been a core dimension of the initial global policy response to the financial turmoil of 2007–2008. At the first G20 summit of heads of state and government in November 2008, more than four-fifths of the action points in the final declaration were about financial regulation (Rottier and Véron, 2010b). Obviously, the crisis is not over at the time of writing, and the cycle of financial reform it triggered is very far from complete. But it can be said confidently that the crisis has been transformational for financial regulatory policy, at least in the US and Europe.[1]

One of the key lessons of the crisis is the close interdependence between the detailed features of financial systems and macroeconomic outcomes. Thus, the tight separation of financial and macroeconomic issues, which is entrenched both in academia and in the policymaking community, needs to

---

[1] The sequence of financial events that started in the summer of 2007 and is still unfolding at the time of writing has been referred to under various monikers including the subprime crisis, the late-2000s financial crisis, the Great Recession, or the global financial crisis. As none of these is fully satisfactory or has been universally adopted, we simply refer to this sequence in this chapter as "the crisis."

be overcome. Initiatives to better analyze "macrofinancial" linkages and to conduct "macroprudential" policy have mushroomed since the start of the crisis, although they generally fall short of a fully joined-up framework. From this perspective, the focus of this chapter is financial regulation in an old-fashioned sense, understood as a cluster of interrelated policies designed to ensure the proper functioning and integrity of financial systems. This scope includes public regulation and supervision of bank capital, leverage, liquidity, and risk management; control of moral hazard and financial industry incentives; protection of the customers of financial services; and regulation of capital markets. Other reform areas such as capital-flow controls, prevention of money laundering, and taxation of financial activities can overlap with this agenda, but are not considered here part of it in a strict sense.

The general impetus of financial reform as a reaction to the crisis, in the US and Europe, has been toward more regulation, or re-regulation. This is admittedly too simplistic a generalization: this policy area is multidimensional and cannot be reduced to a simple choice between less or more regulation. Nevertheless, there was a clear turning point in 2008 with the renewed realization that financial systems, including banking systems, could not be left to their own devices, both because of the large potential economic cost of financial crises and because public expenditure is often a key component of their resolution. This age-old wisdom was neglected in the preceding decade in both the US and Europe, for different reasons, more than in the rest of the world, including Australia, Canada, Japan, and emerging economies.

Financial regulation is a complex thicket of highly technical policy challenges, often subject to the use of mutually incomprehensible jargons even as they are mutually interrelated. The devil is generally in the details, and elegant quantitative modeling of policy trade-offs is rarely available. Analytical frameworks tend to be similarly fragmented across different academic silos, including economics, financial research, accounting, political science, and sociology. From an economic research perspective, this is a less mature field than other policy areas such as fiscal, trade or labor policies. Hopefully, the crisis itself will result in new avenues for research, the results of which might start to become available in a few years' time.

The first section of this chapter examines the dynamics of financial reform as they have unfolded since the start of the crisis. The second and last sections look at the forthcoming challenges and future prospects.

2   The Dynamics of Financial Reform

Systemic financial crises frequently result in major financial regulatory initiatives. The US is a typical example: the key historical milestones of US financial regulation before the current crisis were the creation of the First Bank of the US in 1791, as a consequence of the states' difficulties repaying the debt from the War of Independence; the creation of the Second Bank of the US in 1816 in the wake of the inflation and financial difficulties associated with the war of 1812; the Legal Tender Act of 1862 and National Banking Acts of 1863 and 1864 to deal with the challenges of financing the Civil War; the Federal Reserve Act of 1913 in the aftermath of the banking crisis of 1907; the New Deal legislation, particularly the Securities Act of 1933, the Banking (Glass–Steagall) Act of 1933, and the Securities Exchange Act of 1934 after the Wall Street crash of 1929 and the banking panic of early 1933; the Financial Institutions Reform, Recovery and Enforcement Act of 1989 and the Federal Deposit Insurance Corporation Improvement Act of 1991 as a reaction to the Savings and Loan crisis; and the Sarbanes–Oxley Act of 2002 after the Enron collapse and a string of other financial reporting scandals. Similarly, in Japan much of the current financial policy framework was introduced in the late 1990s and early 2000s following the financial turbulence that accompanied the country's "lost decade."

In the European Union (EU), a distinct driver of financial reform in the two decades preceding the crisis was the effort to create a single market for financial services, particularly after the introduction of the euro in 1999. Landmark corresponding pieces of legislation include the 1989 Second Banking Directive, which encouraged the creation of cross-border branches; the 1993 Investment Services Directive, which established a single "passport" regime for investment banking operations throughout the EU; the 2002 Regulation on International Accounting Standards, which paved the way for the EU's adoption of International Financial Reporting Standards (IFRS) in 2005; the 2004 Markets in Financial Instruments Directive (MiFID), which broke the monopoly of national stock exchanges and established the basis for EU-wide competition among trading platforms; the 2006 Capital Requirements Directives, which transposed the Basel II Accord and paved the way for a harmonized regulatory framework for bank capital requirements; and the 2009 Solvency II Directive (the preparation of which started long before the crisis), which established a parallel capital regulation framework for insurance companies.

EU harmonization efforts have themselves been a powerful stimulant or enabler for global regulatory projects. The two most prominent pre-crisis examples in this respect are IFRS and the Basel II Capital Accord. In the case of accounting, the EU's decision to adopt IFRS, made at the political level in 2000, finalized through the above-mentioned 2002 regulation and implemented in 2005–2006, was the trigger for their subsequent adoption by a significant number of jurisdictions that now represent about half of the aggregate market capitalization of large companies worldwide (Véron, 2011). In the case of Basel II, the EU was instrumental in the negotiation of the accord in the first place, and was among the first to implement it with the adoption of the Capital Requirements Directives and subsequent rulemaking in individual member states. According to the Basel Committee on Banking Supervision, by September 2011, implementation of the Basel II Accord was complete in 21 of the committee's 27 member countries, with at least two more countries planning to join in 2012 (BCBS, 2011b).

Since the start of the crisis, financial reform has resulted from a sometimes complex and iterative combination of discussions and initiatives, at both at the individual jurisdictions and international levels.[2]

2.1   *The G20*

The emergence of the G20 as the "premier forum for [...] international economic cooperation"[3] is a significant development that crystallized in the first few weeks following the collapse of Lehman Brothers and the ensuing wholesale market panic (Price, 2009). The G20 format traces its origins back to the aftermath of the Asian crisis of 1997–1998, but it was adopted as a forum for meetings of heads of state and government only in 2008. G20 summits have been held in Washington (November 2008), London (April 2009), Pittsburgh (September 2009), Toronto (June 2010), Seoul (November 2010), and Cannes (November 2011). In the area of financial regulation, the G20's impact can be observed in two ways.

First, the inclusion of large emerging countries into the "premier forum" of political leaders has triggered parallel expansion or rebalancing of most of the global financial authorities that play a role in financial regulation. This included the April 2009 transformation of the Financial Stability Forum,

---

[2]See Chapter 5 in this volume.
[3]Final declaration of the G20 Summit in Pittsburgh, September 25, 2009.

which like the G20 was created in 1999 following the Asian crisis, into the Financial Stability Board (FSB) and the expansion of its membership from 11 countries (8 Western countries plus Japan, Hong Kong and Singapore) to 24 countries, of which 10 are emerging economies in addition to Hong Kong, Singapore and South Korea. Similarly, in March 2009, the Basel Committee for Banking Supervision expanded from 13 member countries (all developed economies) to 27 (of which 10 are emerging economies, plus Hong Kong, Singapore and South Korea). The Committee on the Global Financial System, also in Basel, expanded at the same time from 13 to 22 countries including Brazil, China, Hong Kong, India, Mexico, Singapore and South Korea. The Monitoring Board of the IFRS Foundation, which oversees IFRS standard-setting by the International Accounting Standards Board (IASB), was initially established in January 2009 with only the US, the EU and Japan directly represented, but the addition of large emerging economies is actively under consideration at the time of writing (Monitoring Board, 2011). Perhaps most prominently, the IMF in December 2010 adopted a significant realignment of its quota shares resulting in the presence of the four largest emerging economies (Brazil, China, India and Russia) among its ten largest shareholders.

Second, beyond its impact on the landscape of global financial institutions, the G20 launched a series of individual initiatives in the area of global financial regulation. As previously mentioned, this was particularly the case during the first G20 summit in Washington, in which 39 out of 47 items in the final declaration were about financial regulation in the sense used in this chapter. The specific impact of the G20 in this field is not easy to assess precisely. Some initiatives were given G20 endorsement but would probably have gone ahead anyway. In other cases, the G20 set deadlines that the authority of the heads of state and governments effectively made binding. This was seen in the negotiation of the Basel III accord on bank capital, leverage, liquidity, and risk management, which was published in 2010 after less than two years of negotiations, compared to its predecessor (Basel II) which took six years to complete. In other cases, however, the G20 set deadlines that were not met, and it is unclear to what extent it had an actual impact on the related work of specialized global financial authorities. For example, the Pittsburgh Summit declaration included a call for the IASB and the US Financial Accounting Standards Board (FASB) to complete their convergence program between IFRS and US Generally Accepted Accounting Principles (GAAP) by June 2011; in the Toronto and Seoul summit declarations, the same aim was mentioned, but with the completion scheduled before the end of 2011; and the Cannes summit declaration acknowledged that even this delayed schedule would not be met by the standard-setters. Rottier and Véron (2010a) suggest that the success of the G20's financial regulatory initiatives is highly dependent on — by decreasing order of effectiveness — whether their implementation was entrusted to treaty-based international institutions, to other global standard-setters, to the FSB as coordinator of individual jurisdictions, or to individual jurisdictions directly.

2.2   The IMF and the FSB

While the G20 is by its very nature a political body, the coordination of the global financial regulatory agenda during the crisis has been mostly the joint preserve of the IMF and FSB, these being "the principal institutions of governance of the global financial architecture" (Schinasi and Truman, 2010). The IMF has played a significant role through its Financial Sector Assessment Program (FSAP). The FSAP, which is conducted by the IMF alone in developed economies and jointly with the World Bank in developing and emerging economies, is a comprehensive assessment of a country's financial-sector stability (and for developing and emerging economies, also of its financial development). In September 2010, the FSAP was made a more regular feature for 25 jurisdictions,[4] for which the assessment will be conducted at least every five years. This meant an end to the de facto exception under which some large countries escaped the scrutiny of the FSAP until the crisis: the first FSAP of the US started in June 2008 and was completed in July 2010; and the first FSAP of China started in August 2009 and was completed in June 2011.

The FSB's role is multifaceted and still, to a large extent, a work in progress. It has set up numerous working groups and coordinates work on multiple fronts, often at the explicit request of G20 leaders. However, the actual work of standard-setting and rulemaking generally remains at the level of specialized global authorities. One case in point is the FSB's report on the "shadow banking system," published a week before the 2011 G20 summit in Cannes (FSB, 2011a). Many of this report's recommendations are addressed not to individual jurisdictions but to global bodies that are

---

[4]Australia, Austria, Belgium, Brazil, Canada, China, France, Germany, Hong Kong, Italy, Japan, India, Ireland, Luxembourg, Mexico, the Netherlands, Russia, Singapore, South Korea, Spain, Sweden, Switzerland, Turkey, the UK, and the US.

FSB members, particularly the Basel Committee and IOSCO. Such patterns mean that assessing the FSB's contribution to the policy process is far from straightforward. In some cases, the FSB's work can be little more than reporting initiatives of its members into which it has had essentially no input; in other cases, FSB leadership is essential for pressing other bodies into taking action. In practice, there appears to be a continuum of situations between these two extremes.

2.3 *Individual jurisdictions*

The pattern of financial reform initiatives has been extremely different from one jurisdiction to another, notwithstanding the coordination efforts deployed in G20 summit and FSB initiatives. Multiple factors converge when explaining the differences of approach, including longstanding variations of institutions, culture, and economic structures, as well as different patterns of impact of the crisis itself.

The US has had a comparatively linear sequence of crisis management and resolution, legislative debate and decision, and implementation of new legislation by specialized authorities. Following the ad hoc rescue of Bear Stearns (March 2008), the *de facto* nationalization of Fannie Mae and Freddie Mac (early September 2008) and the collapse of Lehman Brothers and the rescue of AIG (mid-September 2008), the US introduced the Troubled Asset Relief Program (TARP) as the main instrument of the executive branch's crisis management strategy through the Emergency Economic Stabilization Act, enacted on October 3, 2008. After the November 2008 elections and change of administration in January 2009, the phase of crisis management and resolution was essentially completed with the publication on May 7, 2009, of the results of the Supervisory Capital Assessment Program (commonly referred to as "stress tests") which imposed significant capital-raising requirements on ten out of nineteen participating banks. This step marked the beginning of a gradual normalization of financial conditions. Smaller bank failures, as reported by the FDIC, peaked in the third quarter of 2009 and have been on a downward trend since, even though their numbers remain high. The US Federal Reserve gradually phased out its exceptional liquidity provision, and the main corresponding program, the Term Auction Facility, expired in March 2010. This sequence of crisis management initiatives was followed by more than a year of legislative debate, from the publication of the administration's blueprint for financial reform in mid-June 2009 (US

Treasury, 2009) to the enactment of the Dodd–Frank Wall Street Reform and Consumer Protection Act in July 2010. Thereafter, individual authorities started a protracted phase of rule-making on the basis of the parameters set by the Dodd–Frank Act, a process that is still ongoing at the time of writing.

In the EU, there has been no similar sequence, and crisis management and legislative reform have both been continuous processes with overlapping consequences. Successive rounds of stress tests were completed in September 2009, July 2010 and July 2011 but have not resulted in the return of trust in the European banking sector, and from late 2009 onwards the difficulty has been compounded by sovereign credit fragility affecting first Greece and then Ireland, Portugal, Spain, Italy and others. Simultaneously, the European Commission's Internal Market Directorate-General (DG MARKT), which oversees financial regulation at the EU level, has actively proposed new legislation in multiple areas: capital requirements (proposed in October 2008, adopted in various steps in 2009), deposit insurance (proposed in October 2008, adopted in March 2009), rating agencies (proposed in November 2008, adopted in November 2009), hedge funds and private equity (proposed in April 2009, adopted in June 2011), revision of capital requirements (proposed in July 2009, adopted in November 2010), new EU-level supervisory authorities (proposed in September 2009, adopted in November 2010), revision of credit rating agencies (proposed in June 2010, adopted in May 2011), revision of deposit insurance (proposed in July 2010, discussion ongoing), market infrastructure (proposed in September 2010, discussion ongoing), revision of capital requirements (proposed in July 2011), revision of the 2004 directive on markets in financial instruments (proposed in October 2011), revision of 2003 directive on market abuse (proposed in October 2011), another revision of credit rating agencies (proposed in November 2011), and framework for bank crisis management and resolution (forthcoming), to name only the most prominent pieces. Inevitably, the fact that so many different pieces of legislation are debated and decided upon while the financial crisis continues raises risks of legislative inconsistency and of short-term considerations prevailing over longer-term ones.

Moreover, in the EU important financial legislation is also set at the national level, under various patterns of coordination with EU-level legislative initiatives. This has been particularly the case with moves to introduce special resolution regimes for troubled banks, on the model of FDIC-managed receivership, which did not exist in most European countries until the crisis. The UK, Germany, Belgium, Ireland, Sweden and other EU member states have adopted such legislation, well in anticipation of any European Commission proposal in this area. The UK has distinguished itself with a more in-depth debate on banking structures than its EU peers through the Independent Commission on Banking chaired by John Vickers, which delivered its final report in September 2011 (ICB, 2011). Likewise, the imposition of new taxes or levies on the financial sector has been the preserve of individual member states, even though the possibility of an EU-level or Eurozone tax on financial transactions is being actively debated at the time of writing.

Beyond the EU and the US, Switzerland stands out for its decision to demand capital requirements for its largest banks, which go well beyond the minimum set by Basel III, which itself is tougher than Basel II. This is ostensibly linked to the discovery in 2008 of major risk-management shortcomings at UBS, which had a durable impact on Swiss public opinion. Other jurisdictions, including Canada, Australia, and countries in Asia, the Middle East, Africa, and Latin America, were generally less impacted financially by the crisis. Their financial reform initiatives since 2007, if any, have generally not risen to a level of prominence comparable to those in the US, the EU and Switzerland.

2.4 *Crisis-induced shifts*

In comparison to the preceding two decades, the crisis has induced shifts in the interplay between the public and private sectors, between political and technical factors, between the global and jurisdictional levels, and between developed and emerging jurisdictions. Generalization is difficult in this analysis because reform dynamics vary widely across specific issue areas and jurisdictions, before and after the start of the crisis. Nevertheless, a few trend changes can be identified at a general level.

First, the crisis has marked a relative retreat of the private sector's influence over the financial policy process. At the global level, this change is perhaps best exemplified by the contrast between Basel II and Basel III. The negotiation of Basel II was, to a significant extent, a collaborative exercise between large banks, partly through the agency of the Washington-based Institute of International Finance (IIF) and the Basel Committee and its members. The Basel II Accord ended up giving wide discretion to banks to assess the riskiness of their asset portfolios, under the control of supervisors (Tarullo, 2008). By contrast, Basel III was an initiative of the supervisors and the Basel Committee secretariat under close monitoring by G20 leaders, and resulted in a partly public — and at times bitter — controversy between the Committee and the IIF over the assessment of the Accord's macroeconomic consequences (BCBS, 2010a; IIF, 2010). Similarly, in some jurisdictions, including the US, UK and Switzerland, and at the EU level, financial reform initiatives elicited a level of opposition from the financial industry without equivalent in recent memory. Among other episodes, this shift was illustrated when JP Morgan Chase CEO Jamie Dimon described the Basel Committee's proposed capital surcharges on Global Systemically Important Banks as "anti-American,"[5] or when the Director General of the Confederation of British Industry, John Cridland, referred to the proposals of the UK Independent Commission on Banking as "barking mad."[6] This is not an absolute shift: there were instances of autonomy of public financial policymaking from the private sector before the crisis, including the US Sarbanes–Oxley Act of 2002; and there are examples of private-sector capture of the policy process since the crisis started, such as when the European Commission in October 2008 forced the IASB to amend its IAS 39 standard on financial instruments to help banks escape the early recognition of crisis-induced losses, or when the US FASB eased its criteria for asset impairment in early 2009 under pressure from Congress. There are also many grey areas. Nevertheless, the general trend so far appears to have been a sharp reduction of the private sector's influence over the financial policy process.

Second, within public policy decision-making there has been a general shift toward more politicization. Policy issues that were previously the preserve of a narrow community of technicians and practitioners have tended to climb up the agenda and be directly affected by the political concerns of elected officials. For example, accounting issues have repeatedly been discussed at length among G20 leaders, and featured prominently in political discourses, such as French President Nicolas Sarkozy's first speech at the World Economic Forum in Davos, which contained no fewer than seven references to accounting standards (Sarkozy, 2010). The crisis has elevated financial issues to matters of concern for the general public, as the Occupy Wall Street movement of 2011 in the US and similar initiatives

---

[5]Stephen Mangan, "Jamie Dimon, CEO of JPMorgan Chase, Calls International Bank Rules 'Anti-American,'" *Reuters*, September 11, 2011.
[6]Elizabeth Rigby, "Rush to ringfence banks 'barking mad,'" *Financial Times*, August 29, 2011.

in Europe have shown. Even though it is generally difficult to disentangle the influence of political and technical concerns in the policy process, there is little doubt, for instance, that the restless opening of multiple regulatory fronts by the European Commission successively on hedge funds and private equity, credit rating agencies, remuneration policies, short-selling, regulation of audit firms, and the introduction of a Financial Transaction Tax, responds in part to a politically motivated urge to act, even though the Commission's civil servants have duly produced a technical rationale for each initiative. The evidence of past failures of oversight or excessive regulatory forbearance, such as the US Federal Reserve's failure to properly supervise mortgage originators, the UK Financial Services Authority's inability to anticipate the bank run at Northern Rock, or German supervisors' tolerance of large Irish-based off-balance-sheet conduits at since-failed banks IKB, SachsenLB or WestLB, has also diminished the autonomy of financial authorities. Financial regulators and supervisors, like central bankers, have acted under the general public's eye since the start of the crisis to an extent that was rarely seen in the previous era.

Third, the crisis has affected in multiple ways the boundaries between global and local financial policymaking, even though this transformation cannot be described as a uniform trend. On the face of it, the creation of the G20 has appeared, at least initially, to be a significant shift toward the empowerment of global decision-making in the financial regulatory area. Many political leaders, particularly those from large Western European countries, heralded the need to define "global solutions" to a crisis that was described as a "global problem." Indeed, the G20 agreements to adopt the Basel III accord or to move the clearing of over-the-counter derivatives to central counterparties, even though they are not yet fully implemented, were landmark instances of international joint regulatory action with few precedents in the preceding two decades. However, there have also been crisis-related setbacks in terms of the regulatory underpinnings of global financial integration. This particularly applies to the European Commission, which was a determined champion of global regulatory harmonization throughout the 1990s and 2000s but has shifted markedly since 2008 towards a more unilateralist stance in many areas. At play has been the fact that it is intrinsically more difficult to achieve international regulatory convergence in an era of financial reregulation than in an era of liberalization (Rottier and Véron, 2010a). The UK Independent Commission on Banking's suggestion to "ring-fence" the retail operations of international banks is another illustration of the way the crisis is shifting the limit between globally integrated and jurisdiction-specific regulatory and supervisory approaches.

Fourth, the crisis has accelerated the transition from a Western-dominated financial world toward a more globally-balanced one in which large emerging countries play an increasingly significant role, with consequences for financial regulation that remain difficult to predict. To various degrees, the memberships and/or governance structures of the IMF, the FSB, the Basel Committee and other committees hosted by the Bank for International Settlements, and the IFRS Foundation, have been or are being expanded to include large emerging economies. It will certainly take time for this to translate into a rebalancing of these authorities' senior leadership. IOSCO gave itself a non-Western head in April 2011 with the selection of Brazil's Helena Santana as its chair, but most post-crisis senior appointments have gone to Westerners. At the IMF, Christine Lagarde was appointed Managing Director in June 2011. At the Basel Committee, Australia's Wayne Byres was appointed Secretary General, Sweden's Stefan Ingves Chairman, and Britain's Mervyn King Chair of the Group of Governors and Heads of Supervision in June 2011. At the IASB, the Netherlands' Hans Hoogervorst was appointed Chair in October 2010 (effective in July 2011), and IFRS Foundation's Trustees was announced in December 2011. At the FSB, Canada's Mark Carney was appointed Chair in November 2011. And the next president of the World Bank, to be appointed in 2012, is expected to be an American. Plainly, the shift from G7 to G20 has not yet translated into these selection processes, and the same is true at less visible levels: for example, half of the FSB's member countries are emerging economies, but the vast majority of its working groups and task forces are headed by Westerners. It appears likely that the wider diversity of participants should gradually result in leadership roles being taken by emerging economy representatives, at least in some areas. Even so, it remains to be seen how keen these new entrants will be to empower global financial authorities and effective international cross-border regulatory convergence, in absolute terms and in comparison with the western incumbents.

3   Challenges and Outlook

It is far too early to present a settled picture of post-crisis financial reforms and their impact on the global financial system. Huge challenges remain and it is still unclear how they will be met. First and foremost, the crisis has not yet been resolved, and the interaction between crisis management and longer-term reform creates uncertainties of its own. Second, in spite of widespread calls for "macroprudential" approaches, the interaction of financial-sector policy with other dimensions of economic policymaking remains largely unsettled. Third, how to effectively regulate cross-border financial firms remains a fundamentally unsettled question. Fourth, other reforms will be difficult to implement in an internationally consistent manner, raising concerns about the possible fragmentation of the global financial space. Fifth, the reforms will affect the financial system's contribution to economic growth in multiple ways, which on the whole remain poorly understood.

3.1 Ongoing crisis management

The most obvious uncertainty is that the financial crisis is far from over. Although it was partly overcome in the US in 2009, it is still worsening in Europe and could again spill over to other parts of the world. This creates a triple risk of forbearance, populism, and irrelevance.

Concerns about financial instability in jurisdictions where the financial crisis remains unresolved, including much of continental Europe at the time of writing, can easily lead to excessive forbearance as has been the case in several past episodes of systemic banking fragility, such as in Japan in the 1990s. For example, large continental European countries such as Germany and France were widely reported as being reluctant to tighten the definition of capital and impose higher minimum capital requirements in the negotiation of the Basel III Accord and in the subsequent discussion of SIFI surcharges. Similarly, the first draft of the EU legislation transposing Basel III softens some of the Basel Committee's tightening of the definition of capital, and prohibits the voluntary application of higher capital requirements by individual member states. The same factor was at play when European policymakers forced the IASB in October 2008 to amend the IAS 39 standard on financial instruments and allow more flexibility in the classification of financial instruments by struggling European banks. This is especially important as the EU prepares to introduce legislation on banking crisis management and resolution, for which a proposal is expected from the European Commission in early 2012. It is arguably impossible to eliminate moral hazard from banking sector policy frameworks, but it is arguably even more difficult to prevent it when such frameworks are prepared in a climate of systemic instability.

The risk of populism complements that of forbearance, and the two can be simultaneous. As the ongoing crisis creates a political demand for action, and action at a fundamental level is prevented by the bias towards forbearance, policymakers can be tempted to adopt a punitive attitude toward the financial sector, in response to popular perceptions rather than in-depth policy analysis. This has arguably been the case with initiatives, particularly in the EU, to put hard limits on the scope of remuneration practices in the financial industry and to impose specific taxation on aspects of financial activity. In certain cases, such impulses can be aligned with strategies of "financial repression," namely the forced investment of domestic savings in government securities, or in other forms of repression of market mechanisms for price-setting and capital allocation, such as the attempts to discourage some forms of hedging against sovereign risk or to suspend the publication of credit rating decisions affecting troubled countries. Given the complexity of financial regulation, it can be difficult to disentangle such populist motivations from other drivers of financial reform. Nevertheless, they are likely to gain in prominence if the European crisis worsens and leads to more financial and economic dislocation.

Furthermore, embarking in long-term financial reform while a major financial crisis is still ongoing and unresolved creates a risk of irrelevance of the corresponding legislative and regulatory initiatives, to the extent that the eventual crisis resolution can be expected to usher in a new round of reform to ensure that "it never happens again." Examples in the EU are the successive rounds of amendments to the Capital Requirements Directive of 2006 (introduced respectively in October 2008, July 2009, and July 2011), or the three consecutive regulations to create a tighter legal framework for the activity of credit rating agencies (the first two were respectively finalized in November 2009 and May 2011, and the third set of proposals was published in November 2011).

Each of these three factors, in certain circumstances, can contribute positively to the quality of policymaking. Forbearance can be a rational calculation to minimize financial dislocation, even though it increases moral hazard. Populism can help assert the autonomy of financial reform against pressure from the financial industry. Successive rounds of regulatory reform can result in gradual improvements of the regulatory framework and correction of past missteps. But each of them can also easily have negative consequences in terms of the sustainability and efficiency of the financial policy framework.

3.2 *Macroprudential approaches*

Events since 2007 have revealed embarrassing blind spots in the pre-crisis understanding of the financial system by policymakers but also by the academic community. Thus, there has been an understandable drive to introduce a more comprehensive and joined-up approach to financial regulation. This has resulted in an emphasis on "macroprudential" policies and institutions, using an expression developed well before the crisis by the Bank for International Settlements (Clement, 2010).

Perhaps the most visible consequence has been the creation of new bodies with a mandate to contribute to system-wide financial stability in most jurisdictions affected by the crisis. In the US, the Dodd–Frank Act of 2010 created a Financial Stability Oversight Council (FSOC), chaired by the US Treasury Secretary, and an Office of Financial Research with autonomous resources within the Treasury Department. In the EU, the string of institutional reforms known as the "supervisory package," adopted in November 2010, created a European Systemic Risk Board as an autonomous EU institution hosted by the European Central Bank in Frankfurt and chaired by the ECB's President. In the UK, the Bank of England in 2011 established a Financial Policy Committee, pending forthcoming legislation that will specify this new body's exact role and mission. Similar bodies were created in France (Financial Regulation and Systemic Risk Council), Belgium (Committee for Systemic Risks and System-relevant Financial Institutions), and other jurisdictions. However, this list itself illustrates a diversity of views about the relationship between financial stability policy and the wider aim of economic and price stability, which is typically the preserve of central banks (White, 2012). In the UK, the macroprudential body is part of the central bank and chaired by the bank's governor, even though its membership is distinct from that of the Monetary Policy Committee. At the EU level and in Belgium, it is also chaired by the central bank's governor but is legally autonomous and includes representatives of multiple public entities. In the US and France, it is chaired by the Treasury Secretary/Finance Minister, suggesting further distance from monetary policy.

The macroprudential concept, as described by one of its early promoters (Borio, 2010), has a time dimension (how risk in the financial system evolves over time) and a cross-sectional dimension (how risk is allocated among financial-system participants at a given point of time). Beyond the institutional machinery, there are challenges in both dimensions. On the

first, policies to adjust some financial regulatory instruments over the
financial cycle in order to mitigate their pro-cyclical effect or to make
them counter-cyclical remain tentative at best. Specifically, the Basel III
framework envisages that regulated entities will be required to build up
counter-cyclical capital buffers, but supervisory authorities may be reluctant to take a stance on the shape of the financial cycle that could be proved
inaccurate by future developments. The cross-sectional dimension has given
rise to more follow-up, with the crisis-induced recognition that all financial
firms have a potential impact on system stability, and that regulatory silos
that separate the respective policy frameworks for depository institutions,
insurers, investment funds, etc., can be irrelevant or even counterproductive
from a systemic stability standpoint. This concern partly underlies the new
processes for registration of long unregulated or lightly regulated actors
such as private equity and hedge funds in both the EU (Alternative Investment Fund Managers Directive of 2011) and the US (Dodd–Frank Act).

The same concern also underlies the explicit designation of some
financial firms as systemically important. At the global level, the FSB in
November 2011 published a list of 29 Global Systemically Important Banks
(G-SIBs) on the basis of criteria set by the Basel Committee (BCBS, 2011c).
The FSB intends to enlarge that list in 2012 to include global systemically
important non-bank financial institutions; additional capital requirements
are expected to be applied to G-SIBs from 2016 onwards, on the basis
of the update of the list to be published by the FSB in November 2014
(FSB, 2011b). At the level of individual jurisdictions, Belgium, as early as
October 2010, identified 15 systemic financial firms, including four credit
institutions, four insurers, three holding companies, and three entities of
the Brussels-headquartered Euroclear securities settlement and custodian
services group. In the US, the Dodd–Frank Act prescribes the FSOC to
do the same, even though no such list has been published at the time of
writing. Other individual jurisdictions will follow suit, but some may be
reluctant to single out specific firms as systemically significant, partly out
of concern about creating competitive distortions in the domestic financial
environment, and also because of different perceptions about the specific
risks associated with "too-big-to-fail" financial institutions (Goldstein and
Véron, 2011).

Beyond these two dimensions, macro-prudential concerns have also been
invoked to justify controls imposed on external capital flows in order to

mitigate the risks associated with "hot money." In particular, the crisis has triggered a reversal of the IMF's position on capital controls, which are now viewed as an acceptable tool of financial stability policy if correctly wielded (Ostry *et al.*, 2011). This illustrates the elasticity of the macroprudential concept and of its boundaries with, on the one hand, monetary policy run by central banks, and on the other hand, microprudential supervision of individual financial firms by prudential supervisors. While the crisis has clearly underlined the need to monitor not only individual regulated institutions but also the financial system as a whole, the best way to reach this objective is unlikely to become a matter of universal consensus in the short or even the medium term.

3.3 *Regulating multinational financial firms*

The crisis has brought a sense of urgency to another longstanding challenge: the resolution of the difficulties posed by multinational financial firms. These can shift risks across borders in ways that escape the oversight of national supervisors, as was illustrated by the concentration of risk in the London-based operations of AIG Financial Products, which precipitated the downfall of the entire AIG Group. Moreover, when such firms collapse, the absence of a centralized resolution process creates the scope for considerable uncertainty and cross-border contagion, a striking example of which was provided by the Lehman Brothers bankruptcy.

This challenge relates to an emerging policy debate about the structure of financial firms, in which the UK has taken an early lead with the consultations and conclusions of the Independent Commission on Banking chaired by John Vickers (ICB, 2011). The ICB's most prominent recommendation is to ring-fence the domestic retail activities of UK financial firms in order to more easily separate them from international wholesale activities in the event of a crisis. This raises the possibility of protecting depository operations from the knock-on effects of international financial failures. However, it does not tackle the problem posed by cross-border failures of pure wholesale operations, as was the case with Lehman Brothers.

The FSB has attempted to foster coordination of contingency planning and resolution efforts for global systemically important financial institutions, and has initiated the development of common processes and tools by national supervisory and resolution authorities (FSB, 2011b). However, the European experience suggests caution over the operational relevance of such coordination efforts. When the Fortis financial group collapsed in late

September and early October 2008, in particular, pre-existing arrangements among national regulators, enshrined in memorandums of understanding and other non-binding endeavors to promote constructive cooperation, were largely swept away by the urgency of the situation and the national mandates and accountability frameworks of the main public authorities involved. Some policymakers such as Liu (2010) have suggested the possibility that more binding international approaches to addressing this challenge should be considered, possibly through international law. However, such approaches remain likely to give rise to significant political resistance and are therefore widely considered as being no more than a remote possibility.

3.4   *Consistent implementation of global standards*

While the supervision and resolution of international financial firms is an area in which cross-border interactions are particularly difficult to manage, the comparably less intractable aim of consistency in implementing standards agreed at the global level is not itself assured of being satisfactorily met. This carries risks of competitive distortions, regulatory arbitrage, and to some degree, fragmentation of the international financial space.

A prominent case is the forthcoming implementation of the Basel III Accord (BCBS, 2011a and 2010b), which tightens the definition of capital and raises capital requirements (with a phased introduction to be completed in 2019); introduces a maximum Leverage Ratio (mandatory from 2018); and ushers in liquidity requirements for banks to withstand liquidity stress over periods of one month (Liquidity Coverage Ratio, to be introduced in 2015) and one year (Net Stable Funding Ratio, to be introduced in 2018). The G20 leaders endorsed Basel III at the Seoul Summit in November 2010 and committed to implement it in their respective jurisdictions. At the time of writing, most jurisdictions are still at a relatively early stage of this process, but concerns have already emerged about the consistency of implementation in jurisdictions including the EU, where the proposed legislation (fourth Capital Requirements Directive and Capital Requirements Regulation, adopted by the European Commission on July 20, 2011) diverges from Basel III on some aspects of the definition of regulatory capital. Conversely, there are widespread doubts in Europe about the extent to which Basel III will be implemented by the US.

Comparable concerns exist about accounting standards, with the difficulty of maintaining consistent endorsement and implementation of IFRS as more jurisdictions decide to adopt them. While the IFRS Foundation tries to promote the universal use of all IFRS, some jurisdictions including the EU and to a greater extent China and India, have adopted standards that vary from IFRS in ways that can have significant impact for some issuers, resulting in what can be described as "IFRS dialects" (Véron, 2011). The US has not yet determined its position on eventual IFRS adoption, but is likely to include a strong "dialectal" component as well. If such dialects multiply, the risk is that the central promise of IFRS, namely the cross-border comparability of corporate financial statements, will not be delivered.

3.5 *Financial systems and growth*

Finally, one of the most open questions of all is how the post-crisis financial reform agenda might affect the ability of the financial sector to contribute to overall economic growth. This issue too has multiple dimensions.

As mentioned above, the consequences of tighter capital requirements on economic growth has been a matter of heated controversy in the context of the preparation of Basel III, with a stark contrast between simulations conducted by the financial industry that predicted a devastating effect of the proposed rules on future output (IIF, 2010), and those of the supervisory community that forecasted a much milder impact (MAG, 2010 and BCBS, 2010a). Ultimately, the G20 leaders implicitly endorsed the Basel committee's more sanguine assessment when they adopted Basel III at the November 2010 Seoul Summit.

However, this quantitative argument fails to capture the complexity of the impact of financial reform on growth. In most countries, in the developed world at least, large companies have fairly easy access to international capital markets, and their funding conditions are not overly affected by domestic regulatory frameworks. Smaller companies and other borrowers, by contrast, including younger firms which have the greatest growth potential (Haltiwanger *et al.*, 2010), have no such access, and their ability to mobilize external finance is likely to be most affected by financial reforms. What is at stake is not just the aggregate volume of credit, but how this credit is allocated by heterogeneous intermediaries towards heterogeneous firms and other borrowers. Regulated banks are only one part of this picture, which includes the loosely defined "shadow banking system" (FSB, 2011a) and interacts with the broader economy in ways that existing economic models generally fail to describe comprehensively.

In particular, the impact of the ongoing movement towards reregulation on global financial integration could materially impact economic trends, to the extent that financial openness is associated with higher levels of economic growth (Cline, 2010). Also, how regulation might encourage or limit competition among financial intermediaries, innovation in financial services, and the allocation of capital to risky new ventures, remains poorly understood, especially given the large number of interrelated recent or ongoing financial reform initiatives.

References

BCBS (2010a). An assessment of the long-term economic impact of stronger capital and liquidity requirements. Basel Committee on Banking Supervision (Basel: Bank for International Settlements), August.

BCBS (2010b). Basel III: International framework for liquidity risk measurement, standards and monitoring. Basel Committee on Banking Supervision (Basel: Bank for International Settlements), December.

BCBS (2011a). Basel III: A global regulatory framework for more resilient banks and banking systems. Basel Committee on Banking Supervision (Basel: Bank for International Settlements), June.

BCBS (2011b). Progress report on Basel III Implementation. Basel Committee on Banking Supervision (Basel: Bank for International Settlements), October.

BCBS (2011c). Global systemically important banks: Assessment methodology and the additional loss absorbency requirement. Basel Committee on Banking Supervision (Basel: Bank for International Settlements), November.

Borio, C. (2010). Implementing a macroprudential framework: Between boldness and realism. (Basel: Bank for International Settlements), July.

Clement, P. (2010). The term "macroprudential": Origins and evolution. *BIS Quarterly Review* (Basel: Bank for International Settlements), March.

Cline, W. (2010). *Financial Globalization, Economic Growth, and the Crisis of 2007–2009* (Washington DC: Peterson Institute for International Economics), May.

FSB (2011a). Shadow banking: Strengthening oversight and regulation. Financial Stability Board, October.

FSB (2011b). Policy measures to address systemically important financial institutions, November.

Goldstein, M. and N. Véron (2011). Too big to fail: The transatlantic debate. PIIE Working Paper WP11-2 (Washington DC: Peterson Institute for International Economics), January.

Haltiwanger, J., R. Jarmin and J. Miranda (2010). Who creates jobs? Small vs. large vs. young. NBER Working Paper 16300 (Cambridge, MA: National Bureau of Economic Research), August.

ICB (2011). Final Report: Recommendations. (London: Independent Commission on Banking), September.

IIF (2010). Interim Report on the Cumulative Impact on the Global Economy of Proposed Changes in the Banking Regulatory Framework. (Washington DC: Institute of International Finance), June.

Liu, M. (2010). Financial regulation: Why reform must go further. *Emerging Markets*, October 7.

MAG (2010). Interim Report: Assessing the macroeconomic impact of the transition to stronger capital and liquidity requirements, Macroeconomic Assessment Group established by the Financial Stability Board and the Basel Committee on Banking Supervision (Basel: Bank for International Settlements), August.

Monitoring Board (2011). Consultative Report on the Review of the IFRS Foundation's Governance. IFRS Foundation Monitoring Board, February.

Ostry, J., A. Ghosh, K. Habermeier, L. Laeven, M. Chamon, M. Qureshi and A. Kokenyne (2011). Managing capital inflows: What tools to use? IMF Staff Discussion Note SDN/11/06 (Washington DC: International Monetary Fund), April.

Price, D. (2009). Recovery and reform. *Italy G8*, July.

Rottier, S. and N. Véron (2010a). Not all financial regulation is global. Bruegel Policy Brief 2010/07 (Brussels: Bruegel), August.

Rottier, S. and N. Véron (2010b). An assessment of the G20's initial action items. Bruegel Policy Contribution 2010/08 (Brussels: Bruegel), August.

Sarkozy, N. (2010). Address to the 40th World Economic Forum in Davos, January 27. Available at www.elysee.fr.

Schinasi, G. and E. Truman (2010). Reform of the global financial architecture. Bruegel/PIIE Working Paper WP-10-14 (Washington DC: Peterson Institute for International Economics), September.

Tarullo, D. (2008). Banking on Basel: The future of international financial regulation. (Washington DC: Peterson Institute for International Economics), August.

US Treasury (2009). Financial regulatory reform — A new foundation: Rebuilding financial regulation and supervision. US Department of the Treasury, June.

Véron, N. (2011). Keeping the promise of global accounting standards. PIIE Policy Brief PB11–11 (Washington DC: Peterson Institute for International Economics), July.

White, W. (2012). "Macroprudential Regulatory Policies: The New Road to Financial Stability?" In S. Claessens, D. Evanoff, G. Kaufman and I. Kodres (eds.), *Macroprudential Regulatory Policies: The New Road to Financial Stability?* Sinapore: World Scientific, pp. 357–370.

CHAPTER 3

Did WTO Rules Restrain Protectionism During the Recent Systemic Crisis?

Simon J. Evenett[1]

"The multilateral trading system was instrumental in helping governments successfully resist intense protectionist pressures during the recent global recession. It is vital to preserve this system to be able to face future crisis. Any weakening of the multilateral trading system and the insurance policy that the WTO represents would provide grounds for renewed calls to retreat into protectionism." (WTO, 2011:3)

1 Introduction

According to surveys of the profession, economists favor free trade and more open markets to the alternative, protectionism — and by large majorities. Almost by implication, many are predisposed to believe an international organization that advances across-the-board trade liberalization, such as the WTO, must be doing good. Perhaps unsurprisingly then, when a global economic crisis unfolds and there are no Smoot–Hawley-like increases in

---

[1]The views represented in this chapter are those of the author alone and should not be attributed to anyone else associated with the Global Trade Alert. I thank Kamala Dawar and Johannes Fritz for their reactions to a first draft of this chapter. Other comments on this chapter are most welcome.

tariffs, many economic analysts are inclined to give the WTO plenty of credit.

Using evidence on the range of protectionist measures employed by governments during the crisis era, the incentives created for trade policy and diplomacy during a systemic economic crisis, and information on the actual state of WTO rules and dispute settlement procedures, this chapter seeks to challenge the final inference in the previous paragraph. Readers are essentially being challenged to think through precisely how the WTO might have affected actual state behavior during a global financial crisis, when policymakers are under considerable pressure to intervene. Doing so allows some realities to intrude on the more stylized theory-motivated accounts of the WTO. Moreover, this approach might reveal weaknesses in the current multilateral trading system that could be taken up in future international negotiations.

Being confronted with the realities of contemporary protectionism and the incentives created by global economic crises leads to a more qualified view of what the WTO can accomplish during times of systemic economic duress. The objective here is not to rubbish the WTO but rather, in terms of the quotation from the latest WTO monitoring report reproduced above, to question the contention in the first sentence and downplay the claim made in the second, without encouraging the weakening of the multilateral trading system mentioned in the third sentence. As the evidence presented here casts doubt upon whether WTO rules actually constrained protectionism during the recent systemic crisis, the credit for any restraint should go elsewhere.

This subject matter is important for reasons other than assessing the contemporary impact of the WTO, which, as noted above, has tended to get very good press from economists.[2] It will be interesting to see whether recent developments conform to patterns witnessed in the past and the extent to which lessons learned from previous bouts of protectionism can inform our understanding of the incentive to resort to protectionism. For example, one reaction to the current systemic crisis might be to call for more demanding multilateral trade disciplines. However, in extremis, governments have been known to abandon cast iron constraints

---

[2]As an example of that good press, Bagwell and Staiger (2010) note in a recent survey article on the WTO: "The GATT/WTO is widely acknowledged to be one of the most successful international institutions ever created." (p. 224).

on their policymaking, witness the fate of the Gold Standard in the 1930s (Eichengreen and Irwin, 2009; Irwin, 2012). At what point would a strengthened set of WTO rules risk suffering a similar fate in a future global systemic crisis?

A related theme is the extent to which international institutions actually constrain sovereign governments, especially during times of extreme stress (Mearsheimer, 1994). Realist scholars in international relations have tended to be skeptical, thereby asserting the importance of national factors over regional and multilateral obligations. What, if anything, does the experience with WTO's rules during the recent global economic crisis imply about the validity of Realists' claims?

Another significant theme is to what extent policymakers "learn from history" and adjust their behavior accordingly. After the Great Depression, protectionism has had a very bad name and many public officials have not wanted to be associated with it. Yet the stigma associated with introducing protectionism cannot be that bad because it has continued, often in new and less transparent forms. Do the "lessons from history" affect more the composition of protectionism rather than the amount implemented?

Moreover, the set of policy instruments that analysts perceive as protectionist may differ from that of some public officials, allowing the latter to deny that they have engaged in less well-known forms of protectionism.[3] There was plenty of such double-talk in the recent global economic crisis, so much so that Richard Baldwin and I introduced the phrase "murky protectionism" precisely to identify forms of state intervention that discriminated against foreign commercial interests, were often hard to document (and therefore, easier to deny or ignore), and typically only lightly regulated by WTO rules.[4] These comments raise the deeper question as to what is the best way to characterize protectionism in the 21st century and therefore what policies should fall within the scope of monitoring exercises and research on contemporary protectionism.

The rest of this chapter is organized as follows. Sections 2 and 3 describe the key concepts and elements of the factual record. Since the goal is to assess what role the WTO could have played, it is essential that consideration is given beforehand to the appropriate definition of

---

[3]This practice of policymakers has a long pedigree. Irwin (2012:27, footnote 16) quotes from a discussion on the "new protectionism" described by a 1933 League of Nations Report.

[4]Baldwin and Evenett (2009).

protectionism and to the manner in which global economic crises (as opposed to national recessions) might affect the incentives of governments.

Section 3 provides an overview on contemporary trade protectionism and liberalisation based on the independent protectionism monitoring initiative, the Global Trade Alert. The design of the Global Trade Alert reflected many of the considerations raised in Sections 2 and 3 as well as those pertinent to understanding the sharp global economic downturn in the early 1980s. Variation across country, time, and sector, as well as across G20 membership, is exploited to provide a detailed account of contemporary protectionism. This account may be of use to scholars for other purposes.

The assessment of the contribution of the WTO to the resort to protectionism is presented in Section 4. Implications for the reform of the WTO are considered. The likelihood of those reforms being implemented given the deadlock over the Doha Round will be considered as well.[5] Concluding remarks are presented in Section 5.

2   Twenty-First Century Protectionism During a Systemic Financial Crisis: Some Preliminary Considerations

The starting point is to acknowledge the diverse nature of cross-border commercial movements in the early 21st century. Cross-border movements of goods are now complemented by similar movements of services, financial payments (associated with current and capital account transactions), people (short-term and migration), as well as intellectual property. Moreover, the development of cross-border supply chains has further raised demands for short-term finance (to cover the period between production and revenue receipt) as well as the increased reliance on transportation and telecommunications infrastructure.

---

[5] In this respect, the sharp global economic downturn in the early 1980s may well have a greater long-run effect on the development of multilateral trade rules than now. The former era also had an official GATT monitoring exercise which produced, at the start at least, some pretty tough reports. The facts described in those reports — especially as they relate to newer forms of protectionism — were taken up by some trade delegations when the agenda for the Uruguay Round was decided in the mid-1980s. This time around, however, there appears to be little appetite to complete the ongoing multilateral trade negotiation (the Doha Round), let alone start a new negotiation.

Almost every type of cross-border movements can be the target of discrimination by government. Sometimes the discrimination directly targets the transaction or individual as it crosses the border. In other cases, domestic regulations are used to reduce the commercial prospects of actual or potential suppliers that, initially at least, are based abroad. Utilities and managers of transportation facilities could, upon the instruction of government, treat domestic firms differently from foreign firms as well. Surely one criteria for a sensible definition of contemporary protectionism is that it covers all types of cross-border commercial transaction?

If so, then long-standing characterizations of trade policy intervention may not be sufficient. Irwin (2012) usefully distinguishes between "protectionism" and "mercantilism." Import restrictions are taken to be an example of the former because, he argues, they increase domestic production of those goods that compete with the imports that comply with the restriction. Irwin claims that, because this protectionism is often in response to pressures from special interest groups, it can be quite targeted. Tariffs, quotas, and antidumping duties would fall under this definition of protectionism. Export restrictions and subsidies would not as they do not relate to imports. Nor would visa restrictions as their imposition may actually reduce industry output, not increase it. Limitations on domestic banks to lend to overseas customers might fall under this definition of protectionism if the alternative borrowers were domestic firms seeking to expand output. Put simply, defining protectionism as import-restrictions-leading-to-domestic-output-expansion does not cover all of the 21st century forms of commerce.

Mercantilism, on the other hand, has been motivated by macroeconomic considerations. Improvement in the trade balance, which under the Gold Standard was associated with gold inflows or less gold outflow, provides another rationale for trade policy interventions (Irwin, 2012:160). This rationale typically calls for across-the-board measures (as seen in the 1930s) and could apply to export promotion as well as import restriction. For countries heavily reliant on imported resources, parts, or components, a naïve application of mercantilism would see large tariffs applied on imports even though they could ultimately reduce exports and the trade balance. Other forms of mercantilism include export-promoting trade-related investment measures and export credits. The relationship, however, between migration policy and mercantilism is unclear as well as the relationship between the latter and the protection of foreign intellectual property.

The very diversity of 21st century commerce calls for a definition of protectionism that moves beyond trade in goods and the balance of trade in goods. For the purposes of this chapter, a state measure is said to be protectionist if its implementation discriminates against one or more foreign commercial interests. The latter can be foreign importers, exporters, customers (including borrowers), workers, owners of foreign direct investments, and owners of foreign intellectual property. A state measure is not protectionist, then, if it does not discriminate between competing domestic and foreign commercial interests and between competing foreign commercial interests. The implicit, motivating assumption is that discrimination worsens the competitive position of at least one commercial party and so distorts market outcomes.

Several comments about this definition of protectionism are in order. First, the range of potential discrimination envisaged goes well beyond those state measures covered by existing WTO agreements. Compliance with WTO agreements in the early 21st century need not imply the absence of discrimination. Confining the monitoring or analysis of protectionism to state measures covered by WTO accords may miss commercially significant forms of discrimination.

Second, a state measure may include discrimination against foreign commercial interests but be motivated by some other, perhaps reasonable, policy objective. During the recent global economic crisis, some of the discriminatory measures in the financial sector were discriminatory but were motivated by the desire to stabilize financial markets. What is important here is to discern whether the discrimination was absolutely necessary to achieve financial market stabilization. Just because a discriminatory component was included in a state measure, it does not imply that discrimination is central to solving the market failure in question.[6]

Indeed, one might ask what evidence is there that non-discriminatory alternatives were considered to the discriminatory alternative and the appropriate comparisons concerning effectiveness made. Without these justifications, there probably ought to be a presumption that the state decision-makers in question were acting as if they wanted to secure a non-discriminatory policy objective partly or wholly at the expense of foreign commercial interests.

---

[6]On this view, then, a state measure could include more than one component with some being discriminatory and others being non-discriminatory.

Third, if it could be shown that a discriminatory state measure was the first best response of a government to a market failure then there might be a case for excluding such a measure from the definition of protectionism, or at least differentiating between those discriminatory measures that are first-best policy responses and those that are not. It has yet to be established how much contemporary discrimination can be so defended. Now that there is a substantial paper trail on contemporary protectionism,[7] it is not enough to note the logical possibility that some discrimination could be first best. It would be all the more convincing to show that much contemporary discrimination is first best.

Overall, a discrimination-based definition of protectionism better meets the realities of 21st century commerce than one based on restricting imports or improving the trade balance. A shift towards a broader definition is not without its costs (in terms of data availability) and opponents (the innate conservatism of researchers and policymakers). With respect to the researchers, it is understandable that the risk-averse prefer to analyze policy instruments for which there is an established literature and easily downloadable datasets. With respect to the policymakers, it may be convenient to narrowly define protectionism if that discourages the media, international organizations, and others from looking for discrimination elsewhere. For some the choice of the width of definition of protectionism is quite possibly a strategic matter.

In addition to a broader notion of protectionism, in considering the performance of the WTO due account should be taken of the nature of the systemic financial crisis facing governments. The working assumption here is that the recent systemic financial crisis saw a substantial contraction in many leading macroeconomic aggregates, was almost simultaneous in its timing, and started with the freezing up of financial markets and associated short-term lending to commercial enterprises, including those engaged in cross-border commerce. Such crises are unlike ordinary business cycles, industry-specific collapses, or one-off sharp movements in nominal exchange rates that motivate many analyses of commercial policy choice. Arguably the demands upon and constraints faced by policymakers are different during systemic crises and this ought to be taken into

---

[7]To facilitate research on such matters, the data source used in this chapter states in its publicly available reports when a neutral public policy objective is used to justify the implementation of a discriminatory measure and, wherever available, the official source describing the state measure.

account when considering the impact of international accords, such as
the WTO.

The first important point to be made here is that the financial nature of
the systemic crisis had important implications for the form of help sought
by firms and the discrimination employed by governments. It is now widely
accepted that the real consequences of the failure of financial markets to
advance funds began in 2008. Firms faced being starved of short-term
finance, which in a modern monetary economy allows them to cover the
period between cost outlays and the receipt of sales revenue. Unable to
pay their staff or suppliers, firms with limited cash reserves found they
had to sell off assets, lay off staff or, in the limit, shut down. The system-
wide nature of the financial market collapse meant that the real economy
quickly faced substantial bankruptcies, output declines, and employment
losses unless governments intervened. Associated fears caused firms and
employees to retrench, cutting aggregate demand. The fall in imports and
exports was reinforced by a collapse in trade finance.[8]

The economy-wide demand for cash by firms at the beginning of the systemic crisis made import-restricting measures a particularly blunt instrument for transferring resources from foreigners to local firms, not least
because local buyers of imports would take time to complete or cancel existing contracts and switch to domestic suppliers.[9] Far faster was to offer cash
to firms operating within a government's jurisdiction, either through loans,
subsidies, credit guarantees paid for directly by governments or through
national banking systems instructed to advance funds (sometimes in return
for bailouts received by those same banks).

Where does the potential for discrimination against foreign commercial
interests arise in offering short-term finance? In two ways, inadvertently and
deliberately. With respect to the former, recall that domestic firms' motives
in seeking state aid was to prevent or limit capacity and employment reductions. Even those governments that did not impose conditions on recipients
of financial aid ought to have realized that slowing down capacity reduction

---

[8]See Baldwin (2009) for an account of the collapse of world trade during the recent
systemic crisis.

[9]Furthermore, the falling imports at the beginning of the crisis would have made it
particularly difficult to show that foreign rivals to domestic firms had "materially" injured
the latter, as is required in most national antidumping and countervailing duty laws.
At the onset of the crisis only across-the-board import restrictions would have helped
domestic firms generate cash, but as argued in the main text advancing funds directly
or through the banking system was a more effective alternative.

at home will keep more goods on world markets, shifting the burden of supply contraction (demand had contracted during the crisis) to rival firms in other jurisdictions.[10]

In other cases during the recent systemic crisis, on certain occasions, "strings" were deliberately attached to the receipt of financial aid.[11] Some strings called for repatriation of production from abroad, others to limit or avoid job losses at production plants at home, and others for greater sourcing of inputs and materials for domestic suppliers. Indeed, other than collect revenues, much of what could be accomplished by the imposition of headline-catching tariffs could be delivered far more quietly through financial aid injections with strings attached.

In sum, while short-term financial aid stabilized production at low prices, sector-by-sector it also stalled the reduction of over-capacity and thereby hampered the restoration of profitability. The demand for short-term cash injections from domestic firms provided governments with plenty of leverage over applicants for state aid, leverage that could be far more targeted than imposing tariffs. Some governments used that leverage to force firms to retreat from their longer-term strategies of integration into the world economy. Combined with the depth and uncertain length of the systemic crisis, even those firms that did not need financial injections initially thought twice about criticising any discrimination, lest their firm too need aid in the future. Under these circumstances, corporate opposition was muted, probably far more so than if tariffs had been employed. The financial nature of the recent systemic crisis, and the fears it induced, shaped the form of government intervention sought and created plenty of opportunities for discrimination against foreign commercial interests.

---

[10]Sharp demand falls in a sector may have resulted in a market price below the minimum levels of average variable costs of numerous domestic firms. Faced with the prospect of widespread shutdowns in sector, with its associated knock-on effects on unemployment and business confidence, government subsidies related to variable costs or output may have kept firms producing when they would have otherwise terminated production in the short run. The impact of the subsidies will be to effectively steepen the world supply curve in the sector in question, causing prices to fall further and possibly below the shutdown conditions of firms operating in jurisdictions where governments are not offering such subsidies or offering less generous subsidies. In this manner, the apparently innocuous short-term financial assistance of governments to firms during the recent crisis may have shifted the burden of adjustment to jurisdictions unable, less able, or unwilling to offer comparable subsidies.

[11]It is possible that special interest groups influenced governments in the design of these conditions.

Once the crisis got under way, other opportunities for discrimination against foreign commercial interests presented themselves. Three come to mind. First, the fiscal stimulus packages enacted in the first half of 2009 afforded an opportunity to shift demand away from foreign suppliers. Second, as imports began to stabilize in 2009 and then rebound in 2010, the rising level of imports made it easier for domestic firms to show they had been "materially injured" by foreign sales, thereby making filing trade defence cases more attractive. Third, as unemployment levels rose, discrimination against foreign workers or against foreign migrants became more politically attractive in some jurisdictions.

The second important feature of the systemic crisis is its simultaneous effect on trading nations, in particular, the larger trading nations. A systemic crisis is, by definition, far reaching and affects many national economies at the same time. Given the highly interconnected nature of financial markets and bank linkages, those affected economies faced the same financial market freeze at roughly the same time. As a result governments almost certainly faced similar, acute pressures for state intervention and the temptation to discriminate when initially designing financial aid packages and, subsequently, fiscal stimulus packages.

Most game theoretic models of trade policy choice consider deviations by a single government. Typically, the assessment of the effectiveness of a proposed international trade rule turns on whether the short-term gains to a party deviating from such a rule are less than the longer-term losses once retaliation by other parties is taken into account. The techniques used to assess international trade rules ought to be revised for systemic crises when many, possibly every, government has an incentive to deviate from a given rule at the same time.[12]

Under these circumstances, an alternative to punishing unilateral deviations presents itself. It is not beyond the wit of the larger players to either turn a blind eye to other players' deviations in return for similar treatment. The recognition also that "those who live in glass houses do not throw stones" is important in that it reminds each player that every other player has evidence on the former's transgressions, evidence which can be used to great effect later. Under such an alternative scenario governments might

---

[12]Those trained in game theory will recognise the distinction being made here as that between Nash deviations and Coalitional deviations, and the solution concepts Strong Nash Equilibrium and Coalition-Proof Nash Equilibrium associated with the latter (see Aumann, 1959 and Bernheim *et al.*, 1987, respectively).

also take another step. Such players may deliberately adopt and promote a definition of protectionism — such as tariffs and quotas or even "compliance with existing WTO rules" — that conveniently excludes much of the meaningful discrimination being undertaken. In a systemic crisis, then, it is not clear that "tough" unilateral enforcement of each party's rights is the only outcome. Conspiracies of silence may be an attractive alternative.

Having said this, is it not clear that a tacit agreement to refrain from complaining about each other's discrimination is a particularly robust outcome. If every player has plenty of information about everyone else's misdeeds, then a set of accusations (perhaps triggered by some external foreign policy or other circumstance) might quickly degenerate into mutual recrimination.[13] The considerations in this paragraph and the last one suggest that absence of bitter recrimination at the WTO during the recent systemic crisis may not be such a mystery after all and may not last either.

In short, that the simultaneous nature of systemic crises and the fact that the potentially sharp economic contractions create similar incentives for governments to intervene in markets may call for a rethink in how to model the incentives to deviate from WTO accords and the incentives to engage in dispute settlement or other forms of conflict management (including outright denial). Knowing how these incentives play out during a systemic crisis might affect the types of binding multilateral trade accords governments are willing to sign in the first place, bearing in mind those governments will anticipate that from time to time there may be a systemic economic crisis.[14]

The purpose of this section has been to reorient the discussion of protectionism towards 21st century circumstances. Once due account is taken of the various characteristics of contemporary cross-border transactions and of the recent systemic economic crisis, in particular its simultaneous nature, then it is possible to rationalise some of what has been observed over the past few years and to understand the importance of much of what is to be documented in the section to come. Ultimately, these considerations

---

[13]The recent (October 2011) compilation by the US of a list of crisis-era subsidies that China has allegedly implemented and the official Chinese response, both communicated through the WTO, might signal the start of mutual recriminations. Likewise, the growing number of disputes concerning subsidies to solar power, which has involved disagreements among China, the European Communities, India, and the US, is another example. See the 10th report of the *Global Trade Alert* (Evenett, 2011a) for details.

[14]Barrett (1999) takes some interesting first steps in this regard.

and others that follow will shape the assessment of the effectiveness of the WTO's obligations during the recent global economic downturn.

3 The Resort to Discrimination Against Foreign Commercial Interests Since the First Crisis-Era G20 Summit in November 2008

This account of contemporary protectionism is based upon the data collected by the independent trade policy monitoring initiative, the Global Trade Alert (GTA).[15] Launched in June 2009, this initiative has sought to document as many state measures as possible that may affect foreign commercial interests and that were implemented during or after November 2008. This start date coincides with the first crisis-era heads-of-government G20 summit in Washington DC, when government leaders pledged to eschew protectionism. As such the Global Trade Alert initiative was able to monitor compliance with the G20 pledge and, consistent with that role, ten reports have been issued by the GTA team and a website that can be accessed by all. By November 2011, over 16,800 distinct visitors had visited this site 15 times or more since its creation, a number which represents a large share of the (admittedly informal) initial estimates of the likely interested expert audience.[16] A more extensive account of the GTA database and practice can be found in Evenett (2009) and on the initiative's website.

The work of the Global Trade Alert has received considerable attention since it was launched in June 2009. Senior policymakers, including the President of the World Bank, the President of the European Central Bank, the President of Switzerland, among others, have mentioned the GTA in their speeches, as have Ministers and Ambassadors from developing countries. According to one academic citation website[17], in its two-and-a-half year history the phrase "Global Trade Alert" had by November 2011 been mentioned in 281 papers. One of the earlier phrases used to characterise contemporary protectionism, namely, "murky protectionism," that was based on evidence collected by the GTA and introduced by Baldwin and Evenett

---

[15] As indicated earlier, the author is the coordinator of the GTA initiative.

[16] When the GTA was launched its associates were asked to estimate the likely number of repeat users of the website. Every estimate lied between 10,000 to 20,000. It is, of course, possible that these initial estimates were wrong or that the community interested in commercial policy matters has expanded during the crisis.

[17] *Harzing's Publish or Perish.*

(2009), has also been mentioned in 294 academic papers. *Factiva* identifies 282 distinct reports in national and international media referring to the Global Trade Alert's work.

In the GTA database, the unit of analysis is the announcement of a state measure. The announcement could contain a single change in government policy or many changes. Rather than arbitrarily chop up each state measure into component parts, the GTA team seeks to identify which policy changes are associated with an announcement and whether those policy changes alter the relative treatment of any potentially competing domestic and foreign commercial interests. Consistent with the arguments made in the previous section concerning the diverse nature of 21st century cross-border commerce, the GTA does not confine itself to a predefined set of possibly relevant policy measures, nor to the policy measures that are covered by WTO accords.

Announcements of intentions to change policies are included in the GTA database as well as implemented measures, the former being consistent with the goal of shedding light on government plans as well as their acts. By November 2011, just over 2000 state measures had been investigated by the GTA team and reports published on the GTA website, www.globaltradealert.org. Table 1 provides an annual breakdown of measures investigated by the GTA team.

It is important to bear in mind that the less transparent forms of discrimination (which it turns out that governments have resorted to frequently in recent years) take longer to discover, document, and analyse. As a result, there are reporting lags which tend to yield unduly low initial estimates of the quantum of protectionism in the most recent quarters and years. As many GTA reports have shown, initial estimates of the number of protectionist measures implemented per quarter have had to be revised substantially upwards over time. Consequently, little can be learned from a low first estimate of protectionism in any given quarter.[18] On the contrary, a high first estimate (as was found in Q1 2009 and Q3 2011) may be much more serious for, if anything, quarterly totals get substantially revised upwards over time.

---

[18]Little faith should therefore be placed in news or international organization reports that claim loudly that they have found few protectionist measures in a recent quarter. As argued in the main text later, such instant assessments in 2010 may have lulled some into a false sense of security.

Table 1. Total Number of State Measures Reported in the GTA Database, by Year.

Statistic	As of November 2011		November 2008 – October 2009		November 2009 – October 2010		November 2010 – October 2011	
	Total	Total except unfair trade and safeguards investigations	Total	Total except unfair trade and safeguards investigations	Total	Total except unfair trade and safeguards investigations	Total	Total except unfair trade and safeguards investigations
Total number of measures in GTA database	2001	1484	664	496	606	469	463	354
Total number of measures coded green	484	397	129	94	167	147	133	123
Total number of measures coded amber	490	282	96	56	110	59	89	54
Total number of measures coded red	1027	805	439	346	329	263	241	177

The GTA employs a traffic light system to characterize the likely discriminatory impact of a state measure, should it be implemented. A state measure that has been implemented and is "almost certainly" harmful to some foreign commercial interests is classified "red." An amber indicator is given in the following three circumstances: when a state measure is implemented and is "likely" to harm foreign commercial interests; when a state measures is implemented and includes two or more policy changes, one of which when implemented will "likely" harm a foreign commercial interest; and those state measures that are pending and, if implemented, would be "almost certainly" discriminatory. In what follows, the total number of protectionist or discriminatory measures is referred to as the sum of the implemented red and amber measures (bearing in mind that not every amber measure is an implemented measure). A state measure is labelled green if its implementation involves an improvement in the treatment of a foreign commercial interest or no change.

A state measure is tracked over time and its classification can change as the evidential base changes. For example, the announcement of an investigation of an antidumping investigation is initially listed as amber (as the measure has yet not been implemented). Should the investigation result in duties being imposed the measure switches to red; if the investigation results in no duties being imposed the measure switches to green.[19]

Tables 1–3 provide summary statistics by year and by traffic light classification (discriminatory impact) for all the measures in the GTA database, for the implemented measures in the GTA database, and for the measures implemented by the G20 countries in the GTA database (the latter being of interest given the pledges concerning protectionism made at successive G20 summits.) The differences in totals between Tables 1 and 2 reflect the fact that nearly 20 percent of the entries in the GTA database (around

---

[19]This has important implications for the interpretation of the total number of "green" measures in the GTA database. Table 2 reports 406 green measures have been implemented as of November 2011. It would be wrong to conclude that these were all measures that benefit foreign commercial interests. Some of the 406 measures are trade defence investigations that have concluded with no duties being imposed. For this reason, as well as the disagreement among the trade policy community as to whether trade defence measures are discriminatory, Tables 1–3 reported in this chapter include totals with and without trade defence investigations. Table 2, therefore, reports that 355 state measures not involving trade defence were implemented by November 2011 and were classified as green. This is a more accurate estimate of the total number of liberalizing measures implemented during the crisis era.

Table 2. Total Number of Measures Implemented Worldwide, by Year.

Statistic	As of November 2011		November 2008 – October 2009		November 2009 – October 2010		November 2010 – October 2011	
	Total	Total except unfair trade and safeguards investigations	Total	Total except unfair trade and safeguards investigations	Total	Total except unfair trade and safeguards investigations	Total	Total except unfair trade and safeguards investigations
Total number of measures in GTA database	1593	1309	606	483	537	458	435	349
Total number of measures coded green	406	355	122	92	154	143	131	121
Total number of measures coded amber	160	149	45	45	54	52	63	51
Total number of measures coded red	1027	805	439	346	329	263	241	177

Table 3. Total Number of Measures Implemented by the G20 Countries, by Year.

Statistic	As of November 2011		November 2008 – October 2009		November 2009 – October 2010		November 2010 – October 2011	
	Total	Total except unfair trade and safeguards investigations	Total	Total except unfair trade and safeguards investigations	Total	Total except unfair trade and safeguards investigations	Total	Total except unfair trade and safeguards investigations
Total number of measures in GTA database	1046	805	359	258	336	266	342	273
Total number of measures coded green	265	229	70	49	93	84	103	97
Total number of measures coded amber	103	97	19	19	36	35	47	42
Total number of measures coded red	678	479	270	190	207	147	192	134

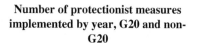

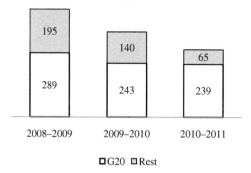

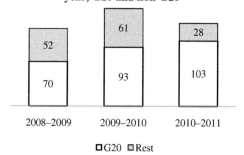

Fig. 1.   The G20's Rising Share of Protectionist Measures.

400 state measures) concern pending state measures, announced but not implemented. Over half of the state measures reported by the GTA team are classified red or almost certainly discriminatory (see Table 1). Of the total number of implemented measures, the share of almost certainly discriminatory measures rises over time to two-thirds. Comparing Tables 2 and 3, and examining Figure 1, it is clear that the proportion of contemporary protectionism accounted for by the G20 countries has actually risen through the crisis.

While the focus during the recent crisis has tended to be on protectionism, in fact a number of state measures to liberalise state commerce have been implemented. Table 2 and Figure 1 summarize some of the key evidence in this regard. Three-hundred-and-fifty-five liberalizing measures have been undertaken as compared to 954 measures involving some discrimination. If anything, the ratio of liberalizing to discriminatory measures has been rising over time, as has the G20's share of the world total. The last two paragraphs suggest that there is interesting within-crisis variation in the resort to protectionism that could be subject of further analysis.

The quarter-by-quarter variation in the resort to protectionism is plotted in Figure 2. Experience has shown that the reporting lags associated with finding and documenting the less transparent forms of protectionism produced a downward bias in the reported totals for later quarters. For example, by November 2011 the GTA had documented 150 discriminatory measures implemented in Q1 2009, when fears about protectionism were acute. The GTA's first estimate of Q1 2009 protectionism, published in September 2009, was only 77. It has been quite remarkable how much some

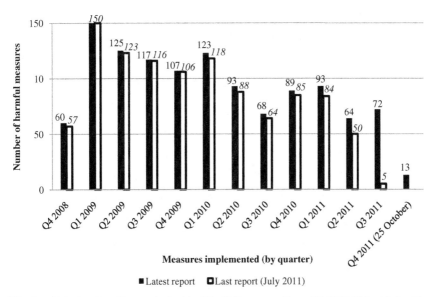

■Latest report   ◻Last report (July 2011)

Fig. 2.   Deteriorating Prospects for the World Economy Since Q4 2010 Coincided with an Increased Resort to Discrimination in 2011.

Notes: The total quarterly number of harmful measures for Q1–Q3 2011 is converging quickly to the 100–120 range seen in 2009. Q3 2010 seems more anomalous as time goes by. In Figure 2, a harmful measure is taken to be one that has been implemented since November 2008 and is almost certainly discriminatory (coded red) or likely to be discriminatory (coded amber).

quarterly totals have been revised upwards over time, and this has complicated the interpretation of the intertemporal record. At first, it looked as
if 2009 saw a terrible outbreak of protectionism followed by a much calmer
2010, hence the title of the GTA's November 2010 report "Tensions Contained... For Now." However, it now seems that Q3 2010 was an outlier,
coinciding with what turned out to be over-optimistic estimates of the pace
of the global economic growth in the second half of 2010 and expected for
the first half of 2011. The rate implementation of discriminatory measures
jumped in Q4 2010 and Q1 2011. The initial estimates for protectionism
implemented in Q3 2011 are particularly worrying, especially given the
precedent of Q1 2009. Worse, as the latest GTA report has documented,
a number of these protectionist measures were across-the-board measures
taken by larger trading nations.

It would be fair to say that the GTA's reporting on protectionism over
time has been summarised in less sanguine terms than the reports prepared
for the G20 leaders by the World Trade Organization, United Nations Conference on Trade and Development, and Organization of Economic Cooperation and Development. Interestingly, in the first half of 2009 and second
half of 2011 there was little difference in the interpretation of the factual
record between the GTA and official reports (both reports expressed considerable concern about protectionism.) During the intervening period (second
half of 2009 to first half of 2011), in particular in 2010, differences emerged
in interpreting the falls in initial totals of protectionism from the 2009
highs. With the publication of each GTA report, the upward revisions of
the total protectionism imposed in Q1 2010 are such that they do not look
very dissimilar to the quarterly totals in the nadir of 2009. The increases
in the totals for Q2 and Q4 2010, if continued, will soon yield results not
dissimilar from 2009. All of this points to the unusual dip in protectionism
in Q3 2010, which some may have over-interpreted.

One underlying factor that probably contributed to differences in views
as to the seriousness of protectionism in the recent is that the range of
state measures that the GTA considers is wider than that of certain official
reports. Some of the official reports included estimates of the total amount
of trade covered by selected trade barriers (typically tariff changes and trade
defence measures), and even reputable media sources, such as *The Financial
Times*, occasionally reported the total trade affected *as if* that accurately
reflected the sum of the trade affected by *all* crisis-era protectionism. It
was for this reason that in 2010 Johannes Fritz and I assembled data on
the likely trade impact of 22 deliberately discriminatory, wide-ranging state

interventions[20] that fell outside the narrow range considered by the official organizations. We were confident of the data collected on 15 of these 22 measures. Together, these 15 discriminatory measures alone affected over US$1.6 trillion of trade, more than 10 percent of total world imports in 2008. Given that many other discriminatory measures have been imposed during the crisis era, the total amount of commerce affected will be larger. To date, no one has challenged the estimates of "jumbo protectionism" found in Evenett and Fritz (2010). Those estimates are summarized by measure in Appendix Table A1.

One of the most significant findings of the Global Trade Alert monitoring concerns the composition of discriminatory measures that governments have resorted to since November 2008. Tables 4 and 5 provide information on the composition of discrimination and its inter-temporal variation. While 416 reports in the GTA database relate to tariffs, only 188 of those involve restrictions on trade. In contrast, 273 state measures involved some form of discriminatory bailout or subsidy (see Table 4).[21] The top 10 most used discriminatory state measures include non-tariff barriers, export taxes and restrictions, migration measures, and public procurement measures, all of which are subject to limited or no multilateral trade rules. Taken together, tariff increases and trade defence measures account for no more than 37 percent of all the protectionist measures taken since November 2008.[22] In the light of this finding, the emphasis on the former two measures in many official reports and in much recent research purporting to analyse contemporary protectionism is bewildering.

---

[20]The list of 22 state measures, therefore, includes three currency devaluations where the implementing government publicly stated that the purpose of the devaluation was to help domestic commercial interests at the expense of importers, etc. Not every government that devalues its currency makes blatant statements in this regard. The GTA team took the view that only where the stated intention of the government to devalue its currency was to harm foreign commercial interests would such a competitive devaluation be listed in the GTA database. For this reason, as of November 2011, only 5 competitive devaluations are listed in the GTA database. Given the difficulties interpreting exchange rate movements, it is quite possible that other perfectly reasonable analysts might have adopted a different classification system.

[21]Let's set to one side one possible concern. In the GTA database, 201 of the 273 discriminatory bailouts and subsidies were paid to firms outside of the financial sector. The extent of discriminatory subsidisation of the manufacturing sector in a number of industrialised countries is perhaps one of the least appreciated facts of contemporary protectionism.

[22]See also Figure 5.

Appendix Table A1.   The List of Jumbo Discriminatory Measures Prepared in 2010, Presented in Descending Order of Trade Covered.

No.	Implementing jurisdiction: Title of measure	Tariff lines affected	Percentage of total tariff lines	Trading partners affected	G20 members affected	Implementer is G20 member?	Total trade value (2008, billions US$) potentially affected	Share of relevant national trade flow (percent)	Trade flow used to compute last column	Included in conservative estimate of trade coverage?
1.	China: Export tax rebates.	243	22.17	155	17	Yes	412.0	28.80	Total exports	
2.	United States of America: Buy American provisions in stimulus package	113	9.63	106	16	Yes	337.8	15.60	Total imports	No
3.	China: Implementation of State Council Opinions on imported goods	80	7.64	61	15	Yes	243.2	21.47	Total imports	No
4.	Russia and Belarus: Increase in export tariffs on crude oil and oil products	5	0.90	78	15	Yes	243.0	48.51	Sum of total exports for Russia and Belarus	
5.	UK: Temporary aid for the production of green products	121	10.65	98	18	Yes	161.1	25.49	Total imports	
6.	China: Adjustment of import tariffs policy on key technical equipment	82	7.83	52	15	Yes	112.4	9.92	Total imports	

(Continued)

Appendix Table A1. (*Continued*)

No.	Implementing jurisdiction: Title of measure	Tariff lines affected	Percentage of total tariff lines	Trading partners affected	G20 members affected	Implementer is G20 member?	Total trade value (2008, billions US$) potentially affected	Share of relevant national trade flow (percent)	Trade flow used to compute last column	Included in conservative estimate of trade coverage?
7.	Venezuela: Devaluation of the Bolivar	784	100.00	71	17	No	108.6	82.97	Total imports plus total exports	
8.	Kazakhstan: Announced 25% devaluation of the national currency	716	100.00	96	19	No	106.5	97.76	Total imports plus total exports	
9.	Nigeria: Deliberate devaluation of the Naira	561	100.00	105	19	No	104.8	95.26	Total imports plus total exports	
10.	Russia: The programme of the anti-crisis measures of the Russian Government — 2009	120	12.33	95	18	Yes	70.0	26.21	Total imports	
11.	Japan: State endorsement of private initiative to raise food self-sufficiency	130	11.67	110	15	Yes	53.4	7.00	Total imports	
12.	Brazil: New credit line for exports of consumer goods	196	25.49	131	18	Yes	50.6	25.55	Total exports	

(*Continued*)

Appendix Table A1. (*Continued*)

No.	Implementing jurisdiction: Title of measure	Tariff lines affected	Percentage of total tariff lines	Trading partners affected	G20 members affected	Implementer is G20 member?	Total trade value (2008, billions US$) potentially affected	Share of relevant national trade flow (percent)	Trade flow used to compute last column	Included in conservative estimate of trade coverage?
13.	Russia: Subsidized loans to producers of certain type of machineries	87	8.94	62	15	Yes	48.4	18.14	Total imports	
14.	India: Extension of service tax refund for exporters	146	17.40	122	18	Yes	45.0	24.73	Total exports	
15.	India: Pre- and post-shipment export credit	146	17.40	122	18	Yes	45.0	24.73	Total exports	No
16.	Indonesia: Import tariff increases on certain products that compete with locally manufactured products	216	24.00	92	17	Yes	33.7	26.04	Total imports	
17.	Indonesia, Malaysia, and Thailand: Limiting rubber exports to 915,000 tons during 2009.	26	3.48	105	18	Yes	26.3	5.14	Sum of total exports for all 3 implementers.	
18.	Argentina: Extension of tax exemptions for locally produced capital goods	194	24.84	63	17	Yes	25.0	43.49	Total imports	No

(*Continued*)

Appendix Table A1. (*Continued*)

No.	Implementing jurisdiction: Title of measure	Tariff lines affected	Percentage of total tariff lines	Trading partners affected	G20 members affected	Implementer is G20 member?	Total trade value (2008, billions US$) potentially affected	Share of relevant national trade flow (percent)	Trade flow used to compute last column	Included in conservative estimate of trade coverage?
19.	Russia: Public procurement price advantage to domestic producers	180	18.50	89	17	Yes	23.0	8.62	Total imports	No
20.	Russia: Preferences to domestic producers in ammendments to Government Procurement Law	174	17.88	88	17	Yes	21.8	8.17	Total imports	
21.	Russia: Temporary import tariff introduction on certain type of machinery	26	2.67	57	16	Yes	20.6	7.71	Total imports	
22.	France: More restrictive public procurement rules for construction work tenders	24	2.08	60	15	Yes	12.3	1.76	Total imports	No

Source: Evenett and Fritz (2010).

Table 4.   Ten Most Used State Measures to Discriminate Against Foreign Commercial Interests Since the First G20 Crisis Meeting (Ranked by the Total Number of Discriminatory Measures Imposed Since November 2008).

Statistic	As of November 2011		November 2008 – October 2009		November 2009 – October 2010		November 2010 – October 2011	
	Total	Total except unfair trade and safeguards investigations	Total	Total except unfair trade and safeguards investigations	Total	Total except unfair trade and safeguards investigations	Total	Total except unfair trade and safeguards investigations
Total number of measures in GTA database	1046	805	359	258	336	266	342	273
Total number of measures coded green	265	229	70	49	93	84	103	97
Total number of measures coded amber	103	97	19	19	36	35	47	42
Total number of measures coded red	678	479	270	190	207	147	192	134

Table 5. Ten Most Used State Measures to Discriminate Against Foreign Commercial Interests, by Year (Ranked by Total Number of Discriminatory Measures Imposed Since November 2008).

State measure	Number of discriminatory (red and amber) measures implemented.				
	As of November 2011	November 2008 – October 2009	November 2009 – October 2010	November 2010 – October 2011	
Bailout/state aid measure	274	168	84	24	
Trade defence measure (AD, CVD, safeguard)	236	93	68	76	
Tariff measure	188	72	75	41	
Non-tariff barrier (not otherwise specified)	111	26	20	65	
Export taxes or restriction	91	14	43	34	
Investment measure	64	15	27	22	
Migration measure	53	19	18	16	
Export subsidy	49	26	15	9	
Public procurement	47	29	13	5	
Local content requirement	33	12	13	8	

Another important difference concerns the estimates of the number of jurisdictions that the GTA team estimates are harmed by each type of measure. Trade defence measures target specific products and named trading partners, whereas tariff measures — like discriminatory bailouts, export taxes, and export subsidies — can distort the trade in many products and harm many trading partners' commercial interests. The last column in Table 4 highlights how few trading partners have been affected by trade defence measures in contrast to other forms of contemporary protectionism, with the exception of investment measures.

The variation in protectionism implemented in the three years since November 2008 is summarized in Table 5. For the first two years, discriminatory bailouts were the most frequently used form of protectionism. Only in the third year of the crisis (November 2010 – October 2011) did trade defence measures become the most resorted to discriminatory measure, whereas that year saw a collapse in the number of bailouts and tariff increases. In fact, non-tariff barriers come a close second to trade defence measures in the third year of the crisis. Overall, in none of the three years since November 2008 have the number of tariff increases and trade defence measures accounted for more than 40 percent of the protectionism imposed.

The fact that no countries have appeared to have broken their tariff bindings at the WTO seems to have deflected attention away from the question as whether the crisis has induced patterns of defensive behaviour by governments towards imported goods. Evenett (2011b) examined changes in various characteristics of national tariff regimes between 2005/2006 and 2009/2010, as reported in the relevant editions of the WTO publication *World Tariff Profiles*. While average tariff rates applied did not change much, those WTO members that tended to lower their tariffs during the crisis also tended to adopt a less uniform tariff regime (see Figure 3). The implications for welfare are ambiguous as the latter is known to lower welfare and the former is typically associated with improved resource allocation. Moreover, WTO members that tended to impose more tariff peaks during the crisis era (that is, tariffs above 15 percent) also tended to reduce the number of tariff lines where goods were imported duty-free (see Figure 4). Interesting cross-country variation in tariff responses requires further analysis — all the more interesting for such variation was accomplished within the constraints of WTO membership.

Important differences were found between the composition of protectionism implemented during the crisis and those pending measures, the potentially protectionist impact of which overhangs the multilateral trading

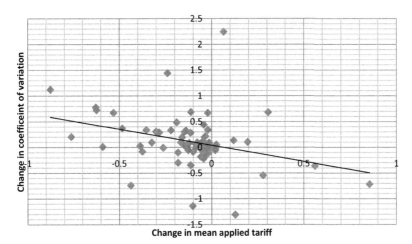

Fig. 3.   During the Crisis-Era Liberalization of Tariff Regimes Was Confined to Lowering Applied Tariff Rates, not the Variance in Those Tariff Rates.
Source: Evenett (2011b).

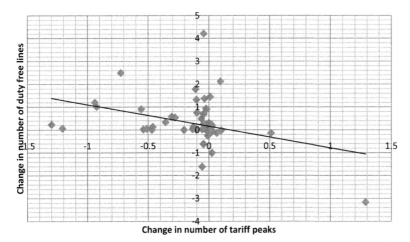

Fig. 4.   Of Those Countries That Altered Their Average Tariff Rates During the Crisis, Those That Created more Tariff Peaks also Extended Duty Free Market Access to Fewer Products.
Source: Evenett (2011b).

system (see Figures 5 and 6). While the composition of implemented protectionism has already been discussed, the composition of pending protectionism is heavily skewed towards trade defence measures. As counted by the number of state measures, 51 percent of pending measures are trade

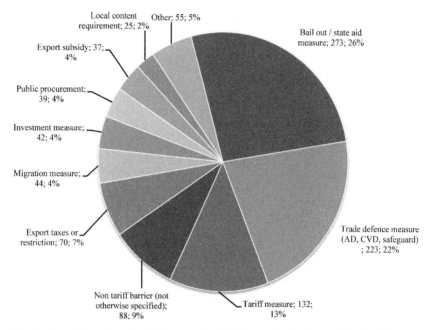

Fig. 5.   Top 10 Implemented Measures Used to Discriminate Against Foreign Commercial Interests Since the First G20 Crisis Meeting.

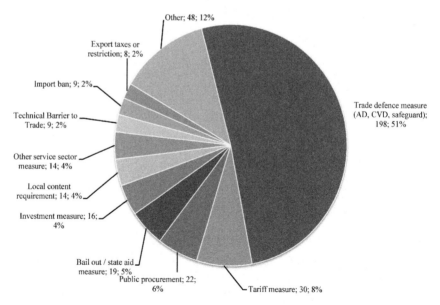

Fig. 6.   Top 10 Pending Measures That Target Foreign Commercial Interests.

defence measures. Given the targeted nature of trade defence measures and the propensity for other measures to affect more products and trading partners, it is quite possible that the pending public procurement, state aids, and other less traditional state measures would, if implemented, still have greater effect on resource allocation, trade flows, and welfare.

Turning from the form of protectionism to its perpetrators, Tables 6 and 7 and Figure 7 report the principal findings. Because the GTA initiative did not have the resources to conduct econometric analyses of every reported state measure, it was decided to report information that could be aggregated into (intermediate) indicators of harm done by each jurisdiction. Four such indicators were calculated for each jurisdiction: the number of almost certainly discriminatory measures implemented; the number of tariff lines affected by almost certainly discriminatory measures (where appropriate, zero otherwise); the number of sectors affected by almost certainly discriminatory measures; and the number of trading partners affected by almost certainly discriminatory measures. The methodology used to compute the final three measures is very conservative and is available from the author upon request. What has proved to be of some comfort is that the rankings of countries on all four metrics have proved to be highly correlated (Evenett, 2011c).

Table 6 ranks countries on all four metrics, listing the top 10 worst performers. The G20 countries are well represented in those lists. What is more the lists of top 5 worst jurisdictions are dominated by the EU 27 (that is, the combined effect of the measures taken by the European Commission and the 27 member states), China, and Argentina. One piece of good news implied by the data in Table 6 and on the GTA website is that only 11 nations have implemented discriminatory measures that cover more than a quarter of the possible product categories (and there are a number of larger trading nations not among this 11). This is in marked contrast to the Great Depression when many countries are said to have raised tariffs on all of their imports.

Interesting inter-temporal variation is reported in Table 7 and Figure 7 for individual jurisdictions and for certain groups of countries. The worldwide share of discriminatory measures imposed by the G20 countries has risen in each of the three years since their leaders declared their intention to eschew protectionism! Over time there has been a marked tendency to downplay trade policy matters at the G20 and perhaps the G20's growing worldwide share should be interpreted as evidence of weakened resolve against protectionism. No doubt defenders of the G20 will argue the "pledge

Table 6. Which Countries Have Inflicted the Most Harm?

Metric, Country in Specified Rank, Number

Rank	Ranked by number of (almost certainly) discriminatory measures imposed	Ranked by the number of tariff lines (product categories) affected by (almost certainly) discriminatory measures	Ranked by the number of sectors affected by (almost certainly) discriminatory measures	Ranked by the number of trading partners affected by (almost certainly) discriminatory measures
1	EU 27 (242)	Vietnam (927)	Algeria (62)	China (195)
2	Russian Federation (112)	Venezuela (786)	EU 27 (58)	EU 27 (181)
3	Argentina (111)	Kazakhstan (729)	China (47)	Argentina (175)
4	UK (59)	China (698)	Nigeria (45)	Germany (161)
5	Germany (58)	Nigeria (599)	Kazakhstan (43)	India (154)
6	India (56)	EU 27 (550)	Germany (42)	UK (154)
7	China (55)	Algeria (476)	USA (42)	Belgium (153)
8	France (51)	Russian Federation (439)	Ghana (41)	Finland (153)
9	Brazil (49)	Argentina (429)	Indonesia (40)	Indonesia (151)
10	Italy (47)	Indonesia (388)	Russian Federation (40)	France (150)

Note: There is no single metric to evaluate harm. Different policy measures affect different numbers of products, economic sectors, and trading partners. GTA reports four measures of harm.

Table 7. Protectionist Measures Implemented by Leading Trading Jurisdictions, by Year (Ranked by Total Number of Discriminatory Measures Imposed Since November 2008).

Implementing jurisdiction or group	As of November 2011	Number of discriminatory (red and amber) measures implemented		
		November 2008 – October 2009	November 2009 – October 2010	November 2010 – October 2011
G20	786	289	243	239
BRICs	313	120	93	101
EU 27	252	141	59	36
Russian Federation	127	53	46	28
Argentina	123	18	37	67
India	73	28	12	18
UK	62	18	15	22
Germany	61	27	13	18
Brazil	57	17	23	17
China	56	22	12	38
France	56	22	12	21
USA	29	9	12	7

worked" because the share would have been higher or possibly risen more. To be credible such a defence would have to account for the significant variation across the G20 in the resort to protectionism (shown in part in Figure 7). For example, the EU 27 group appears responsible for a falling share of measures implemented over time, while the BRIC nations account for a rising share.[23]

The frequency with which a jurisdiction's commercial interests have been harmed by contemporary protectionism is summarised in Table 8 and Figure 8. No single jurisdiction has been harmed more often than China,

---

[23]Leaving aside the matter of whether the G20 pledge on protectionism had any effect, the intertemporal changes witnessed are important. In terms of the number of measures implemented, the EU 27 group were quick to impose protectionism, whereas the BRICs only ratched up their share of worldwide protectionism well into the crisis. Whether this reflected tit-for-tat behaviour or emulation by the BRICs nations or differences in the degree or extent of economic harm felt between the BRICs nations and the EU 27 group is certainly worthy of further analysis. More generally, the differences with the G20 group and over time again reinforce the subtle point that it is most unlikely that the same factors drove protectionism before and during the crisis.

**Percentage of worldwide total of protectionist measures
implemented by jurisdiction(s) and year**

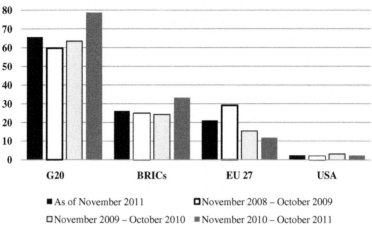

■ As of November 2011   □ November 2008 – October 2009
□ November 2009 – October 2010   ■ November 2010 – October 2011

Fig. 7.   The G20 Are Responsible for a Growing Share of Contemporary Protectionism.

Table 8.   Number of Times a Leading Trading Jurisdiction's Commercial Interests Have
Been Harmed, by Year (Ranked by Total Number of Discriminatory Measures Imposed
since November 2008).

Affected jurisdiction or group of jurisdictions	Number of discriminatory (red and amber) measures implemented that harm the jurisdiction in question.			
	As of November 2011	November 2008 – October 2009	November 2009 – October 2010	November 2010 – October 2011
G20	835	328	267	232
BRICs	684	267	227	184
China	574	229	190	151
EU 27	557	226	200	127
USA	457	193	154	108
Germany	425	184	153	86
France	370	161	134	71
UK	367	151	136	77
Italy	365	152	132	78
Korea	352	133	109	107
Netherlands	330	144	110	72
India	325	111	112	99
Brazil	250	116	82	49
Russia	195	88	74	31

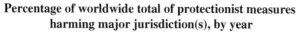

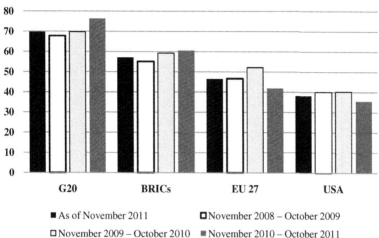

Percentage of worldwide total of protectionist measures harming major jurisdiction(s), by year

■ As of November 2011   ☐ November 2008 – October 2009
☐ November 2009 – October 2010   ■ November 2010 – October 2011

Fig. 8. The BRICs and Some Other G20 Members, but not the EU 27 and USA, Are the Target of a Growing Proportion of Contemporary Protectionism.

with a total of 574 measures harming at least some Chinese commercial interests. The numbers reported in Table 8 reveal that, with the exception of Brazil and India, every major trading jurisdiction has seen its commercial interests harmed over 300 times in the three years since the November 2008 summit. The fact that trade wars have not broken out does not mean that trading nations interests are unharmed. Water does not have to be at boiling point to cause considerable harm.

Approximately 70 percent of all measures harm one or more G20 country's trading interests. In fact, over time the proportion of discriminatory measures implemented that harm at least one G20 country has risen (Figure 8), a pattern found for the BRICs nations too. Interestingly, in the third year of the crisis (November 2010 – October 2011) the proportion of measures harming the EU 27 group and the USA fell.

Last, but not least in this overview of contemporary protectionism, is the sectoral incidence of discriminatory measures. That the financial sector is at the top of the list of beneficiaries of discrimination is perhaps not surprising, a finding that is almost entirely the consequence of bailouts given during November 2008 – October 2009 (see Table 9). In terms of number of discriminatory measures, what is striking about Table 9 is that so many of the most frequent recipients of contemporary protectionism are the very

Table 9. Number of Times Commercial Interests in an Economic Sector Have Been Harmed, by Year (Ranked by Total Number of Discriminatory Measures Imposed Since November 2008).

Sector	Number of discriminatory (red and amber) measures implemented that harm the sector in question.			
	As of November 2011	November 2008 – October 2009	November 2009 – October 2010	November 2010 – October 2011
81 (Financial intermediation services and auxiliary services therefore)	106	66	19	8
01 (Products of agriculture, horticulture and market gardening)	132	43	57	32
34 (Basic chemicals)	127	47	49	30
49 (Transport equipment)	124	61	45	18
41 (Basic metals)	123	62	37	23
44 (Special purpose machinery)	116	57	38	20
21 (Meat, fish, fruit, vegetables, oils and fats)	103	46	35	22
42 (Fabricated metal products, except machinery and equipment)	91	44	30	16
23 (Grain mill products, starches and starch products; other food products)	91	38	31	21
26 (Yarn and thread; woven and tufted textile fabrics)	91	33	36	22

smokestack and agricultural sectors that have traditionally been shielded from international competition by their governments. So while much has been made in policy circles of measures to support "green growth" and other new "economic growth poles." In fact, on some metrics, much contemporary protectionism has been captured by those sectors that have been successful in securing protectionism in the past (Aggarwal and Evenett, 2009). This finding is a useful reminder that while some aspects of contemporary protectionism may be different, not every aspect has changed. Sorting out explanations that account for what has changed (the composition of protectionism) and what has not (the sectoral composition of protectionism) may keep analysts busy for some time.

The purpose of this section has been to give a comprehensive overview of crisis-era protectionism. These facts will partially inform the assessment of the effectiveness of multilateral trade disciplines that follow.

While the focus here has been on contemporary protectionism, the finding that the composition of recent protectionism differs from that seen previously is both old and new. "New" in the sense that most recent protectionism was not in the form of tariff increases and trade defence measures, as has been the focus of so many studies of trade policy over the business cycle. "Old" in the sense that the historical pattern that in crises "new" forms of protectionism come to the fore — witnessed in the 1930s and documented then by the League of Nations and witnessed in the slump of the early 1980s and documented then by the GATT secretariat — has reasserted itself.

4 An Assessment of the Impact of WTO Rules During the Recent Systemic Crisis

The arguments made in this section will be principally qualitative, although they are informed by the quantitative evidence discussed earlier. Given the global economic crisis is not over, it is also appropriate to add that the assessment here is best thought of as one that is informed by the first three years of the recent systemic crisis. Subsequent events may confound the points that follow. Moreover, more data will undoubtedly be collected on behavior before and after the crisis, and this may facilitate the type of statistical examination that some find persuasive. Still, there are a number of useful points that can be made at this juncture.

One starting point is to ask on what basis could the WTO influence government behaviour during a systemic crisis? Here it will be useful to quote Irwin (2012:171) at length, for the argument presented is fairly representative of the views of many economists who follow WTO matters:[24]

> In the early 1930s, countries could impose higher tariff barriers unilaterally, without violating any international agreements or necessarily anticipating much of a foreign reaction. Today, WTO rules constrain the use of discretionary trade policy interventions. Countries may be tempted to violate WTO agreements for domestic political reasons, but they will have few illusions that they will escape from retaliation if they do. The WTO's dispute settlement mechanism has been a deterrent to the imposition of new trade barriers, forcing countries to think twice about taking actions that will reduce imports.

This quotation nicely distinguishes the 1930s situation from the incentives at work now, incentives that are based on binding WTO disciplines and dispute settlement. Some build upon this argument by noting that tariff barriers were raised across the board in the 1930s but not in the recent crisis, and then conclude that the WTO has stopped an economically destructive trade war. But does this story really hang together? What follows are some doubts.

The first doubt concerns the statement "WTO rules constrain the use of discretionary trade policy interventions." For many WTO members, for all intents and purposes this is simply not the case. Much has been made of the 1930s that saw the imposition of the infamous Smoot–Hawley tariffs which raised US tariffs by approximately 6 percent. Readers may be surprised to learn that in 2006, one year before the financial crisis began, no less than 85 members had average maximum allowed (that is, bound) tariff rates on manufactured goods that were 6 or more percentage points higher than their applied rates (*World Tariff Profiles*, 2006).

These 85 WTO members, representing more than half of the WTO membership and including important trading nations such as Australia, Brazil, India, Indonesia, Mexico Nigeria, South Africa, and Turkey, could all implement a Smoot–Hawley-like tariff without breaking their WTO obligations.[25] This is a matter of fact, not opinion. For 85 of the WTO's members the legal constraints on discretionary trade policy are so weak that

---

[24]Fairness to Irwin requires noting that a few pages later he offers some, in my view, realistic caveats to this starting view.

[25]So long as they organized each tariff increase that it did not exceed the bound level for the product in question.

they could not stop the return of 1930-style global protectionism![26] Readers might want to bear in mind that the above finding applies to manufactured imports, where it is widely acknowledged that multilateral trade rules are more stringent.[27] For most governments, the potential to discriminate in agricultural and service sector commerce without violating WTO obligations is even greater.

One could repeat the same exercise for circumstances that might be more appropriate to a systemic crisis. In a crisis a government may not want, or need, to raise tariffs across the board. Rather, the government might want to raise tariffs above 15 percent — normally associated with a "tariff peak" as it conveys a lot of protection to the import-competing firms in question — for a select group of industries. One might be interested in asking how many governments have such weak WTO limits on their tariffs that they could raise 15 percent or more tariffs on product categories equal to 5 percent or more of that country's tariff lines? On the eve of the crisis, the answer is that 67 WTO members were in the position to create so many tariff peaks without breaking their WTO obligations.

In sum, when it comes to their tariff regimes, the quintessential element of discretionary trade policy, it is not enough to look for violations to tariff bindings during the recent crisis and, having found none, conclude that all is well with WTO rules. Given the latitude in existing WTO bindings on tariffs, surely the correct question to ask is to what extent those rules *could ever* have been a constraint on tariff setting by many governments during the recent crisis?[28] If preventing the implementation of a Smoot–Hawley tariff is the right metric (and many making comparisons to the 1930s implicitly raise this standard), then for over half the WTO membership, their tariff obligations could not prevent a determined government

---

[26]For many of these WTO members, what has led to this outcome is that, since they last negotiated their maximum bound tariff rates on imported manufacturers in the Uruguay Round, they have unilaterally lowered their applied tariffs and this creates a larger gap between the average tariffs that they do charge and the maximum tariff rate that they are allowed to charge. In short, something other than WTO tariff bindings in manufacturing, has encouraged many WTO members to refrain from sizeable tariff increases during the recent crisis.

[27]Even with manufactured goods casual inspection of the WTO's *World Tariff Profiles* publication reveals that there are a large number of WTO members that have not agreed to bind 100 percent of their tariffs on imported manufactures.

[28]In this sense, the question posed in the title of this chapter may already cede too much ground to those who believe that the current multilateral trade disciplines have substantially constrained protectionism.

from repeating the mistakes of the 1930s. If governments chose not to raise tariffs much during the recent systemic crisis, then it is because those governments had other reasons not to restrict imports. The WTO cannot be credited with inducing such tariff restraint.

Two other important institutional considerations ought to be borne in mind when considering the bite of WTO rules. Both considerations relate to the WTO dispute settlement procedure, which is arguably much weaker than many realise. One less well-known feature of the WTO dispute settlement mechanism is that should a WTO member have a case brought against it for violating its trade obligations, and should that WTO member lose the case before the Panel, and subsequently lose an appeal before the Appellate Body, then that WTO member faces no sanctions and need offer no compensation to its harmed trading partner(s) so long as the WTO member withdraws the state measure that was found to have broken WTO rules.

What is the significance of this provision? Whether in a crisis or not, it is now far from clear that governments will, as Irwin puts it, "have few illusions that they will escape from retaliation if they do" break WTO rules. A cynical government could deliberately break the WTO's rules, knowing that it will take between several years before, ultimately, the Appellate Body ruling is handed down and the government has to withdraw the illegal measure. Factor in the allowed time to withdraw the offending measure and effectively a government is allowed to break WTO rules for three years without facing any threat of retaliation. Until the WTO Dispute Settlement Understanding is reformed, multi-year respite from any WTO rule is possible.

Worse, a deeply cynical government could implement illegal measure A, obtain relief from competition for some domestic commercial interests for around three years, withdraw measure A and then replace it (after a small period of time not to look too suspicious) with a different measure B, which may or may not be contested by trading partners at the WTO. If the cynical government has anything to fear, it is not the retaliation but rather the expectation that their measures will be challenged.[29]

---

[29] And possibly gaining a reputation as a serial flouter of WTO rules. But even the latter argument raises the awkward question that it is something other than the WTO dispute settlement understanding that may be effectively discouraging governments from flouting multilateral trade rules.

These are not hypothetical considerations. Such loopholes in the WTO's Dispute Settlement Understanding have already been exploited by governments needing a medium-term respite from multilateral trade rules. The leading example is surely the US government's imposition of a blatantly WTO-illegal safeguard action on steel imports in the early part of the first administration of President George W. Bush. That measure was withdrawn after the WTO ruled against the US in a ruling handed down in November 2004 that came well after the midterm elections of 2002, an election that the illegal measure was supposed to have influenced. It is unfortunate that President Bush said at the time the measure was removed "... these safeguard measures have now achieved their purpose... it is time to lift them." In sum, only a poorly briefed government need worry about retaliation under the current WTO Dispute Settlement Understanding.

The second consideration is that whatever threat the WTO Dispute Settlement Understanding constitutes, it requires another WTO member to bring a case against an errant government. There are plenty of reasons in normal business conditions why some governments do not bring cases against others (foreign policy considerations, risking aid flows, doubts about ultimate compliance, as well as a reluctance to raise tariffs on its own imports to "punish" a trading partner). While these reasons may well apply during a systemic crisis, another factor alluded to earlier comes into play. The simultaneous and deeply painful nature of a systemic crisis may mean that governments want to deviate from any international rules, including WTO rules, in similar ways.

Under these circumstances, governments do not have to go so far as to suspend the WTO's rules when they can just quietly agree not to bring dispute settlement cases against one another. With a relatively small number of large trading nations, orchestrating a policy of "turning a blind eye" to each others' infractions may not be that difficult and might appeal to the sensibilities of diplomats who do not want inter-governmental disputes during a time of adverse economic circumstances. In this manner a collective deviation from the WTO rules could be effected while the polite fiction could be maintained that multilateral trade rules are being adhered to.

The last argument, however, cannot quite account for the contemporary protectionism documented in the last section. The argument in the last paragraph would allow for collective violations of the most transparent WTO rules, and these have not been observed in recent years. One countervailing factor is the media, whose reporting would probably expose any serial attempt to blatantly break WTO rules, pose difficult questions, and so make it hard to sustain the polite fiction of compliance. Instead, the final piece of the puzzle is provided by the financial origins of the recent systemic crisis.

As argued earlier, once financial markets froze and the real sector could not rollover their loans, then the principle demand of business from government was for cash not customers (the latter of which the traditional forms of protectionism can deliver to import-competing interests.) The simultaneous nature of the crisis meant that many governments faced pressure to bail out firms around the same time. As some started giving bailouts, these measures forced the burden of adjustment on to trading partners' firms and employees, whose governments then retaliated by granting bailouts of their own. For sure, some governments added blatantly discriminatory strings (often unofficially) to the bailouts.

The demands for bailouts become so frequent that by the time each major trading nation appreciated the damage being done to their commercial interests by the bailouts of others, each had implemented so many discriminatory bailouts that the less confrontational approach was to adhere to the rule that "people who live in glass houses don't throw stones."[30] Add to this the facts that the WTO rules on subsidies are not that far reaching, that no organization was in place to actively monitor this less-than-conventional form of discrimination, and that therefore there was no smoking gun that the media could report on without doing a substantial amount of research on its own. Taken together, this meant that all the preconditions for a collective deviation from WTO principles could be affected. A similar dynamic almost certainly developed with respect to discriminatory stimulus packages, implemented in 2008 and 2009, where WTO rules again remain underdeveloped.

That so many governments simultaneously wanted to counter the credit freeze, provide stimuli to national economies and create employment opportunities probably accounts for the drive to exploit the looseness (or absence) of the WTO rules on subsidies, public procurement and migration, respectively (combined with many developing countries' worries about commodity

---

[30]Plus, once each government had offered subsidies to the firms in a given sector then they had a strong disincentive to be the first to withdraw those subsidies, doing so would inflict most of the adjustment on own firms. Essentially, once the subsidies were imposed a game of chicken followed in which each party waited for the other to blink or fold, which in this case meant withdraw their subsidies first. The subsequent emphasis on austerity packages in 2010 and 2011 may have brought some of these games to an unexpected end.

prices and pressures to exploit weak WTO rules on export taxes and quotas together account for much of the composition of recent protectionism).

A crucial part of the argument in the previous paragraphs is that the WTO rules in many areas of government policy where discrimination is possible are weak, remain underdeveloped, or do not exist at all. Furthermore, since the WTO tends to systematically collect information in the areas where its rules are strongest, there is relatively little monitoring of other areas of policymaking. What this implies is that at most the WTO rules affected the composition of crisis-era protectionism, with pressures for discrimination channelled towards those areas where the WTO rules are weaker. With such a patchwork of strong, weak, and missing multilateral trade rules, why would a government refrain from using a less regulated protectionist tool to help a desperate domestic commercial interest, just because some other tools have been banned by WTO rules? A good answer is needed to this question before a plausible story can be told that the current WTO rules limited the total amount of crisis-era protectionism.

In drawing implications from the above arguments for the potential reform of the WTO rules so as to better cope with systemic economic crises, certain considerations should be borne in mind. One reaction is to repeat what GATT members did after the sharp slump of the 1980s, namely, to put reforms to multilateral trade rules on some of the "newer" forms of protectionism witnessed on to the agenda of the next round of global trade negotiations. Following this approach would imply, in current circumstances, strengthening the WTO's subsidies code, expanding the scope and membership of the WTO Agreement on Public Procurement, and developing a set of disciplines on export taxes and the like.

However, there are good reasons for doubting that this path will be taken or, even if it is, whether it will fundamentally alter state behaviour during systemic economic crises. First, and it cannot be avoided, the lessons from the *de facto* failure of the Doha Round have yet to be agreed upon, let alone digested. Furthermore, there must be real doubts as to whether some of the BRICs are willing to subject their governments to international disciplines that they will regard as intruding further on their national sovereignty.[31] Second, so long as only WTO members (and not some advocate independent of government) can bring cases to the WTO dispute settlement mechanism,

---

[31]The BRICs may not be alone in this regard.

there must be some skepticism that when a systemic crisis occurs a collective, unofficial deviation from WTO rules will not be orchestrated.

Third, even if new rules could be negotiated and unofficial deviations cannot be pulled off, then the new WTO rules are still likely to be incomplete and so will afford opportunities for circumvention should domestic pressures mount up on governments to deliver discrimination. And, finally, even if new WTO rules were complete — that is, covering every possible form of discrimination — and for some reason unofficial deviations don't happen, then surely the lesson of the Gold Standard's demise in many countries during the Great Depression is relevant. During a severe systemic crisis where governments are under substantial pressure to intervene, then should binding rules be seen to be preventing governments from implementing measures that are thought to have major (even short-term) benefits, then there is a serious risk that the rules are repudiated.[32]

The depressing conclusion to draw is that either future WTO rules remain substantially incomplete, in which case during future systemic crises governments will merely circumvent those WTO rules, or future WTO rules become complete and when faced with the pressures of a systemic crisis, governments may openly repudiate them. Put this way, the fate of the WTO's rules during future systemic crises is to be either circumvented or violated outright. In the light of these circumstances, perhaps less should be expected of binding WTO rules when desperate politicians are taking steps to counter systemic economic crises.

The arguments made in this section were based on observations from the factual record as well as consideration of certain often-overlooked institutional features of the WTO. Once the incentives associated with the latter and with systemic economic crises are taken into account, the current multilateral trade system is not as strong as much writing on the WTO leads one to believe. Worse, should the set of WTO disciplines expand over time then there may come a point where, during a systemic economic crisis, some governments openly repudiate them. The pessimistic conclusions reached in this section do not arise from any differences in normative view from most international economists (such as the merits of an open trading system),

---

[32]In his account of the fate of the Gold Standard in the 1930s, Irwin (2012) observes: "Despite the gold standard's importance and the efforts to keep it intact, the pressures on financial crises and deflation became so strong that eventually every country was driven off it." (p. 42).

rather they arise from considering the implications of incentives that to date few have chosen to consider.

5 Concluding Remarks

Since its creation, analysts broadly sympathetic to the benefits of an open world trading system have lauded the World Trade Organization. This adulation has gone too far, or at least too far for the factual record and for logic to bear. The recent global economic crisis affords an excellent opportunity to revisit the effectiveness of the WTO, examining how much it really affects behaviour when member governments are under tremendous pressure to restore health to national economies. It should be understood, however, that the contribution of the WTO to an open trading system may differ between systemic economic crises and less strained economic circumstances, and only the former was examined here.

During the recent global economic crisis much has been made of the fact that governments have not resorted to Smoot–Hawley-like tariff increases that were condemned after the Great Depression. Contemporary analysts of protectionism have thus been lectured on the lessons of history, notably by those wanting to credit the WTO. Unfortunately, the Smoot–Hawley tariff argument cuts both ways and is not the only important historical point of reference. At least two others are relevant. First, during dire economic circumstances governments create new forms of protectionism that circumvent existing multilateral trade rules and are not picked up by monitoring exercises whose scope are typically circumscribed by prevailing trade rules. In any systemic crisis sticking rigidly to inherited notions of protectionism will almost certainly create a misleading, incomplete understanding of contemporary protectionism.

The second historical lesson of relevance is that when a policy choice (such as being on the Gold Standard) becomes the ultimate constraint preventing desperate policymakers from taking certain actions thought to provide sizeable relief, then the odds are that the constraint gets overthrown. What this means for the WTO is that those who view binding multilateral trade rules as the best way to prevent discrimination against foreign commercial interests had better ensure that every redesign of those rules allows for non-discriminatory means to be available to tackle each future systemic crisis. Moreover, since the nature of the latter are unknown and potentially unknowable, one might question whether such redesigns are possible and, therefore, the wisdom of relentlessly pursuing ever more multilateral trade disciplines. Practical considerations in times of extremis overturn the tidy visions of an ever-expanding architecture of legally binding commercial rules. Rather than banning every form of discrimination perhaps revisions to multilateral trade rules should channel discrimination into less harmful and shorter-lived forms.

To the extent that governments have shown restraint toward protectionism during the recent global economic crisis, it is difficult to give much credit to existing multilateral trading obligations for the reasons presented above. So weak and easy to evade are those obligations that other factors had to have been more important. Noting in addition the regrettable breakdown of the Doha Round negotiations, it is just as well that the medium-term health of the world trading system does not rely solely on multilateral trade rules and the international organization established to administer them. The ultimate conclusion of this paper is that in times of systemic economic crisis, the prevailing patchwork of multilateral trading obligations is much weaker than many realize. Expectations need to be realigned accordingly.

Appendix: Estimates of Total Trade Covered by Jumbo Measures

1) Most conservative estimate: All five public procurement measures (where the total import numbers include sales to the private sector) and one of the Indian export promotion measures (see measures 14 or 15) are excluded from the calculation. The total trade coverage of the remaining jumbo measures is US$1.618.1 trillion, or 10.45 percent of total world imports in 2008.

2) Least conservative estimate: The total trade coverage of the all the jumbo measures listed above is US$2.304 trillion, or 14.77 percent of total world imports in 2008.

References

Aggarwal, V.K. and S.J. Evenett (2009). Have long established patterns of protectionism changed during the crisis? A sectoral perspective. In Simon J. Evenett (ed.), *Broken Promises: A G20 Summit Report*, (Global Trade Alert), pp. 124–131.

Aumann, R.J. (1959). Acceptable points in general cooperative *n*-person games. *Annals of Mathematics Studies*, 40, 287–324.

Bagwell, K. and R. Staiger (2010). The World Trade Organization: Theory and practice. *Annual Review of Economics*, 2, 223–256.

Baldwin, R.E. (2009) *The Great Trade Collapse: Causes, Consequences and Prospects*, ed. VoxEU.org. Available at http://www.voxeu.org/index. php?q=node/4297.

Baldwin, R. and S.J. Evenett (2009) *The Collapse of Global Trade, Murky Protectionism, and the Crisis: Recommendations for the G20*, eds. VoxEU.org. Available at http://www.voxeu.org/index.php?q=node/3199.

Barrett, S. (1999). A theory of full international cooperation. *Journal of Theoretical Politics,* 11(4), 519–541.

Bernheim, B.D., B. Peleg and M.D. Whinston (1987). Coalition-proof Nash equilibria. I. Concepts. *Journal of Economic Theory*, 42, 1–12.

Eichengreen, B. and D.A. Irwin (2009). The slide to protectionism in the Great Depression: Who succumbed and why? NBER Working Paper no. 15142. July.

Evenett, S.J. (2009). What can be learned from crisis-era protectionism? An initial assessment. *Business and Politics*, 11(3), 1–26.

Evenett, S.J. (2011a). *Trade Tensions Mount: The 10th GTA Report*. Available at www.globaltradealert.org.

Evenett, S.J. (2011b). Did tariff regimes on manufactured goods change during the recent global economic crisis? In J. Evenett (ed.) *Trade Tensions Mount: The 10th GTA Report*, pp. 27–43.

Evenett, S.J. (2011c). Indicators of the harm done by discriminatory measures: Many indicators, one message. In J. Evenett (ed.) *Resolve Falters as Global Prospects Worsen: The 9th GTA Report*. Available at http://globaltradealert.org/sites/default/files/Chapter4. pdf.

Evenett, S.J. and J. Fritz (2010). "Jumbo" discriminatory measures and the trade coverage of crisis-era protectionism. In S.J. Evenett and J. Fritz (eds), *Unequal Compliance: The 6th GTA Report*, pp. 49–58. Available at http://www.globaltradealert.org/sites/default/files/GTA6_Evenett_Fritz.pdf.

Irwin, D.A. (2012). *Trade Policy Disaster: Lessons from the 1930s*. Boston, MA: MIT Press.

Mearsheimer, J.J. (1994). The false promise of international institutions. *International Security*, 19(3), 5–49.

WTO (2011). Report to the TPRB from the director-general on trade-related developments, September 7, 2011, Document number WT/TPR/OV/W/5/Rev.1.

CHAPTER 4

The International Monetary System after the Financial Crisis

Barry Eichengreen

For fully half a century, ever since observers began worrying about the shortcomings of the Bretton Woods System, the phrases "reform of" and "international monetary system" have gone together. It is hard to think of another aspect of the global economic and financial landscape for which the perception of shortcomings is as immediate and discussions of reform are as continuous.

That said, these long-standing concerns acquired new salience with the emergence of large international imbalances after the turn of the century and then with the global financial crisis. Those imbalances, epitomized by the enormously large current account deficit of the US and surplus of China, showed financial capital to be flowing in the "wrong" direction, uphill from low- to high-income economies. Even if global imbalances did not cause the crisis, they contributed to its severity.[1] Foreign purchases of US treasury and agency securities which financed the US deficit while at the same time meeting the desire of other countries for additional international reserves put downward pressure on yields on safe assets in the US, encouraging investors to move into riskier investments.[2] By reducing the cost of borrowing, they encouraged reliance on leverage. When bad news then arrived,

---

[1] See Obstfeld and Rogoff (2010) and Eichengreen (2011).
[2] As documented by Warnock and Warnock (2009).

triggering deleveraging and flight to quality, the resulting disruptions were correspondingly more severe.

Yet, ironically, the country at the center of the crisis, the US, was protected from the worst effects. The dollar, as the world's ultimate source of liquidity and dominant funding currency for international banks, strengthened when problems erupted in the market for securitized subprime mortgages in September 2007 and then again with the failure of Lehman Brothers in September 2008. This buffered the impact of the crisis on US financial markets. The opposite was however true of other countries that used dollars for international transactions. They suffered even larger disruptions to their trade and production when dollar liquidity dried up and then when they found themselves on the receiving end of a tsumani of financial capital once the Federal Reserve embarked on quantitative easing to offset the weakness of demand in the US. The US's exorbitant privilege as the issuer of the only true global currency thereby enabled it to shift some of the costs of the crisis onto other countries.

These observations about global imbalances and the crisis point, in turn, to the problems with the international monetary system as currently configured. That system is conducive to chronic imbalances whose pattern is not obviously consistent with an efficient allocation of savings and investment across countries. There is no adjustment mechanism adequate for narrowing those imbalances when they arise. There is persistent reserve accumulation by emerging markets, which is costly (since reserve assets bear low returns), inefficient (insofar as insurance against contingencies is held in the form of noncontingent claims), and dangerous (insofar as it contributes to the build-up of other risks). There is the inconsistency of exchange rate regimes and capital account regulation across countries and the failure of central banks to adequately take into account the cross-border repercussions of their policies. There is the unreliability of the global supply of liquidity. Above all there is the volatility and fragility of global financial markets and flows and the threat these pose to financial stability and economic growth.

For all these reasons, international monetary reform is again in the air. South Korea placed the construction of a global safety net — as officials refer to alternatives to reserve accumulation at the national level for countries requiring emergency liquidity and balance-of-payments insurance — at the top of its agenda when chairing the G20 in 2010. France, on assuming the chairmanship of the G20 in 2011, made reform of the exchange rate and reserve systems its focus. The US has trained attention on China's exchange rate regime as a problem for international adjustment and stability. China and Brazil have berated the US for neglecting the cross-border repercussions of its policies. The International Monetary Fund (IMF) continues to commission studies and issue papers addressing these and other deficiencies of the international monetary system.

That said, there is still no agreement on the nature of a reformed system. In this chapter, I therefore seek to describe the essential elements of a more stable and smoothly functioning international monetary system. I focus on four aspects of the international monetary architecture: the global reserve system, the emergency provision of liquidity, the regulation of international financial flows, and the role of the IMF. Other observers would no doubt emphasize still other issues. But, as I show below, these are four aspects of the reform agenda about which disagreement is greatest. They are four areas where further convergence of views is needed if we are to fashion an international monetary system suitable for the circumstances of the 21st century.

1 The Global Reserve System

For more than 50 years the global reserve system has been dollar based. Countries other than the US seeking to accumulate reserves have had to accumulate dollars. Only the US, the one country with both liquid financial markets open to international investors and the fiscal capacity to backstop a large quantity of treasury securities, has been in a position to supply a significant volume of reserve assets to the rest of the world. Middle-sized countries like Germany and Japan have historically resisted the internationalization of their currencies for fear that this would complicate their economic policies. Smaller countries like Switzerland for their part are not in a position to supply reserve assets on a meaningful scale. Supplements to national currencies like the IMF's Special Drawing Rights have played only a minor role in central bank reserve portfolios, reflecting their limited utility in market transactions together with political constraints on their issuance.

This aspect of the monetary landscape is now changing as other economies, starting with the Euro Area and China, acquire the size and engage in the volume of international transactions needed to create reserve assets on a meaningful scale. Prior to its descent into crisis, the euro had begun making inroads into the dollar's dominance of central bank reserve portfolios and even faster progress as a currency in which to invoice and settle merchandise transactions and denominate international bonds. Once Europe's debt and banking crisis is resolved, its currency will resume doing so, given the economic scale of the Euro Area, the development of its financial markets, and the extent of its external transactions. The renminbi's emergence as a reserve asset remains, for now, a thing of the future; realization of this prospect will have to wait on the further liberalization of China's capital account, on the adoption of a more flexible exchange rate, and on the country's progress in developing deep and liquid financial markets. But there is no longer any question that internationalization of the renminbi is in the cards or that currency internationalization and its concomitants are part of Beijing's strategy for rebalancing Chinese growth away from exports of manufactures.

For all these reasons, a global reserve system based on multiple national currencies — the dollar, the euro and the renminbi in the first instance and perhaps the Brazilian real and Indian rupee in the longer run — is coming. This multiple-reserve-currency system will have both advantages and disadvantages relative to the dollar-based system that preceded it. The advantages will include more regular discipline on reserve-currency countries. If the US again shows a tendency to fall prey to financial excesses — if it again uses foreign credit to engage in frenzied real estate speculation, for example — then central banks seeking to accumulate additional reserve assets will have sources other than the US from which to acquire them. As a result they will buy US fixed-income securities less freely. US interest rates will rise at an earlier stage in the credit cycle, curtailing America's financial excesses. Foreign central banks for their part will not be as vulnerable to capital losses on their reserve portfolios.

This new system will have the further advantage, in addition, of ensuring a steadier rate of growth of the global supply of reserve assets. The supply of reserves will not depend on economic and financial conditions in any one economy to the same extent as under the current system. Financial problems in a reserve-issuing country like the US that create a sudden dollar shortage will not cause a global reserve shortage to the same extent as in the past, insofar as reserve assets will still be provided by other national suppliers. Hyper-loose monetary policies in any one key-currency country (like the Fed's QE2) will not blow up the global supply of reserves as dramatically in a world where the growth of reserve supplies depends on the policies of more than one central bank.

A multiple-reserve-currency system, moreover, will not be susceptible to the 21st century analog of the Triffin Dilemma. The original Triffin

Dilemma, formulated before the current period of high international capital mobility, held that the reserve-currency country, in practice the US, had the choice of either avoiding current account deficits, which would starve other countries of reserves, or of continually running such deficits, thereby supplying adequate reserves but ultimately undermining confidence in its ability to convert its foreign-held dollar liabilities into gold. The 21st century differs by virtue of international capital mobility and the fact that foreign exchange reserves are no longer convertible into gold at a fixed price. Capital mobility, in particular, means that countries can accumulate dollar reserves without running current account surpluses and without the US running current account deficits to the same extent as before. In our world of high capital mobility, a sufficiently high level of US foreign direct investment can finance foreign purchases of US treasury securities. This is what we see in practice: the US supplies US treasury securities to official foreign holders both by running current account deficits and engaging in net direct investment abroad.

But the confidence problem of which Triffin warned can still arise if the stock of US treasury securities in foreign hands grows large relative to the capacity of the US to service them. It is that fiscal capacity that allows the prompt payment of debt service on US debt securities and that therefore ensures the liquidity and stability making them an attractive form of reserves. But with growth in emerging markets running faster than growth in the US, the US accounts for a progressively smaller share of global GDP; this means that the fiscal capacity of the US to backstop the market in treasury securities and to supply other countries with adequate reserves is shrinking relative to the size of the global economy. Eventually, in other words, a 21st century variant of the Triffin Dilemma will bind. But this limit on the global supply of reserves can be relaxed if the United States is no longer the only country whose fiscal capacity backstops the liquid foreign reserves of other economies.

A final advantage of a multiple-reserve-currency system is greater exchange rate stability. Insofar as all three reserve assets — the dollar, the euro and the renminbi — are viewed as safe havens and thus as close substitutes for one another, their relative prices cannot vary widely (Farhi, Gourinchas and Rey, 2011).

This property depends, however, on confidence that the central banks issuing reserve assets are committed to preserving the stability of their currencies and that their countries' respective fiscal authorities are committed to the same. In turn, this brings us to the principal disadvantage of a multiple-reserve-currency system: the potential for instability owing to doubts about the policies of one of the reserve-currency-issuing countries. Were such doubts to arise, there could then be mass flight away from its currency by official as well as private holders. This reaction could be more violent than under the present system in which foreign official holders of dollars have nowhere to run. The result could be massive financial dislocations. The exchange rate of the offending country would crash, catching important investors, private as well as official, wrong-footed; other reserve currencies, and the currencies of countries shadowing those reserve units, would go through the roof, creating competitiveness problems and threatening recession. The importance of stable policies for the operation of this new system will be, if anything, even greater than for that of its dollar-based predecessor.

There is thus discomfort about the prospect of a global reserve system organized around national currencies insofar as its stability will hinge on the policies of a handful of not-always-reliable countries. Other economies will depend on them for stability even more than before. This has prompted disgruntled observers to contemplate alternatives, notably a global reserve system organized around a supranational unit like the IMF's Special Drawing Rights (SDRs).

While we are likely to see limited amounts of additional SDR issuance, there are multiple reasons for thinking that the SDR will not replace national currencies as the principal form of reserves. For starters, there is no obvious formula for allocating them. Under current rules the vast majority would go to high-income countries. Actually following this procedure would be tantamount to foreign aid in reverse. But agreeing on a new allocation formula under which high-income countries transferred their SDR allocations to developing countries would be politically difficult, to say the least.

Another problem is that there is no liquid market in SDRs. This would not be a constraint for countries with more reserves than they can ever conceivably use for market intervention. Their central banks could tie up those excess reserves in SDRs, just as their sovereign wealth funds tie up their portfolios in illiquid investments. But this comparison suggests that more attractive investments — in oil refining capacity, timber reserves or industrial shares — will continue to dominate SDRs.

Central banks actually seeking to use their reserves in market transactions — for intervening in the foreign exchange market, financing essential imports, and related purposes — have to go through the cumbersome process of requesting their conversion into national currencies at the IMF. The Fund then must find another country willing to supply a usable currency. Failing that, it must invoke what is known as the "designation process" to compel other members to provide usable currencies. Doing so could have financial implications for those members, not all of which will be to their liking. Significant additional SDR issuance could expose the US, the Euro Area and China to significant additional financial obligations, for example, assuming that their currencies are those used in the bulk of international financial and commercial transactions.

In the long run these problems could be addressed by creating private markets in SDRs, obviating the need to go through a cumbersome conversion process. But commercialization of the SDR is at best a long-term project (as reviewed in IMF 2011). There is the need to create a market infrastructure to support transactions: this would have to include a clearing mechanism, hedging instruments, and so forth. Interested governments could encourage this by issuing their own SDR bonds. But the first SDR-denominated instruments would not trade in deep and liquid markets by definition. IMF staff predicts that the first SDR issuers would pay an 80–100 basis point liquidity premium.

Moreover, for the SDR to become attractive globally, the unit would have to include more than just the dollar, the euro, the pound sterling and the Japanese yen, the four currencies currently constituting the SDR basket. At a minimum the basket would have to be expanded to include a weight on the renminbi, given that currency's growing role in intra-Asian transactions. But while this would make the SDR more attractive in the long run, it would also make it less liquid in the short run, given the significant restraints that remain on using the renminbi for international financial transactions.

Then there is the fact that the IMF will not be able to respond in a crisis with the speed of a reserve-currency-issuing national central bank that provides emergency swap lines and credits to its partners. Recall how the Federal Reserve moved quickly following the failure of Lehman Brothers to provide $30 billion swap lines to Mexico, Brazil, Singapore and South Korea and more generally how the Fed and the European Central Bank rushed emergency credits to countries that used dollars and euros for the bulk of their international transactions. For the IMF to respond similarly, it would first have to secure the approval of governments accounting for 85 percent of voting power in the Fund, this being the threshold for new SDR issuance. (IMF members did agree to an "emergency" SDR allocation of $250 billion in 2009 but only after discussion, debate and delay.)

Under the Articles of Agreement, issuing new SDRs requires the Fund to show that this is not only useful under currently prevailing circumstances but also that doing so meets "the long-term global need... to supplement existing reserve assets." This burden of proof may not be easy to meet. From this point of view, it would be desirable to amend the Articles of Agreement to allow SDRs also to be issued under other circumstances so long as those temporary allocations are withdrawn subsequently (as suggested by Cooper, 2009). More ambitiously, IMF management could be given the power to act under its own authority rather than requiring approval from 85 percent of membership or, for that matter, from the executive board. But this would be tantamount to giving the Fund the powers of an independent central bank, something for which there is no appetite given that there is no global government to hold it accountable for its actions.

For all these reasons, an international reserve system based mainly on national currencies will be with us for the foreseeable future. The question, to repeat, is: which currencies. For a national currency to play a consequential role in the global reserve system it must possess three characteristics: scale, liquidity and stability. Scale means that a currency is issued by the central bank of a country that engages in a large volume of international transactions; otherwise, foreign central banks and governments will not find holding it useful and attractive. Markets in that currency must be deep and liquid, enabling foreign official investors to alter their holdings without moving prices. And stability is the sine qua non of a reserve currency. If foreign official investors develop doubts about the readiness of an issuer to honor its liabilities, they will have an incentive to limit the share of their reserve portfolios allocated to its currency.

These observations in turn suggest what the US, the Euro Area and China can do to smooth the transition to a multiple-reserve-currency system. The US possesses the liquid markets needed in order for the dollar to retain its reserve currency status but has lagged since the financial crisis in terms of economic growth. This has reduced its share of global commercial and financial transactions and threatened to render dollar reserves correspondingly less attractive, if not now, then in the future. But the country's most urgent task far and away is to restore confidence in its commitment to maintain the value of its foreign official liabilities. The dollar has depreciated substantially since its post-Lehman Brothers peak. Chronic budget deficits implying an ever-rising debt/GDP ratio do not engender confidence in the country's commitment to honor its debts. The same can be said of the political noise surrounding the decision to raise the federal government's debt ceiling in the summer of 2011. To be sure, the US is still far from the point where it is economically incapable of servicing its debts. But as debt service in general and debt service to foreigners in particular claim growing shares of federal government expenditure, questions are sure to develop about whether it possesses the requisite political will.

Although the sovereign debt problems of Greece and other Southern European countries have attracted considerable attention, the debt problems of the Euro Area as a whole are no more serious than those of the US. Indeed, European countries have shown if anything an even greater commitment to fiscal consolidation. And for better or worse, the European Central Bank has an unmatched commitment to price stability. But for the euro to acquire a meaningful reserve-currency role, Europe will have to draw a line under its crisis. It will have to solve a growth problem rooted in unfavorable demographics and chronic slow productivity growth in Italy and elsewhere in the south. If the Euro Area fails to address its painfully slow rate of economic growth, it will be left in the dust by the US and China. After a few decades, the euro will be to the dollar and the renminbi what the Swiss franc now is to the euro.

Finally, for the renminbi to emerge as a major reserve currency, China will have to create deep and liquid financial markets open to the rest of the world. This will imply moving to a more flexible exchange rate in order to accommodate a larger volume of capital inflows and outflows. The government will have to continue distancing itself from the banks and the banks from state-owned enterprises. All this implies far-reaching changes in China's development model. In fact, policy is already moving in this direction. In only a couple of years, the renminbi has come to be used significantly for cross-border trade settlements, mainly in Asia but also in other parts of the world. Nearly a tenth of all bank deposits in Hong Kong are denominated in renminbi. International corporations have tapped that pool of renminbi liquidity by issuing dim sum bonds for use in funding their Chinese operations. A growing number of Hong Kong-based banks have been authorized to invest their renminbi funds on the interbank bond market in China. It would be a mistake to overlook China's commitment to internationalizing its currency or to underestimate its progress.

2 The Emergency Provision of Liquidity

A smoothly operating reserve system will require facilities for the emergency provision of dollars, euros and renminbi when there is a spike in the demand for international liquidity. Governments and central banks have traditionally prepared for this eventuality by accumulating reserves. Now there is a growing recognition that this strategy is less than ideal. Holding reserves as insurance creates a temptation to take on risk: the authorities may allow banks to incur additional foreign exposures in the knowledge that the official sector possesses reserves with which to pay them off, or they may allow corporations to raise additional funding offshore in the knowledge that the official sector can backstop the companies in question. In assessing the adequacy of reserves, the markets consider not only absolute levels but also how they compare across countries; this beauty contest compels governments to accumulate excessive levels of reserves overall. Finally, there is the fact that relying on foreign reserves entails holding noncontingent claims as protection against contingent events. Governments and central banks are required to hold low-yielding assets at all points in time as insurance against risks that materialize only periodically.

An alternative is to utilize the IMF as a de facto reserve-pooling arrangement, allowing countries without a current need for international liquidity to make their reserves available to others. Members deposit their currencies when subscribing their quotas, and some of those currencies — dollars and euros, for example — can be made available to other members in times of need. But quotas designed for a world of limited cross-border capital flows and the heavy policy conditionality associated with standby arrangements are poorly suited to a world of capital-account crises. This observation has led the Fund to create a number of new, lightly-conditioned, front-loaded, quick-disbursing lending facilities. It has established a Flexible Credit Line (FCL) for countries with strong policies and a Precautionary and Liquidity Line (PLL) for countries with moderate vulnerabilities.[3] Under the FCL, countries have large, assured, up-front access to IMF credit without having to satisfy ongoing conditions. Under the PLL, prequalified countries are assured of being able to draw up to 500 percent of their quotas and twice that after a year of satisfactory performance, more than triple the 300 percent of quota associated with the Fund's traditional lending

---

[3]The PLL is a generalization of the earlier Precautionary Credit Line, the principal difference between the Precautionary and Liquidity Line and the Precautionary Credit Line being that the latter was only for countries with potential future needs at the time of approval while the former can also be extended to countries with actual needs (that may wish to draw the line immediately).

windows. They are subject to simplified ("streamlined") conditionality (Moghadam, 2010).

But there have been few takers, potential borrowers evidently worrying about stigma effects. Only Mexico, Colombia and Poland have applied for FCLs as of the time of writing; no Asian country has applied. Macedonia became the first and only recipient of a Precautionary Credit Line in January 2011. Some observers have suggested that the IMF could encourage simultaneous application by groups of countries as a way of solving the stigma problem. It could go further and prequalify such countries unilaterally without their applying. The Fund is exploring the idea of a so-called Global Stabilization Mechanism under which it would extend credit facilities to multiple countries while relaxing the criteria governing qualification in the event of problems in global financial markets. For the time being, however, there is no agreement on the structure of this mechanism.

Overall, then, efforts to create at the IMF a quick-disbursing, unconditional facility — an effective reserve-pooling arrangement — continue to disappoint. The problem, as Goldstein (2011) notes, is that the model commits the Fund to lending large amounts of money on the basis of judgments about the quality of country policies that may no longer be current. Either the IMF will have to be prepared to place itself in financial jeopardy, or else it will be forced to limit access to members with impeccably strong policies. The idea that the Fund should be authorized to unilaterally prequalify a substantial set of members as a way of dealing with the stigma issue runs up against this same constraint: it exposes the institution to an open-ended financial liability. Finally, the difficulty of disqualifying a previously prequalified country without precipitating the very crisis that the credit facility was designed to avert, something pointed to by critics of these schemes since they were first envisaged, remains unsolved.

Another option suggested by critics of the IMF is relying on the kind of bilateral swaps and credits made available by the Federal Reserve System and, to a lesser extent, other leading central banks in the recent financial crisis (see McGuire and von Peter, 2009). These swaps played a key role in alleviating shortages of dollar liquidity at the height of the financial crisis (Goldberg, Kennedy and Miu, 2011). Korean observers for example credit the $30 billion swap between the Fed and Bank of Korea as the main factor relieving their country's post-Lehman Brothers financial distress (see e.g., Park, 2009).

The problem with ad hoc swaps and credits is that they are ad hoc. There is no guarantee that dollars and, in the future, euros and renminbi

will again be made available so freely and promptly. The Federal Reserve
Board may not be as appreciative of the need or may be subjected to Congressional pressure "not to lend hard-earned US taxpayer dollars" to foreign
central banks (as was the case in 2010 — see di Leo and Wessel, 2010). This
danger could be addressed by negotiating the relevant swap arrangements in
advance and routinizing their activation. Something similar was done when
negotiating the Gold Pool in the 1960s (Eichengreen, 2006) and in conjunction with the New and General Arrangements to Borrow, under which a
number of key-currency countries agreed to make additional resources available to the IMF to be on-lent to other members. But relying on a measure of
market conditions such as the VIX (the Chicago Options Exchange Market
Volatility Index) or the change in foreign exchange swap positions to acti-
vate these pre-negotiated arrangements is likely to be problematic insofar
as market structures are changing continuously. It is also likely to be unac-
ceptable to key-currency central banks, which will be putting real money
on the barrelhead. As a compromise, Goldstein (2011) suggests delegating
decision-making power to a special committee made up of senior officials of
the central banks of the key-currency countries plus the managing director
of the IMF.

Rather than attempting to organize reserve-sharing arrangements globally through the IMF or bilaterally through swap arrangements with
the Federal Reserve System, a third way is organizing them regionally.
ASEAN+3, seeking to shed its dependence on the Fund and the Fed,
took steps in this direction with the creation of the Chiang Mai Initiative (now Chiang Mai Initiative Multilateralization or CMIM) in 2000. The
Euro Area has done likewise, in May 2010 creating the European Financial Stability Mechanism (to be succeeded in the future by the European
Stability Mechanism, or ESM).

The limitation of these mechanisms is not unlike that of the IMF's
new lightly-conditioned lending facilities: in the absence of effective ex ante
surveillance and effective ex post monitoring of country policies, there is a
reluctance to lend. Imposing painful conditions can reawaken historic tensions and conflicts. In 2010, the EU addressed this by outsourcing the negotiation of conditionality for Greece and other crisis countries to the IMF,
which was also junior partner in its lending programs. Goldstein (2001)
argues that European governments, with their diverse priorities and agendas, would not have been able to agree on the structure of a program absent
the IMF's agenda-setting role. Viewed from the side of the IMF, these joint
operations, where the institution takes the lead in negotiating program

conditions but its regional partners provide the majority of the finance, are a way of dealing with the problem of limited financial resources. That said, this kind of systematic cooperation between the IMF and European governments worked only because of special circumstances, specifically that the Fund's managing director was a well-connected senior European politician (Henning, 2011). And, even then, the relationship was fraught with difficulty. It was never entirely clear which of the two parties, the IMF or the EU, would take the lead in negotiations. In the early stages of the Greek program, the Fund was pressured by the EU not to push for debt restructuring, which the Europeans viewed as embarrassing and a threat to the stability of their monetary union (not to mention to the balance sheet of the European Central Bank, the third member of the so-called creditors' "troika"). History suggests that a regional donor is most likely to get its way in a dispute with the IMF when it finances the majority of the rescue package. This was the case in Latvia in 2008, when the IMF recommended devaluation but was overruled by the EU, which provided more than three quarters of the funding. But the idea of a regional entity dictating program conditionality but the Fund nonetheless putting up its own resources makes long-time IMF hands queasy. Goldstein (2011) argues that the solution to this problem is for the Fund to be the principal creditor in all joint programs so that it can have the dominant voice in their design. But achieving this would require a vast increase in IMF financial resources.

The CMIM also includes an IMF link: members currently must negotiate a program with the IMF in order to draw more than 20 percent of their CMIM credits. This has been a factor in the reluctance of Asian countries to utilize the agreement, given the continuing stigma attached to IMF programs in the region. CMIM members are committed to raising this 20 percent threshold and ultimately to removing the IMF link. Whether they can do so will hinge on their ability to substitute effective regional surveillance for multilateral surveillance by the Fund. Establishing the ASEAN+3 Macroeconomic Research Office (AMRO) in Singapore is a first step. But while AMRO has appointed a director, the office is not yet operational at the time of writing. It lacks a legal personality and therefore full authority. Its very name is revealing of the reluctance of the members to delegate meaningful powers of surveillance to a regional entity.

And if effective surveillance of regional neighbors is difficult, the imposition of painful loan conditionality is harder. Asia lacks Europe's commitment to even limited political integration and continues to espouse nonintervention in national affairs. It remains to be seen whether the CMIM countries will be able to engage in firm surveillance and meaningful policy conditionality in the absence of an IMF link.

3   Regulating Capital Flows

In contrast to the situation under Bretton Woods, international capital flows are an integral element of today's global monetary system. Policy makers and independent observers alike may have reservations about their benefits, but capital flows are not going away. The tight regulation of capital movements under Bretton Woods was feasible only because of tight regulation of financial markets generally. With financial liberalization and development and with the progress of information and communications technology, international capital flows are here to stay, like it or not.

Many emerging markets, in particular, do not like it very much. Small countries and countries with shallow financial systems are poorly placed to cope with large capital inflows. Among the problems they experience are surging domestic lending, booming household consumption, deteriorating domestic bank credit quality, bubbly asset markets, and declining competitiveness. They are susceptible to financial dislocations and worse when those capital flows reverse direction, as happens sooner or later.

The dilemma is heightened insofar as the standard policy instruments are not up to coping with the bonanza. If the central bank raises interest rates in an effort to damp down booming consumption and slow the growth of bank lending, this will only attract additional inflows. It may intervene in the foreign exchange market to limit upward pressure on the currency, selling government bonds and central bank bills in order to sterilize the impact on the money supply. But such interventions have significant quasi-fiscal costs, the interest rates on local-currency bonds being high relative to those on the foreign government securities that the authorities are buying. They may also be of dubious efficacy, since they do nothing to eliminate the incentive for foreign investors to purchase high-yielding local-currency securities. Exchange rate flexibility may introduce an additional element of risk that helps to deter the carry trade, but exchange rate volatility has other costs, for export-oriented economies in particular.

Fiscal tightening is the most effective policy response in principle. It leans against the growth of domestic spending and thereby against upward pressure on the currency. By reducing domestic interest rates, it discourages the carry trade. But taking away the fiscal punch bowl is hard. In small economies, very large budget surpluses may be required to begin to neutralize the impact of capital inflows. Chile ran general government budget surpluses on the order of 8 percent of GDP prior to the 2008–2009 financial crisis and even then was unable to contain strong upward pressure on the peso.

These dilemmas have been accentuated by the sharp divergence in monetary policies resulting from the crisis. In particular, the second round of quantitative easing by the Federal Reserve in 2010 was seen as unleashing a tidal wave of capital flows to emerging markets. Brazilian finance minister Guido Mantega accused the US central bank as engaging in a *de facto* policy of "currency warfare."

Emerging markets responded with administrative measures intended to limit the extent and impact of capital inflows. Brazil tripled its tax on foreign inflows into local securities markets to 6 percent and limited the permissible foreign exchange exposures of its banks. Indonesia imposed a minimum holding period for foreign purchasers of central bank money market certificates. Korea capped foreign currency derivatives positions and the growth of its banks' noncore foreign funding; in addition it imposed a 20 percent capital gains tax on foreign-held government bonds. Thailand levied a 15 percent tax on interest income and capital gains earned by foreign investors.

These measures are discriminatory by intent; they are biased against foreign investors by construction. They can be less than transparent; they allow for considerable leeway on the part of the bureaucrats responsible for their administration. They can be used to protect banks and firms from foreign competition. They are not coordinated across countries, giving rise to capital-flow diversion. They are perceived as sending a negative signal about the commitment of policy makers to the pursuit of sound and stable policies. And questions remain about their effectiveness.

Some of these problems can be solved if policy makers do a better job of explaining the purposes for which capital controls have been enlisted. In some cases the measures in question are adopted mainly as a supplementary tool of macroeconomic management: as a way of avoiding excessive real exchange rate appreciation and loss of export competitiveness. In others they are valued for their macroprudential role: they are used as a supplementary form of prudential supervision and regulation in order to limit the build-up of financial risks. Better describing the rationale, whatever it is, will help to limit the danger that market participants misconstrue the policy's intent.

Policy makers should also emphasize the supplementary nature of the policies. Controls cannot substitute for appropriate monetary and fiscal policies as a tool of macroeconomic management; they can only reinforce them. They cannot substitute for standard instruments of prudential supervision and regulation. But they can provide a second line of defense. More generally, it is important for the authorities to explain how controls fit into the broader policy framework.

Here the IMF has leapt into the breach, proposing a code of conduct for countries adopting capital-flow-restricting policies. The resulting guidelines for capital controls would specify the circumstances under which resort to such policies is appropriate and warranted. They would recommend the form or forms of controls that are least likely to have pernicious side effects, either at home or for other countries. To minimize the danger of adverse signals, use of these policies could be monitored by the IMF, which could certify the conformance of countries' policies with global standards.

Progress in this direction will have to surmount several significant obstacles. To start, the IMF lacks authority in this area: while the achievement of current account convertibility is an obligation of members under Article VIII of its Articles of Agreement, the Fund lacks authority over members' financial account policies (Benassy, Pisani-Ferry and Yu, 2011). Vesting it with that authority would be delicate business, given memories of the earlier attempt, in 1997–1998, to amend the Articles to make capital account convertibility an obligation of members. The IMF may have changed its tune on capital controls, but emerging markets remain suspicious that the Fund is a creature of the advanced countries, which will use it as a lever for forcing open emerging financial markets and compelling the abandonment of controls. The European monopoly of the Fund's managing directorship and the fact that the US remains the largest single shareholder reinforces these fears.

Then there is the fact that the global policy community is still far from consensus on the basic issues: under what circumstances controls are appropriate and about what controls work best. IMF papers on these questions offer only vague and general guidelines (see e.g., IMF, 2010). This fuels doubts about whether international standards would in fact be a step forward. The governments of Brazil and India, worrying that their policies would be constrained, opposed the concept of a code of conduct for capital controls at the IMF spring meetings in April 2011. Brazil's Mantega declared his country's opposition to "any guidelines, frameworks or 'codes of conduct' that attempt to constrain, directly or indirectly, policy responses of countries facing surges in volatile capital flows" (Bretton Woods Project, 2011). G20 officials have been able to agree only on "voluntary coherent conclusions" for the use of controls, something that falls far short of a binding code of conduct.[4]

Finally, a code for controls would place the burden of proof on emerging markets seeking to regulate inflows, where in fact equal responsibility for international financial imbalances properly falls on the advanced countries whose policies operate on the "push side" of the equation (Griffith-Jones and Gallagher, 2011). To date, there has been little effective action to address this aspect of the problem, by the IMF or anyone else.

4 The Role of the IMF

Previous sections have already touched on the role of the IMF as a mechanism for reserve pooling, issuer of a supranational reserve unit, and overseer of member's financial account policies. This section now considers the role of the Fund in crisis prevention and exchange rate management.

Since the Asian crisis, there have been ongoing efforts to enhance the IMF's capacity to anticipate and avert financial crises. Recent efforts have highlighted financial vulnerabilities and macro-financial linkages along with the more familiar real imbalances manifesting themselves in the chronic current account deficits that characterized 20th century crises. Results have included the creation of a department within the institution charged with monitoring financial conditions and publication of a biannual *Global Financial Stability Report* to complement the long-established *World Economic Outlook*.[5] The Fund undertakes Financial Sector Assessment Reports jointly with the World Bank; these are now mandatory for the 25 countries with the most systemically significant financial sectors. In the wake of the 2007–2009 crisis, it has added the advanced countries to its regular "vulnerability exercise." It has launched an early warning exercise joint with the Financial

---

[4]See IMF (2011c).

[5]The Fund's triennial review of surveillance, issued in October 2011, suggests integrating the GFSR and WEO and augmenting the WEO to include "multilaterally consistent assessments" of the exchange rates and current accounts of the IMF's principal members. See IMF (2011d).

Stability Board, conducted additional research on macro-financial linkages, and experimented with "spillover reports" designed to highlight the cross-border repercussions of national policies (spillovers presumably being most important in the case of the institution's largest members).[6]

In addition, agreement was reached at the Pittsburgh Summit of the G20 in 2009 to create a Mutual Assessment Process (or MAP) under which the IMF would provide technical assistance to governments seeking to establish the consistency of their policies and compatibility of those policies with the G20's stated goals of achieving "lasting recovery and strong and sustainable growth in the medium term." The Fund's role is to estimate the impact of national policies on global outcomes and to present alternative scenarios. On the issue of imbalances, the IMF's technical analysis is charged with identifying the roots of imbalances and the obstacles to their correction, specifically in the large countries making a major contribution to the problem.

The final step will be for leaders to implement specific actions designed to correct imbalances and secure strong and stable growth. But whether this last step will actually be taken is unclear. The MAP bears a strong resemblance to the ill-fated Multilateral Consultation on global imbalances undertaken in 2006–2007. Under that initiative the IMF brought together a handful of economies (the US, the Euro Area, Japan, China and Saudi Arabia). It provided technical analysis of the problem. It called for corrective action. The governments of the participating countries echoed its call and then proceeded to do precisely nothing.

This failure was symptomatic of the IMF's lack of leverage over countries with current account surpluses or whose currencies are widely used in international transactions and which therefore have no need to borrow from it. The worry is that what was true of the first Multilateral Consultation will be true of the MAP and of whatever implications flow from spillover reports and other multilateral surveillance initiatives.

---

[6]In addition, in 2011 the Executive Board accepted Managing Director Lagarde's proposal that a new framework for IMF surveillance be established that included a focus on not just bilateral aspects of a member's policies — that is, on whether those policies are consistent with its own internal and external balance — but also on multilateral aspects — that is, whether they are also consistent with global economic and financial stability.

Subsequent G20 summits reinforce these fears. At the Seoul Summit in November 2010, the US pushed for numerical targets for current account surpluses, but the surplus countries, led by China and Germany, succeeded in blocking agreement on numerical thresholds that would automatically trigger action. At the next G20 meeting, in early 2011, China was able to block the adoption of specific targets for foreign exchange reserves.

In light of this, the IMF remains understandably reluctant to pursue stronger sanctions on countries with misaligned exchange rates that run persistent current account surpluses and chronically accumulate reserves. This has led to a variety of ideas for finessing the problem. From the Peterson Institute alone there are proposals that the IMF should be obliged to send a mission to any country with a surplus greater than 4 percent of GDP, where that mission would be charged with examining whether its exchange rate is undervalued. Or that the WTO should be given the power to penalize a country for maintaining an undervalued exchange rate by using its dispute settlement system to authorize trade restrictions against an offending country (with the evidence needed to convict being supplied by the IMF). Or that a reserve-currency country should have the right of counter-intervention against a country maintaining an undervalued currency, subject to appeal to the IMF.

The best developed variant is that of Goldstein (2011), who proposes that a current account imbalance equal or greater than 4 percent of GDP or some equivalent number over a year should automatically trigger an exchange rate consultation with the IMF. The Fund's staff report would then specify corrective action. In the event that the action in question was not taken, the IMF would then label a country a currency manipulator, at which point the WTO could permit other governments to impose trade sanctions.

An alternative, harking back to Keynes' clearing-union plan, is for a progressive tax on the reserves of current-account surplus countries that would rise with the size and persistence of those surpluses (Eichengreen, 2009). A country that had run a current account surplus in excess of 3 percent of GDP for three years, for example, might be required to transfer additional resources to the Fund at the end of every year in which that excess persisted. The transfer might equal one-half of the current account surplus in excess of 3 percent of GDP. Alternatively, one can imagine a tax on the increase in foreign exchange reserves when reserves had been rising for 3 years and the increase in the current year exceeded 3 percent of GDP. Under this scheme, nothing would prevent countries from running large and persistent external surpluses if they found it difficult to raise investment or reduce savings. But doing so would entail an additional cost, in turn ratcheting up the pressure on the central bank and government to adopt policies of adjustment.

A variant of this idea appeared in a January 2011 paper prepared by IMF staff for the institution's executive board (IMF, 2011a). The idea there is that SDR allocations could be made contingent on a country's adherence to norms regarding reserve accumulation — chronic surplus countries could be denied their allocations, in other words. But a staff report to the board phrased in noncommittal terms is still very far from policy.

The advantage of this approach is that it is based on rules rather than discretion. The IMF could not be pressured by the shareholder subject to the tax to waive its imposition, something that is a problem with Goldstein's approach. The disadvantage is, similarly, that it is based on rules rather than discretion. Current account deficits occur for both good and bad reasons (Blanchard and Milesi-Ferretti, 2009). A mechanical approach would leave no room for this distinction.

Goldstein's proposal would be a quantum leap for IMF surveillance. By labeling a country a currency manipulator and initiating a process that could culminate in the application of trade sanctions, it would be moving away from the consensual approach that characterizes the deliberations of the Fund's executive board. That Goldstein himself contemplates outsourcing the final stage of the decision to the WTO is indicative of the difficulties involved. That said, it would be consonant with the vision of the institution's founders, who included in the Articles of Agreement a scarce currency clause sanctioning the imposition of discriminatory measures against chronic surplus countries.

But even contemplating this possibility presupposes progress in reforming governance and representation in the IMF. The Fund's shareholders will be prepared to delegate additional powers to the institution only if it is representative of its members. There has been progress in revising quotas and voting shares in the Fund and a few modest changes in board representation since the financial crisis. But change remains slow. The selection of a new managing director in 2011 is a reminder, if one was needed, that governance reform is incomplete. The IMF can be an effective steward of the international monetary system only if its decisions are seen as legitimate. And legitimacy will be possible only if the organization is representative of its members.

5 Conclusion

International monetary reform remains a work in progress. There has been slow but steady progress from a dollar-dominated global reserve system toward a better balanced multiple-reserve-currency arrangement, as evident in the fall in the share of dollars in reported global foreign exchange reserves from nearly 70 percent at the turn of the century to barely 60 percent at the time of writing. A 60 percent share is nothing to sneeze at, but the direction of change is clear. Likewise, there has been the gradual development of regional reserve pooling arrangements in East Asia and Europe. We are beginning to see better integration of capital account regulation with macroeconomic management and macro-prudential supervision. All these are signs of progress in the development of a more stable and smoothly functioning international monetary system.

This progress reflects decisions taken at the national level. National central banks decide on the composition of their foreign exchange reserves. National central banks and governments decide on the imposition and design of capital controls. The nature of the exchange rate regime and degree of intervention are similarly decided at the national level.

But a decentralized reform process organized mainly at the national level inevitably suffers from inadequate coordination. Exchange rate arrangements are inconsistent. The preference of some countries to peg but others to float frustrates both groups. There may be greater appreciation of the importance of capital-account regulation, but the result is still a hodgepodge of controls whose effectiveness, cross-border repercussions and systematic effects are uncertain.

All this points to the need for more systematic international coordination to encourage countries to more effectively internalize the cross-border consequences of their policies. The observation applies equally to the sources and recipients of capital flows. It applies to current account surplus and deficit countries alike. And, in turn, this points to the need for an IMF capable of effective monitoring and surveillance, whether the country that is the subject of that surveillance is in surplus or deficit, big or small, advanced or developing. It points to the need for an IMF that can organize the emergency provision of substantial amounts of international credit, whether from its own coffers or those of its members.

But there will be a readiness to endow the IMF with these additional powers and responsibilities only if the institution is regarded as legitimate.

By implication, meaningful governance reform is a prerequisite for further progress on this agenda.

References

Benassy-Quere, A., J. Pisani-Ferry and Y. Yongding (2011). Reform of the international monetary system: Some concrete steps. *Bruegel Policy Contribution,* No. 2011/03, March.

Blanchard, O. and G.M. Milesi-Ferretti (2009). Global imbalances: In midstream? Available at www.imf.org.

Bretton Woods Project (2011). Brazil, India spurn IMF capital controls framework, Bretton Woods Project (June 13). Available at www. brettonwoodsproject.org/art-568564.

Cooper, R. (2009). Necessary reform: The IMF and international financial architecture. *Harvard International Review,* 30, 52–55.

Di Leo, L. and D. Wessel (2010). Fed extends swaps for foreign banks. *Wall Street Journal,* December 22.

Eichengreen, B. (2006). *Global Imbalances and the Lessons of Bretton Woods.* Cambridge, MA: MIT Press.

Eichengreen, B. (2009). Out-of-the-box thoughts on the international financial architecture. IMF Working Paper No. 09–116, May.

Eichengreen, B. (2011). *Exorbitant Privilege: The Rise and Fall of the Dollar and the Future of the International Monetary System.* New York: Oxford University Press.

Farhi, E., P.-O. Gourinchas and H. Rey (2011). *Reforming the International Monetary System.* Unpublished Manuscript (March 27).

Goldberg, L., C. Kennedy and J. Miu (2011). Central bank dollar swap lines and overseas dollar funding costs. *Federal Reserve Bank of New York Economic Policy Review,* 17, 3–20.

Goldstein, M. (2011). The role of the IMF in a reformed international monetary system. Paper presented to the Bank of Korea Conference on the Future of the International Financial Architecture (May 27–28).

Griffin-Jones, S. and K. Gallagher (2011). *Curbing Hot Money Flows to Protect the Real Economy.* Unpublished Manuscript, Columbia University and Boston University (January).

Henning, C.R. (2011). Coordinating regional and multilateral financial institutions. Working Paper No. 11–9, Washington, DC: Peterson Institute for International Economics, March.

International Monetary Fund (2010). The fund's role regarding cross-border capital flows. Paper prepared by the Strategy, Policy and Review Department and Legal Department. Available at www.imf.org.

International Monetary Fund (2011a). Enhancing International Monetary Stability — A Role for the SDR? Available at www.imf.org.

International Monetary Fund, Independent Evaluation Office (2011b). IMF Performance in the Run-Up to the Financial and Economic Crisis: IMF Surveillance in 2004–2007, Independent Evaluation Office, IMF, Washington, DC, January.

International Monetary Fund (2011c). G20 reaffirms commitment to resolve crisis. *IMF Survey.* Available at www.imf.org.

International Monetary Fund (2011d). Triennial surveillance review. Available at www.imf.org.

McGuire, P. and G. von Peter (2009). The dollar shortage in global banking and the international policy response. BIS Working Paper No. 291, October.

Moghadam, R. (2010). Global safety nets: Crisis prevention in an age of uncertainty. *IMF Direct*, September 9.

Obstfeld, M. and K. Rogoff (2010). "Global imbalances and the financial crisis: Products of common causes." In Reuven Glick and Mark Spiegel (eds.), *Asia and the Global Financial Crisis*. San Francisco: Federal Reserve Bank of San Francisco, pp. 131–172.

Park, Y.C. (2009). Reform of the global regulatory system: Perspectives of East Asia's emerging economies. Paper Presented to the Annual Bank Conference on Development Economics, World Bank, Seoul.

Warnock, F. and V. Warnock (2009). International capital flows and US interest rates. *Journal of International Money and Finance*, 28, 903–919.

CHAPTER 5

The Group of 20: Trials of Global Governance in Times of Crisis

Ignazio Angeloni[1]

Kant's notion of global governance — a philosophical one, yet so concrete and compelling in his view that he even produced a formal proof of its inevitability – did not consist of a world government, a single entity central-ising political representation and policy-making for the planet as a whole. It was a peaceful federation of independent states, bound by consensus to a set of rules designed to prevent antagonism and conflict.[2] One of the "articles" he prescribed for this futuristic agreement was, not unexpectedly, the abolition of all permanent armies. It was a good suggestion that unfor-tunately was not heeded; shortly after he wrote *Perpetual Peace* (1795), Europe was shattered by the Napoleonic wars. Another of Kant's proposals, more surprising and interesting with hindsight, was strict control over the size of financial sectors, which he thought would, if left to grow unchecked, turn into war machines aimed at dominating and oppressing neighbors. He had Britain in mind in this respect.

More than two centuries and many wars later the international commu-nity has embarked on an experiment that in some ways is reminiscent of

[1] I am grateful to Silvia Merler for excellent assistance in analysing the data in Section 3 and to Stephen Gardner for editorial support. This chapter draws heavily from Angeloni and Pisani Ferry (2011); however, the views expressed here involve only the author.
[2] Kant (1795).

Kant's idealistic vision. The motives differ from the philosopher's, though the size of financial systems has something to do with them. Threatened by a financial crisis of intensity equal to, or worse than, the one that led to the Great Depression of the 1930s, the leaders of the largest economies have decided to create a "council" to coordinate their economic and financial actions, with the goal of safeguarding stability and prosperity as a common good, by avoiding, in particular, destructive trade and financial conflicts. The decision to convene G20 summit in November 2008 surprised the world but was not, strictly speaking, without historical precedent as an attempt at global governance. The UN with its constellation of agencies and the Bretton Woods organizations (IMF and World Bank group), all having their near-universal membership, have formed the backbone of global cooperation since World War II. There has been, of course, a G7/G8 process since the mid-1970s, trying with variable success to coordinate the economic policies of the leading industrial nations. The G20 itself existed before 2008, though at a smaller scale. The "new" G20 is different, not just for its loftier ambitions but also because it combines many features in an unprecedented way. The political leaders participate directly, rather than being represented as in the IMF. Advanced and emerging nations are present, unlike the G7/G8. It is representative, not universal; its selective participation (19 members plus the EU), while potentially conflicting with the universality of the interests it claims to represent (we shall return to this), gives the grouping the potential to become a standing "world economic governing board." This possibility is remarkable in itself, though whether it will become reality remains an open question.

During its three-year life (a short time, admittedly, to express any firm conclusion), the G20 has fulfilled its ambitions only in part. After a good start, there have been less dynamic phases, and on some occasions its role has not been as significant as one would have expected or hoped. Recently, observers have expressed outright disappointment over its performance and pessimism about its relevance. Yet the reality is that it is still an evolving entity, driven by circumstances, following a largely unwritten script. Its mission remains to be better understood and defined. The new and recent configuration of world power, in which emerging and advanced nations dialogue and decide on an equal basis, has not yet been internalized in all countries' approaches to policy and foreign relations, nor has it generated sufficient awareness of the responsibilities and the opportunities it entails for each participant. Until this happens, the G20 is likely to produce, in different times, equal doses of hope and disillusion, inspiration and criticism.

What purpose is the G20 supposed to serve? Since its birth, this body has had two souls, one as policy coordinator in good times and another as crisis manager. The G20 was actually born twice: first in 1999, after the Asian crisis, as a forum for finance ministers and central bank governors, and second in the autumn of 2008, when it was lifted to the level of heads of state and government during the great financial scare that followed the Lehman demise. On both occasions, the situation called for a crisis manager, not a fair-weather sailor, and both times the immediate danger was averted. But in both cases, after the risks receded, the G20 turned to the more routine task of crisis prevention, through attempts at economic policy coordination. In this respect, its performance has been less convincing.

The resurgence of turbulence in international financial markets in 2010 and especially 2011, with the epicentre no longer in the US banking system but in the European sovereign sector, has offered the G20 a new opportunity to engage itself again at the centre of policy action. Many questions have arisen in this new phase. Are the financial risks stemming from the euro debt crisis relevant from a global perspective? Is the G20 the right forum to detect and avert them? And if so on both counts, what concretely can and should the G20 do? An interesting and constructive dialogue has developed among observers and policymakers around these issues, with many radically innovative options being actively considered — including that of emerging countries providing a safety net to protect global finance, something unheard of previously. In this context, expectations for the Cannes summit grew very high; many felt that the G20 could help manage the new crisis by striking some kind of "grand bargain" within its membership. Nothing of that happened. With the ink still drying on Cannes' concluding statement, the prevailing sense is of disappointment, and concern for the consequences of what is perceived as a lost opportunity. But work continues, and, as often, excessive pessimism could later prove premature.

It is useful, at this juncture, to revisit some basic ideas: reviewing the reasons for the existence of a G20 at all (not following Kant's demonstration, but using more modern economic arguments and evidence), and examining in some detail how the G20 has acted in the six meetings that have taken place so far, and trying to evaluate systematically its overall performance. These are the main aims of the pages that follow. We take stock

of the at the time of writing very recent Cannes meeting, where the leaders
were forced to deviate from earlier lines of work to focus on the European
debt crisis emergency, and last-minute events that created obstacles to successful negotiation. We conclude that, contrary to what many critics say
and despite some recent setbacks, neither is a global governance forum like
the G20 unnecessary, nor should the judgement on how it has performed
be unambiguously negative. It is true, however, that its effectiveness has
diminished, particularly when it has acted as a policy coordinator (less so
in crisis times). We conclude in the last section with some thoughts on ways
to enhance the relevance and effectiveness of the G20.

1   Benefits from International Coordination: Reviewing the Arguments

In spite of a long stream of research over the recent decades, the scope
of international economic policy coordination, and its benefits and limits,
remain unresolved issues in economics. The research literature has given
us useful insights, elegant models and plenty of empirical evidence (often
ambivalent), but the main questions remain open. Policymakers remain, in
this complex matter, without reliable theoretical guidance.

In principle the issue would seem easy to settle. In an interdependent
world, in which national economic performance and policies influence others, hence generating "externalities" from national policies and outcomes,
there should be collective benefits from coordinating policy actions — that
is: deciding on policies not only on the basis of national interests or objectives, but also in relation to how they affect others. Moreover, since economic interdependence has increased in recent times, due to the surge in
international trade and financial flows, coordination should have become
more valuable over time. In practice, however, economists have never succeeded in measuring these benefits precisely or showing that they are significant, for several reasons. First, the counterfactual is lacking: it is not possible to observe what the outcome would have been, should coordination in a
given circumstance have (or not have) materialized. Second, many empirical
analyses date back several decades, prior to the surge in international trade
and capital flows and long before the rise of emerging economic powers. In
that world, interdependence was limited, and it is not surprising that early
research concluded that benefits from coordination were negligible.

A revival of the literature on international policy coordination occurred after the collapse of the Bretton Woods system — somewhat surprisingly, since, according to some authoritative voices, floating exchange rates should have rendered such coordination unnecessary. Models of strategic interaction among policymakers[3] showed that monetary policy could be used to generate Pareto-superior outcomes. While this finding provided an argument for coordination, the question was how significant this gain was quantitatively. In the 1970s and 1980s, the question was approached with multi-country econometric models, linked by international trade.[4] Capital flows were absent or passive, reflecting the reality of the time. As a consequence, any international spillovers in these models depended on trade integration — also limited at the time, but rising. The central message of this literature[5] was mixed. On the one hand, there was clearly a role for coordination, generated by the fact that domestic policy choices had cross-border effects — in particular, beggar-thy-neighbor policies were possible by manipulating the exchange rate. On the other hand, these effects were quantitatively small, and so were the potential gains from coordination.

More recently, economists have revisited the subject using more sophisticated models,[6] with explicit microeconomic foundations and individual preference functions. The characteristics of the new models permit exact calculations of welfare (within the model, of course) as well as comparisons of it across different policy frameworks. In spite of this precision, this literature has unfortunately not achieved more conclusive results. In the interest of simplicity, the models are very restrictive, often assuming constant balance-of-payments equilibrium and no capital flows, in addition to homogeneous agents. Under these assumptions, these models cannot provide sufficiently reliable descriptions of, and prescriptions for, a world dominated by persistent external imbalances and large, highly volatile capital flows.

When analytical answers are lacking, reasoned conjecture can be helpful. Given that the gains from coordination are found to be small either

---

[3]Hamada (1974, 1979), Canzoneri and Gray (1985).
[4]E.g., Oudiz and Sachs (1984).
[5]See Canzoneri and Henderson (1990) for a review.
[6]Obstfeld and Rogoff (2001), Corsetti and Pesenti (2001), Canzoneri, Cumby and Diba (2002).

because cross-border linkages are assumed to be low, when in fact they have increased in recent years, or because the models disregard other important aspects of financial globalisation, it does not seem unreasonable that coordination may be worth considering in today's economy, particularly if the costs and risks involved are not overwhelming. The financial crisis has provided one important argument for this, showing the existence of substantial international spillovers in the area of financial regulation. Countries with large developed financial sectors act typically, particularly if their money performs a role as reserve asset (such as the US, and to a lesser extent the Euro Area), as financial intermediaries for borrowers and lenders located across borders. Their financial structures adapt to this role. The local banking system typically collects large volumes of short-term funds (bank deposits or securities traded in liquid markets) abroad and re-lends these funds across borders, typically long-term. Since financial regulation is a national responsibility (except for harmonisation of certain rules or standards), usually assigned to the competent authority in the country where the bank is incorporated, the supervisory regulatory frameworks prevailing in major financial centres can have significant international repercussions, affecting financial stability in other countries and even globally. This thus provides an argument in favour of international coordination. This is, in fact, an area in which the G20 has been prominently active since 2008, mainly through the Financial Stability Board.

2   A Narrative of the G20 in Times of Crisis

Table 1 presents a synoptic view of the G20 summit meetings so far, with dates and an indication of the main topics.

2.1   *Washington (November 2008)*

The G20 meeting in the composition of heads of state or government was convened for the first time in Washington on November 15, 2008, at the peak of the financial turmoil in the US, shortly after the failure of Lehman Brothers. Several policymakers later claimed credit for the idea, including the then UK Prime Minister Gordon Brown, the outgoing Bush administration and President Sarkozy of France, which held the rotating EU presidency at the time. The G20 summit on that occasion performed the role

Table 1. From Washington to Cannes: An Evolving Agenda.

Summit	Date	Headline priorities
Washington	November 2008	Reform of financial regulation
London	April 2009	Global stimulus Reform of financial regulation
Pittsburgh	September 2009	Rebalancing of world economy Reform of financial regulation
Toronto	June 2010	Rebalancing of world economy Reform of financial regulation
Seoul	November 2010	Rebalancing of world economy International financial institutions
Cannes	November 2011	Euro crisis International monetary system Financial reform Macroeconomic policies Commodity prices

of a "crisis committee,"[7] an entity that could adopt the urgent measures deemed necessary to contain the immediate risks and, by its mere presence, reassure financial markets and instil confidence in the public at large.

As the US was holding presidential elections, leadership at that time was more than usually exercised by the Europeans, among whom coordination had strengthened after an emergency meeting of Euro Area heads of state and government (and the UK), convened at the initiative of the French on October 12 to define common responses to the banking crisis. That was still a time in which many, in Europe and elsewhere, thought that the trans-Atlantic repercussions of the financial crisis would remain limited, and the euro provided an effective shelter against financial instability.

Regardless of who can legitimately claim credit for the initiative, the Washington meeting achieved its goal. It contributed to the stabilization of financial markets, by conveying to market participants the sense that authorities were on top of events, capable of agreeing on a forceful coordinated response to a likely global financial meltdown.

---

[7]See Woods (2010).

The concluding statement[8] was short by usual standards (5 pages, plus an annex containing the Action Plan on financial regulation) and fully concentrated on the situation in the financial markets and on the actions to be taken to stabilize them. The section on the diagnosis of the crisis mentioned macroeconomic factors only vaguely, mentioning "unsustainable global macroeconomic outcomes." This was reportedly because the Chinese did not want global imbalances to be explicitly mentioned among the root causes of the crisis, as this would have suggested that their surplus was somehow to blame for it. The macroeconomy would come later.

The statement included a concrete action plan, focused on financial markets and financial institutions, with five lines of action: strengthening transparency and accountability; enhancing financial regulation; promoting integrity; reinforcing international cooperation; and reforming international financial institutions (IFIs). The agenda was further broken down between urgent actions to be implemented by March 31, 2009 and medium-term actions. The G20 ministers, supported by an enlarged Financial Stability Forum (FSF), by standard-setting bodies and national supervisors, as well as by the IMF, were entrusted with the task of monitoring and ensuring progress against the action list. In an informal way, a pyramidal governance structure (G20 at the top, supported by FSF and IMF) was taking shape, though it would be enshrined in formal decisions later.

The Washington communiqué conveys a sense of urgency, focus and concreteness that could not be found in the traditional G7/G8 declarations. Instead of broad, often nebulous, open-ended political declarations encompassing a wide range of topics, it reads like what it is — an extremely focused action plan. The traditional set of commitments that can suit every participant, because it merely restates what they are already committed to nationally, cannot be found in the text. Instead, the language is precise, even technical. Specialized institutions in charge of carrying out work — the IMF, FSF, the Basel Committee, national regulators and others — are named and given strict deadlines for implementation.[9]

---

[8]See http://www.g20.org/Documents/g20_summit_declaration.pdf.

[9]For example, the first item of the financial regulation action plan, for implementation by March 31, 2009, reads "The IMF, expanded FSF, and other regulators and bodies should develop recommendations to mitigate pro-cyclicality, including the review of how valuation and leverage, bank capital, executive compensation, and provisioning practices may exacerbate cyclical trends."

2.2   *London (April 2009)*

The London summit on April 1–2, 2009 is likely to remain in history as the moment when the international community united to ward off the risks of recession and protectionism. Indeed, it took place at a time when world output and trade were beginning to stabilize, through this was not yet apparent at the time. Observers were afraid that the world would be heading towards another Great Depression.[10] In the same city where the countries participating in the World Economic Conference of 1933 had failed to find common ground, the London summit provided a major impetus toward cooperation.

The leaders convened in London just after the deadline set for the "immediate actions" on financial markets decided in Washington. A "Progress Report on the Washington Action Plan," published in London on April 2,[11] suggests with hindsight that most of the major areas of financial reform, such as bank capital strengthening, the definition of a new capital framework to avoid pro-cyclicality, new liquidity and risk management standards, IMF surveillance (including the unprecedented decision to conduct a Financial Sector Assessment Program for the US), internal incentives and compensation practices, were underway. Less clear was the progress on transparency and accountability, in particular due to lack of progress towards harmonisation of accounting standards.

On financial regulation the London summit maintained the momentum launched in Washington, and also brought about new results. The final statement was again relatively short and to the point, explicitly indicating concrete actions to be taken. The leaders decided to reshape the FSF, transforming it into a Financial Stability Board (FSB) with broader representation (mirroring that of the G20) and an enhanced mandate. The FSB would, from then on, act as coordinator of all actions taken, in the area of financial regulation and supervision, by national and international standard setters. The leaders also started to establish the broad principles that would characterize, after a transition, post-crisis bank capital standards: in the short term, until the macroeconomic recovery would strengthen, minimum capital requirements would remain unchanged or even decline, to facilitate lending; subsequently, prudential standards would be strengthened, building capital buffers above regulatory minima, increasing the quality of

---

[10]Eichengreen and O'Rourke (2010).
[11]Available at http://www.g20.org/Documents/FINAL_Annex_on_Action_Plan.pdf.

capital, mitigating the pro-cyclicality of capital ratios (including a requirement that banks build up capital buffers in good times), supplementing capital requirements with non-risk based measures, improving risk management incentives, and enhancing liquidity buffers. In addition to capital standards, the London conclusions feature provisions on hedge funds (registration, information gathering), credit derivatives (establishment of central counterparties), executive compensation and bank board risk control responsibilities, credit rating agencies (registration and supervision, according to IOSCO rules). Still tentative were, on the contrary, the initiatives agreed in London concerning systemically important banks (SIFIs), eventually adopted at the Cannes meeting in 2011, shadow banks and accounting standards.

The London summit also broadened the scope for action to include macroeconomic topics. The leaders stated that their countries were implementing fiscal expansion, monetary expansion and banking sector repair, indicating that these actions constituted[12] *"the largest fiscal and monetary stimulus and the most comprehensive support programme for the financial sector in modern times."* They pledged to conduct *"all [their] economic policies cooperatively and responsibly with regard to the impact on other countries"* — a significant commitment for a number of non-G7 countries which were used to regarding sovereignty over macroeconomic policy as nearly absolute. It should be noted, however, that the declaration included no specific commitment in terms of either effort or date.

A major innovation was the strengthening of the resources available to emerging and developing economies through the IFIs. The summit decided on a $750 billion overall increase in the resources available through the IMF (of which $250 billion in immediate, temporary bilateral loans, to be substituted at a later stage by $500 billion in form of an expansion of the Fund's New Agreements to Borrow, plus SDR allocations of $250 billion), and on an increase in the capital endowments of the multilateral development banks, part of which was earmarked for low-income countries. Finally, an increase in trade credit at the global level, to be channelled through the IFC, was agreed. All this amounted to an unprecedented increase in the resources available to multilateral institutions, more than offsetting the restrictions that had been enacted in the benign economic and financial environment of the preceding years.

---

[12]See http://www.g20.org/Documents/final-communique.pdf.

The reason for this massive increase in available resources was the fear that, at a time when advanced economies were struggling with the domestic fallout from the financial crisis, emerging countries would suffer from a major reversal of capital flows. Indeed, these countries, which had mostly been immune to the financial crisis until the Lehman shock, experienced a sudden stop in the third quarter of 2008, especially in emerging Europe and in Asia.

2.3   *Pittsburgh (September 2009)*

Five months later, the summit in Pittsburgh marked what can be regarded as a sort of watershed. In a number of ways, in a climate of low expectations, Pittsburgh achieved important results, but also coincided with a marked slowdown in the productivity of the G20.

By the time the leaders gathered it was clear that a recovery was underway and optimism was on the rise: the October IMF forecast envisioned 3.1 percent world growth in 2010, against 1.9 foreseen by the April forecast. The sense of urgency that had characterised the two previous meetings had abated and the policy focus was shifting to making preparations for more normal times. Nevertheless, the communiqué unambiguously emphasized that it was too early to remove the stimulus:[13]

> *We pledge today to sustain our strong policy response until a durable recovery is secured. We will act to ensure that when growth returns, jobs do too. We will avoid any premature withdrawal of stimulus. At the same time, we will prepare our exit strategies and, when the time is right, withdraw our extraordinary policy support in a cooperative and coordinated way, maintaining our commitment to fiscal responsibility.*

A first important result from Pittsburgh concerned institution-building. The leaders decided that the G20 summit would become a regular event, replacing the G8 at the top of the international financial architecture. In this framework, Finance Ministers would act as deputies, preparing agendas and implementing decisions, supported by the FSB and the IMF — the first responsible for financial markets, the second for macroeconomic surveillance and last-resort lending. The leaders also committed to a strengthening of the voice of emerging and developing countries in the IMF by shifting by January 2011 at least 5 percent of the quotas from over-represented to

---

[13]See http://www.g20.org/Documents/pittsburgh_summit_leaders_statement_250909.pdf

under-represented countries. However, because of US reluctance, they could not agree to appointing without condition of nationality the heads of the Fund and the Bank.

On financial reform, a key challenge in Pittsburgh was to continue to exert guidance and preserve the reform momentum, while at the same time avoiding micro-management and excessive top-down command of what were bound to be increasingly technical discussions. In this area, the leaders struck a reasonable balance between direct guidance and delegation to the FSB and to the national authorities. On risk control the message was clear — strengthen capitalization; extend the focus to leverage and liquidity; avoid pro-cyclical regulation — but implementation was left in the hands of the Basel Committee. A number of broad principles on compensation practices were established, but the task of working out the implications and, most importantly, implementation, was left to the FSB and especially to national supervisors (which *"should have the responsibility to review firms' compensation policies and structures with institutional and systemic risk in mind..."*). On moral hazard, the leaders asked for the establishment of bank resolution procedures and crisis management standing groups in all systemically important institutions, especially those operating across borders.

The G20 made significant headway in Pittsburgh also on global imbalances. The issue had been left aside in the two previous meetings, first to avoid turning the summits into US–China confrontations and second, because the priority was to address financial regulation failures and the common risk of a depression. But it was becoming too important an issue for continued avoidance. First, in discussion on the causes of the crisis, the idea was gaining ground that large and persistent payment disequilibria among currency areas had been among the contributors to systemic risk-building.[14] Second, the IMF was projecting for the medium term a rebound of imbalances (the October 2009 WEO envisaged that they would stabilize at about 2 percent of world GDP — a forecast that has not changed much since — against 2.5 to 3 percent in 2006–2007). Third, it was feared that in the years ahead, demand in the advanced countries would remain subdued because of the extent of deleveraging and the coming fiscal retrenchment,

---

[14]This link was made explicit in two influential European reports by Jacques de Larosière (2009) and Adair Turner (2009) on the reform of financial regulation. However, the idea remained disputed among academics, with some notable exceptions (Eichengreen, 2009; Portes, 2009) and among policymakers.

and that to sustain global growth there was a need to foster demand in the emerging countries.

On the eve of Pittsburgh it seemed unlikely that leaders would enter this contentious territory, but the outcome surpassed expectations. On the initiative of the US, a "framework" for macroeconomic policies was agreed upon, with the aim of making national policies ("fiscal, monetary, trade, structural") consistent with balanced growth, including regular consultations on commonly agreed policies and objectives. Agreement on the Framework represented an ambitious international coordination endeavour, which set differentiated goals for deficit countries and surplus countries.[15] Furthermore, the leaders instructed their finance ministers to put in place a surveillance process, the "Mutual Assessment Process" (MAP) "to evaluate the collective implications of national policies for the world economy." The IMF was asked to give technical support to this exercise in multilateral surveillance, working with G20 ministers and central banks, and to report regularly to the G20 leaders.

Less significant for the short term, but noticeable nevertheless, Pittsburgh was also characterized by a broadening of the agenda: for the first time the communiqué mentioned at length energy security, climate change, poverty, job quality, and trade and investment. All important issues for sure, but on which pronouncements were more verbose than on core G20 business.

2.4   Toronto and Seoul (June and November 2010)

In the year following Pittsburgh, the G20 calendar included two summit meetings under a joint Canadian–Korean chair: Toronto and Seoul. The Toronto meeting on June 27, 2010 marked the lowest point, based on progress made at the meeting, in G20 history. The macroeconomic coordination framework virtually stalled against the test of delivering a joint assessment. The IMF, which was steering the process although its responsibility was in principle one of technical assistance only, was reluctant to move too fast to policy conclusions as it wanted first to educate governments in the process of information sharing. At the same time, specific circumstances contributed to rendering agreement difficult. In spring 2010, it was undisputable that the recovery was underway, but fears of double-dip recession remained widespread. In all countries, monetary and fiscal authorities,

---

[15]See Vines (2011).

while beginning to think about "exit strategies" and to refer to them in public communication, maintained de facto an accommodative stance. But the awareness was increasing that the revenue shortfall provoked by the recession (and to a lesser extent by the stimulus) would give rise, in time, to a historically unprecedented debt explosion. In the midst of the trade-off (expand now, consolidate later), positions were divided. Europeans were especially concerned about fiscal risks after the outbreak of the Greek crisis (which had led, weeks earlier, to what many regarded as a first controversial step towards a fiscal union, the creation of the European Financial Stability Facility), while the US, where unemployment had risen much more, being still decisively positioned in favour of fiscal expansion. The majority of participants in the summit emphasised the fiscal risks and the need for consolidation, as evident in these passages from the final statement[16]:

> *[. . .] recent events highlight the importance of sustainable public finances and the need for our countries to put in place credible, properly phased and growth-friendly plans to deliver fiscal sustainability, differentiated for and tailored to national circumstances. Those countries with serious fiscal challenges need to accelerate the pace of consolidation.*

and

> *Sound fiscal finances are essential to sustain recovery, provide flexibility to respond to new shocks, ensure the capacity to meet the challenges of aging populations, and avoid leaving future generations with a legacy of deficits and debt. [. . .] Those with serious fiscal challenges need to accelerate the pace of consolidation. Fiscal consolidation plans will be credible, clearly communicated, differentiated to national circumstances, and focused on measures to foster economic growth.*

Not least because of a convergence of views between the new British Prime Minister, David Cameron, and German Chancellor Angela Merkel, the tone of the final statement concerning macroeconomic policies was surprisingly emphatic on the need for fiscal consolidation, an orientation that left the US uncomfortably isolated. The advanced G20 countries agreed to halve fiscal deficits by 2013 and to reduce public debt ratios by 2016 if not before. The whole macroeconomic discussion was very much reminiscent of traditional US–European disputes, with the emerging countries playing a secondary role. In this respect, as well as in the fairly general tone of the discussion,

---

[16]See http://www.g20.org/Documents/g20_declaration_en.pdf.

the Toronto G20 summit was closer to a traditional G7 summit than to the meetings in London and Pittsburgh.

At the same time, the financial reform agenda had visibly slipped out of the hands of the heads of state and government. It was left entirely in the hands of the FSB, without much further political stimulus or guidance. This was probably an inevitable development in view of the complexity of the details involved, but contributed to give the impression that the Toronto summit had little to deliver.

The Seoul G20 summit was the first chaired by a non-G7 country, and Korea was especially keen on making it a success. It was not an easy task: on the macroeconomic front, a swift return to normality was reviving old problems. The currency dispute between the US and China was again making headlines and other controversies had erupted as many emerging countries were overwhelmed by capital inflows. "Currency wars," in the words of Brazilian Finance Minister Guido Mantega, was the theme of the day. Simultaneously, the Mutual Assessment Process was proving more cumbersome and controversial than expected.

In this climate, the Korean presidency was not able to achieve breakthrough on the controversial issues. An attempt was made to open a new road towards compromise between China and the US by stating that current account balances should remain below 4 percent of GDP, but no agreement could be found in time for the summit. Heads of state and government could only agree to name the problem (a change from the initial reluctance to mention imbalances) and call for further work by their Finance Ministers. The corresponding sentences in the communiqué[17] were particularly convoluted:

> *Persistently large imbalances, assessed against indicative guidelines to be agreed by our Finance Ministers and Central Bank Governors, warrant an assessment of their nature and the root causes of impediments to adjustment as part of the MAP, recognizing the need to take into account national or regional circumstances, including large commodity producers. These indicative guidelines composed of a range of indicators would serve as a mechanism to facilitate timely identification of large imbalances that require preventive and corrective actions to be taken.*

In this passage, a mandate is given to ministers and governors to identify the set of relevant indicators; interestingly, such a mandate had already

---

[17]See http://www.g20.org/Documents2010/11/seoulsummit_declaration.pdf.

been given at Pittsburgh, and not fulfilled. *Repetita iuvant?* Perhaps. For sure, the reiteration revealed the diplomatic hurdles the new coordination model entailed, with countries on opposite sides of the fence twisting concepts and wordings to pursue momentary interests or reputational concerns. The MAP produced a set of "policy commitments," in which each country indicated its policy goals in several fields (fiscal, financial, monetary and exchange rate, structural, development, other policies) and how they contributed to the Framework goals.[18] The fact that all participants agreed to commit to policy actions *vis-à-vis* partners was a valuable political signal, though the commitments themselves did not entail departures from their pre-existing policy course.

Seoul was more successful on two other fronts: first, it delivered ahead of time on the Pittsburgh commitment to reform IMF governance, with a reform that shifted 6 percent of quota shares toward under-represented countries.[19] Second, it could take stock of an agreement reached in the Basel Committee to revise bank capital adequacy ratios.

Korea had been keen to open two new chapters in the discussion. It had first proposed to discuss "financial safety nets," in other words, mechanisms to give countries access to liquidity when facing capital outflows. This intended to remove a motive for self-insurance through reserve accumulation, itself a potential contributor to global imbalances. Safety nets could consist of IMF facilities, regional agreements and swap agreements with the major central banks. The theme was widely recognized as valid, but achievements and agreement remained limited. The IMF announced in August 2010 a new low-conditionality facility, the Precautionary Credit Line (PCL) to complement the pre-existing Flexible Credit Line (FCL), but no agreement could be found on the more ambitious Global Stabilization Mechanism (GSM). The theme however served as a bridge to discussions under the French G20 presidency on reforming the international monetary system.

The other chapter was development. This was indicative of the broadening of the G20 agenda from an initial focus on financial regulation and crisis management to a broader set of issues. Clearly, Korea had substantive and political motives to open a new chapter, and so would future presidencies.

---

[18]IMF (2010).

[19]Agreement was reached in a Finance Ministers meeting in Gyeongju on October 22–23, 2010.

But the downside was, inevitably, a lack of focus and lower potential for significant deliverables.

2.5   *Cannes (November 2011)*

In 2011, the French G20 presidency started with high ambitions, adding two new elements to the agenda.[20] The work programme for the year was intense, including four ministerial meetings in preparation for the Cannes summit on November 3–4, plus working group meetings and a high-level seminar.

The first new element was a focus on the international monetary system (IMS), and prospects for its improvement and reform. According to the presidency's programme, the theme would have included four chapters:[21]

- a new framework to address the volatility of capital flows, of interest especially for emerging countries;
- the introduction of new financial safety nets, along the lines pursued in the previous year by the Korean presidency;
- a review of the role of the SDR, possibly including the composition of the currency basket;
- a strengthening of IMF surveillance on financial, monetary, fiscal and exchange rate policies.

The activity in the first part of the year — two ministerial meetings (February and April) and a high-level seminar on the "Reform of the International Monetary System" in China in March, with the participation of President Sarkozy — confirmed the central role of this issue in the French agenda. However, in the second part of the year the intensification of the European crisis diverted attention and narrowed down the original ambitions on this front. The IMS did not feature in the communiqué following the September meeting of ministers and governors, and the mention in the subsequent October meeting, the last preceding the summit, was long but insubstantial.[22]

---

[20]See French G20 Presidency (2011).

[21]A more detailed overview of issues is contained in Angeloni *et al.* (2016).

[22]The two final statements are available respectively at http://www.g20.org/Documents 2011/09/G20%20communiqué%20-%20Washington%20DC%2022%2009%202011.pdf and http://www.g20.org/Documents2011/10/G20%20communiqué%2014-15%20October% 202011-EN.pdf.

The second innovative element was a new chapter on commodity markets. The origin of the idea lay in the sharp price fluctuations experienced in recent years, with a particularly dramatic rise in 2008 subsequently reversed after the financial crisis. Some G20 members felt that these movements had to do with the increasing presence in the market of financial investors, speculating in derivatives. A group of experts was asked to execute an in-depth study. The main message from it was that commodity price developments had been driven, in the last 10 years, mainly by the expansion of demand by emerging economies, linked to their fast rate of growth and to the accompanying changes in social structures and consumption patterns (leading to high energy consumption and food demand). According to the study, the uncertain response of supply accounts for the volatility of expectations and prices. Financial factors are deemed to be present, but their overall impact is believed not to be dominant. In light of these conclusions, and of the diverging positions within the G20, the initial desire of some members to agree on concrete interventions to stabilize the market by curbing "speculative" activities was not upheld. The study recommended improving the functioning of markets by increasing transparency, and tackling market abuse, thereby avoiding distortions and creating favorable conditions for investment and an expansion of productive capacity.

Another French programme item, inherited from past agendas, was the further development of the "Framework for Growth." The immediate goal was to agree on a scoreboard of statistical indicators to monitor macroeconomic developments and policies, with a view to coordinating policies to reduce global imbalances. Here progress was made in the ministerial meetings of February and April, with an agreement on a two-step approach. In the first stage, countries whose size and/or conditions may imply systemic risks for the global economy would be singled out, on the basis of a small set of indicators. In the second stage, an in-depth analysis of those countries would be conducted. The negotiation was long and complex, largely around semantics. Reportedly, in the Paris meeting, the drafting came to a gridlock over the acceptable use of the term "current account," and the meeting lasted more than 14 hours. In the end, as reported by the press, the confidential list of countries singled out for second-stage examination includes the US, Japan, Germany, France, the UK, China and India. Even considering these complications, the outcome was valuable because it broke the stalemate prevailing in earlier meetings, in which leaders and ministers had been unable to give shape to their commitment to give operational content to the "Framework" agreed in Pittsburgh.

On financial regulation, ministers and governors continued to give stimulus and guidance to the FSB, mainly in four areas: the prudential regulation of SIFIs, particularly of global relevance (GSIFIs); the regulation and oversight of shadow banking systems; the reform of OTC derivatives, introducing where appropriate central clearing arrangements and margin requirements; and the monitoring and disclosure of compensation practices, in line with the standards and principles agreed in the FSB.

These were the initial goals of the French presidency. In practice, however, starting in mid-2011, the focus of policy discussions was increasingly absorbed by the Euro Area sovereign debt crisis. An extended description of this crisis cannot be given here.[23] A clear alarm bell rang in July, when the tension in sovereign debt markets, already severe since Spring 2010 in smaller countries such as Greece, Ireland and Portugal, extended to Spain and Italy, countries large enough to pose severe threats to the stability of the whole Euro Area, and to render the existing crisis-management instruments, principally the European Financial Stability Facility (EFSF), insufficient to ensure adequate protection. Since then, the situation in European sovereign markets has deteriorated further, a consequence of hesitation on the part of European leaders in putting together a cohesive strategy and the lack of an adequate response by the countries concerned. A Euro Area summit on October 26–27 decided to expand the scale of the EFSF through, *inter alia*, additional capital contributions that according to the concluding statement should come from unspecified "public and private" sources.

The official indication of the possibility of external support, other than that already provided by Euro Area members through their contributions to the fund, came after several weeks during which such a possibility was repeatedly mentioned and explored.[24] Bilateral contacts are reported to have been taken by some Euro Area governments with large emerging countries in surplus, including China. On a number of occasions, Brazil has signalled its willingness to contribute. Immediately following the October Euro Area summit, the CEO of the EFSF, Klaus Regling, travelled to the Far East, reportedly to take soundings about, or perhaps to solicit,

---

[23] A detailed and compelling account is provided in a forthcoming book by Bastasin (2012).

[24] See, for example, Angeloni (2011a).

contributions to the fund. The response was mixed — Japan was more positive, China more prudent. In any event, the most natural occasion for any final decisions and announcement would have been, it was felt, the forthcoming Cannes summit.

Against this background, the expectations for Cannes grew. In the meantime, however, several events complicated the situation and undermined the prospects for a potential agreement. Risk spreads on peripheral bonds, notably those of Italy, deteriorated further, amidst indecisiveness and divisions among the authorities in Rome, with the Italian risk increasingly in the spotlight of European discussions. Three days before the summit, then Greek prime minister George Papandreou announced his intention of calling a referendum on the EU-backed economic programme. The announcement, which stunned markets, European leaders and even Greek cabinet members, was promptly withdrawn following a meeting with Germany, France and the EU hastily convened in Cannes before the beginning of the summit. But the sequence of events in the crucial preceding hours had already given the impression that Europe was not ready to negotiate with external contributors, due to lack of cohesion, hesitation by national leaders in deciding crucial adjustment measures at home and, importantly, lack of clarity on how the enhanced EFSF would effectively function.[25]

In this environment, though leaders discussed the issues openly and explored several options, the outcome of Cannes fell dramatically short of expectations. Not only did the contribution from emerging countries not materialise — the conclusions vaguely refer to the intention of ministers to return to the table in the near future — but the G20 leaders also failed to make significant progress on other areas ministers had been working on during the year. No substantive conclusion was reached on possible improvements to the IMS, a flagship of the French agenda. No new initiatives were mentioned on IMF surveillance or on managing volatile capital flows. On financial reform, the final statement confirms conclusions and intentions already expressed by the FSB on SIFIs, shadow banks and other items. On macroeconomic policies, an announcement was made on a new Action Plan for Growth, rather generic in content. The only exception was an unusual reference to Italy, stressing its decision to "invite the IMF to carry out a public verification of its policy implementation on a quarterly basis." Even this unexpected and potentially important request, however, failed to

---

[25]Reportedly, a near-struck deal on enhancing the EFSF further by, *inter alia*, pooling a fraction of central bank reserves failed because of opposition from Germany.

reassure markets; Italian spreads climbed to historic levels as soon as the summit conclusions appeared on the screens, eventually contributing to the government's fall a few days later.

3 Scoreboards of Success

In this section, we change perspective, moving away from the contingencies of specific events or negotiations and focusing on an alternative way to assess the G20 record. The approach involves the compilation of "scoreboards" to measure success or failure ex-post, using a systematic methodology. Luckily we do not need to build a new dataset from scratch; we can draw on the work of the University of Toronto (UoT), which is accessible through the website of the "G20 Information Center."[26]

The UoT's approach consists of measuring the compliance of G20 nations with their own stated objectives as expressed by official post-meeting statements. UoT researchers have watched, for several years using a consistent methodology, the G8 and G20 processes, and compiled detailed scoreboards after each meeting. There is a fairly long time series of these data for the G8, and a more limited one for the G20. More specifically, the UoT researchers catalogue, for every G20 summit, the commitments expressed in the final statement, and then monitor compliance with these commitments in the period up to the next summit. For each commitment and meeting, each country is judgementally assigned a value of 1 if the commitment was fulfilled fully or nearly, of 0 if the commitment could not be fulfilled or was fulfilled only to a limited extent, and −1 if the country did not act.[27] The next step is to calculate average measures of the degree of compliance, separately for each meeting or each topic. A positive value means that there was at least partial compliance on average with the commitment made, while a value close to 0 or negative signals limited or no compliance. The information conveyed by this type of data is different from that examined in the previous section, because it refers to the extent that stated commitments were fulfilled, without making any judgement about the quality of those commitments.

Table 2 reports simple average scores, divided by topic (upper part of the table) and meetings (lower part). For simplicity we have restricted attention

---

[26]See http://www.g20.utoronto.ca.

[27]See a technical note available on the University of Toronto G20 Information Center website (http://www.g20.utoronto.ca/analysis/index.html).

Table 2. G20 Compliance Scores.

	Macroeconomic policy	Financial Reform	IFI reform	Other	Average
G20	0.55	0.27	0.48	0.31	0.40
Advanced	0.66	0.57	0.89	0.58	0.67
Advanced in deficit	0.67	0.60	0.83	0.62	0.68
Emerging	0.46	−0.06	0.10	0.03	0.13
Emerging in deficit	0.32	−0.04	0.20	0.13	0.15
G7	0.65	0.63	0.93	0.60	0.70
G7 Europe	0.73	0.74	0.88	0.66	0.75
Memo: St-Dev G-20 total	0.31	0.41	0.49	0.35	0.39

	Washington	London	Pittsburg	Toronto	Seoul	Average
G20	0.51	0.23	0.24	0.28	0.50	0.35
Advanced	0.72	0.49	0.58	0.58	0.66	0.61
Advanced in deficit	0.80	0.57	0.56	0.59	0.71	0.65
Emerging	0.19	−0.04	−0.08	−0.02	0.32	0.08
Emerging in deficit	0.28	0.08	−0.08	−0.09	0.36	0.11
G7	0.72	0.54	0.57	0.59	0.65	0.61
G7 Europe	1.00	0.65	0.59	0.61	0.71	0.71
Memo: St-Dev G-20 total	0.59	0.43	0.45	0.34	0.24	0.41

Source: University of Toronto G20 Information Center, author's calculations.

to four topics: macroeconomic policy, financial reform, IFI reform, and others (a heterogeneous mix including trade, development, climate change, terrorist financing and money laundering, etc). The latest summit for which scores are available is Seoul. We calculated simple average scores for the G20 as a whole and for the following sub-groups of members: the advanced countries, the advanced countries with a current account deficit, the emerging countries, the emerging countries with a current account deficit, the G7 and G7 Europe. We have also calculated the standard deviation across the G20, as a measure of the cross-country dispersion of the degree of compliance.[28]

Two messages emerge immediately from the table. First, almost all numbers are positive. This means that, based on the assumed criteria, there was

---

[28]Note that the averages shown in the two parts of the table do not coincide, due to the fact that averages are not weighted and the number of commitments on which scores are calculated in each policy area or meeting are different.

at least some compliance in nearly all cases. For the G20 as a whole, and as an average across all meetings, the score is 0.40, with a standard deviation of 0.39, which means that a large part of the distribution, including that comprised between ± sigma, lies in the positive range. The only negative numbers regard emerging countries in the area of financial reform. Surprisingly, the overall G20 compliance in the area of financial reform is rather low (0.27). This, however, depends entirely on the negative score of emerging countries (where financial reform may be perceived as less urgent than other areas), and on the fact that the averages reported in the table are not weighted by size (which implies for example that the US, with a GDP share in total G20 close to 25 percent and an even larger share in terms of financial market size, is weighted equally to Indonesia, which has a share of 1 percent in total GDP).[29] This suggests that performance in this domain tended to be stronger for large developed countries.

The second finding is that compliance drops after the first meeting (Washington). The London meeting, which, as we discussed earlier, was very successful on the basis of the commitments expressed in the final communiqué, seems to have been less so on the basis of the eventual compliance as measured by the UoT indicators. The decline is visible in both the advanced and the emerging-country groups. However, the two groups are characterized by sharply different levels of compliance, the advanced having a much higher score than the emerging. In essence, the decline in G20 compliance after Washington tends to be largely a problem of emerging countries. To the extent that this concerns financial reform, the signal is not necessarily disappointing, since reform of the financial sector was (and remains) a priority principally for the advanced countries.[30] The G20 financial reform agenda was meant to trigger action in advanced countries and it should be no surprise to observe that it is in these countries that it was most effective.

Note that, after London, the average compliance increased steadily, with a somewhat stronger increase in the scoring of the Seoul meeting. This strengthens the impression that the Seoul commitments, while perhaps not constituting a breakthrough relative to expectations, were realistic and achievable.

---

[29]Weighted scores are presented in Angeloni and Pisani Ferry (2011).
[30]Rottier and Véron (2010) suggest that, in the area of financial reform, the effectiveness of the G20 depends on the implementing agent — national authorities or international agencies. They show that the latter have on average been more effective, especially when they claimed full authority as opposed to a mere coordination role.

Across topics, the highest scores are obtained by macroeconomic poli-cies and IFI reform. Again, advanced countries display a higher degree of compliance.[31] On macroeconomic policies, the positive score, despite slow progress in setting up the "Framework for Sustainable and Balanced Growth," is attributable to the timely enactment of the stimulus policies agreed mainly in the Washington meeting.

Two comments should be made before closing this section. First, despite its novelty, the performance of the G20, based on implementation of the self-assigned objectives, seems encouraging. To be true, commitments may be not very ambitious to begin with, and hence easily achievable. This underscores the need to supplement the score analysis with a judgemental evaluation of the "weight" of the decisions.[32] Second, the data in Table 2 suggests the possibility that the degree of ambition of the G20 commitments may have been inversely related to their subsequent implementation. This hypothesis is unproven at this stage, and would require a deeper analysis. That said, it is interesting to note that the G20 scores are roughly similar to those of the G8, calculated by the UoT researchers following the same approach, despite the much longer experience and the more manageable size of the older formation.[33]

4 Taking Stock and Looking Forward

From November 2008 to November 2011 the G20 has gone through a cycle. The initial period (Washington and London summits), character-ized by a "crisis mode," was marked by success on several fronts: finan-cial reform, coordinated macroeconomic stimulus and the avoidance of protectionist measures. The Pittsburgh summit, while effective in terms of institution building (establishment of a permanent G20, plus the macroe-conomic "Framework") marked the transition to the second stage. Here the

---

[31]The compliance with the IFI reform commitments is calculated with reference to the national ratification of the international accords, and/or with the countries "taking an active stance in addressing the reforms." This explains why compliance scores differ across countries, even if these reforms are collective in nature.

[32]On the other hand, caution is also warranted also in judging summit outcomes on the basis of final statements; they may conceal difficulties in translating them into national decisions.

[33]See Angeloni and Pisani Ferry (2011).

G20 moved toward macroeconomic coordination and progress stalled, in the context of economic recovery, renewed asymmetry between advanced and emerging countries, and reduced financial market tensions. In recent times, there seems to have been some revival of effectiveness, based on compliance with announced goals; however, this was probably due to more limited ambitions. The Cannes meeting, disappointing in all areas where progress was expected, confirms this trend.

That said, the judgement on the overall performance of the G20 summits remains tentative at this stage. The disappointing outcome at Cannes may have been due to specific contingencies — lack of preparedness on the European side — and unfortunate timing. In any event, it seems clear that the G20 is unlikely to fulfil the ambition announced at Pittsburgh to become, by the mere fact of existing, the central forum of global governance. The transition will be a more gradual process, with small steps forward and extensive homework to do, prone to reversals and accelerations.

Looking ahead, three directions of further work seem important. The first is to ensure a higher degree of representation and ownership in G20 deliberations. Political and geographical representation is supposed to be provided by the presence at the table of leading representatives of the largest economies, plus a correction in favour of the emerging world — a distinguishing trait of the G20. This may not be sufficient, and the "representation issue," signaled by some recent critical views, should not be underestimated.[34] In a global community counting nearly 200 independent nations, 19 countries (and one region) can claim universal legitimacy only if there are mechanisms to ensure that decisions are also effectively owned by countries not present at the table. Procedures to ensure this do not exist at present. They could be established within existing international organizations with broader membership (for example, the IMF).

A second point concerns internal organization and effectiveness. The G20 has established good working arrangements with a number of entities that de facto report to it — IMF, FSB, Basel Committee on Bank Supervision — and is assisted by substructures (ministers and governors, plus their deputies). The lack of its own technical expertise does not seem to be a serious limitation. The expert input comes from the bodies just mentioned. A more serious problem, however, has been ensuring continuity of

---

[34]Vestergaard (2010); Åslund (2011).

action over time. As we have noted agenda, setting completely relies on the annual rotating presidencies, often with very different priorities from one year to the next.

Some improvements in working arrangements could help. Long-term (multi-annual) work lines should be agreed, with the aim of providing guidance to the rotating chair. Leaders and ministers should seek, with other sources of expertise, input from independent experts. A steering group, similar to that set up in the FSB, with a mandate extending beyond the annual chair, could be established. A more ambitious possibility in the same direction would be to set up a small permanent secretarial structure at the IMF. Its mandate — ensuring continuity to the process and stronger liaison between the rotating chairs — would not require large staffing, and bureaucracy and red tape should be avoided.

That said, it is clear that organizational changes can never be a substitute for substance and vision. As it stands, the G20 cannot provide such a vision, in part because it lacks a shared philosophy, a common understanding of the economic priorities of our time and the way to approach them. A serious debate has not started yet on many questions of central importance for the global economy, though it would be desirable. How will the global community cope with the limits to global resources in this century and beyond? How will the inescapable aspirations of economic newcomers (the emerging world) be made compatible with the requirements of the veterans, in a balance of interests that benefit all? How can within- and between-country inequalities generated by the globalization process be tackled? How, in the political economy of this balance, should the interests of future generations be considered? What economic system, specifically what position in the multifaceted spectrum between free and regulated markets, offers the best chance of making the reconciliation of this multidimensional set of interests easier? And, neither least nor final, what are the specific orientations to be taken in the key areas facing the global economy — energy, environment, financial regulation, international monetary relations, crisis and natural disaster management, just to name a few?

The increased relevance of these themes stems from the same historical forces (globalization and the new balance in international relations) that gave rise to the G20. These are complex and controversial issues, over which the risk of stalemate is significant. The G20 should become a driving force in developing this dialogue. Until now the G20 has worked on the urgent issues of the moment and on those inherited from the past. While justified given the conditions, this will be hardly sufficient going forward. The G20 needs to make the best of its diversity and set itself a forward-looking agenda.

References

Angeloni, I. (2011a). Back into action: The *Bruegel G20 Monitor*. Available at http://www.bruegel.org/bruegel-and-the-g20/, August 25.

Angeloni, I. *et al.* (2011b). *Global Currencies for Tomorrow: A European Perspective*; Bruegel Policy Brief n. 13.

Angeloni, I. and J. P. Ferry (2012). The G20: Characters in search of an author. Bruegel Working paper.

Åslund, A. (2011). Why the Group of 20 is failing, Peterson Institute for International Economics.

Bastasin, C. (2012). *Saving Europe*. New York: Brookings Institution Press.

Canzoneri, M., R. Cumby and B. Diba (2002). The need for international policy coordination: What's old, what's new, what's yet to come? *Journal of International Economics*, 66.

Canzoneri, M. and J. Gray (1985). Monetary policy games and the consequences of non-cooperative behavior. *International Economic Review*.

Canzoneri, M. and D. Henderson (1990). *Noncooperative Monetary Policies in Interdependent Economies*. Cambridge, MA: MIT Press.

Corsetti, G. and P. Pesenti (2001). International dimensions of optimal monetary policy. NBER Working paper n. 8230.

Eichengreen, B. and K. O'Rourke (2010). A tale of two depressions; what do the new data tell us? Vox EU, March 8.

Eichengreen, B. (2009). The Financial Crisis and Global Policy Reforms. Federal Reserve Bank of San Francisco, Asian Economic Policy Conference.

French G20 Presidency (2011). La Presidence Française du G20 en 2011. Available at http://www.g8.utoronto.ca/summit/2011deauville/2011-g20-g8_dossier_presse.pdf

Hamada, K. (1974). "Alternative exchange rate systems and the interdependence of monetary policies." In R.Z. Aliber (ed.), *National Monetary Policies and the International Financial System*. Chicago: Chicago University Press, pp. 13–33.

Hamada, K. (1979). "Macroeconomic strategy coordination under alternative exchange rates." In R. Dornbusch and J. Frenkel (eds.),

International Economic Policy. Baltimore: Johns Hopkins University Press, pp. 292–324.

Kant, I. (1795). *Perpetual Peace: A Philosophical Sketch.*

International Monetary Fund (2010), "G20 mutual assessment process — IMF staff assessment of G20 policies." Report to the G20 for the Second Summit, November.

Larosière, J. de (2009). *Report of the High-Level Group on Financial Supervision in the EU* (Brussels, February).

Oudiz and Sachs (1984). International policy coordination in dynamic macroeconomic models. NBER Working Paper n. 1417.

Portes, R. (2009). Global imbalances, PEGGED Policy Brief n. 3.

Rottier, S. and N. Véron (2010). An Assessment of the G20's Initial Action Items, *Bruegel Policy Contribution* 2010/08, September.

Turner, A. (2009). *The Turner Review: A Regulatory Response to the Global Banking Crisis*. London: Financial Services Authority.

Vestergaard, J. (2010). The G20 and beyond: Towards effective economic governance. *Danish Institute for International Studies Report* 2011:04.

Vines, D. (2011). The G20MAP, global rebalancing, and sustaining economic growth, mimeo, April.

Woods, N. (2010). The G20 leaders and global governance. GEG Working paper 59, Oxford University.

CHAPTER 6

Emerging Markets in the Aftermath of the Global Financial Crisis

Eswar S. Prasad[1]

1 Introduction

Emerging market economies (EMEs) have come to play a dominant role in the world economy. They now account for a large and rising share of global output and trade. Indeed, by virtually every economic indicator, the prominence of EMEs has increased over the last few decades. This chapter evaluates the empirical basis for this proposition and examines its validity in the aftermath of the worldwide recession that was precipitated by the global financial crisis of 2008–2009.

Before the financial crisis, there was a growing sense among investors and policymakers that EMEs, with their newfound economic might, had become more resilient to shocks originating in advanced economies. This notion of emerging markets decoupling from advanced economies became widely prevalent before the global financial crisis. The high and rising growth gap between the two groups, with EMEs recording consistently higher growth than advanced economies during the period 2000–2007, supported this view.

---

[1]This chapter draws on material from Kose and Prasad (2010) and Prasad (2011). I am grateful to Grace Gu for excellent research assistance.

The global financial crisis seemed to put paid to such notions of "decoupling." As a significant fraction of EMEs followed the advanced countries into recession, the crisis called into question the notion of greater resilience of EMEs to advanced country shocks. This was not altogether a surprising outcome as past episodes of business cycles suggest that deep and highly synchronized recessions in advanced countries tend to have large spillovers to the EMEs. Nevertheless, the growth gap between the two groups had created the hope that EMEs could sustain high growth independent of growth in advanced economies, and perhaps even become the key locomotives of global growth, a hope that seemed to have been dashed by the worldwide recession.

Remarkably, however, the majority of EMEs have bounced back briskly from the global recession since mid-2009 and, as a group, the EMEs have weathered the crisis much better than the advanced economies. This is not to say that all EMEs did equally well in the aftermath of the global financial crisis. There is significant variation in the degree of resilience displayed by different groups of EMEs. For instance, Asian emerging markets, especially China and India, have done far better than the economies of Emerging Europe, while the emerging economies of Africa and Latin America were not as badly affected by this recession in advanced economies compared to previous such recessions.

Overall, the global financial crisis has proven to be a watershed event that has intensified the prominence of EMEs. There is now a striking dichotomy between advanced economies and EMEs in terms of the short-term risks and policy challenges that they face. Among advanced economies, the major concern is about weak growth and deflationary pressures, with conventional monetary policy having reached its limits and the burden of debt having risen to dangerous levels constraining the scope of fiscal policy. In EMEs, by contrast, growth has rebounded sharply. With their strong growth prospects, they now face rising inflation, surges of capital inflows that are creating risks of bubbles in asset and credit markets, and pressures of rapid currency appreciation. This points to another reality, that emerging markets are still buffeted by macroeconomic developments and policy responses in the advanced economies.

In this chapter, I first provide an overview of a number of economic indicators that point to the rising prominence of EMEs in the world economy and then discuss these economies' contribution to world growth. I then briefly summarize the effects that the global financial crisis had on these underlying trends, followed by a discussion of what factors account for cross-country differences in emerging markets' resilience to the aftershocks from the crisis. I will then discuss a looming macroeconomic problem — the growing burden of public debt in the advanced economies — and how this could affect phenomena such as capital flows and the growth bifurcation between advanced economies and emerging markets. Finally, I discuss the nature of external risks now faced by EMEs and whether the resilience they showed during the global financial crisis implies that they have become less vulnerable to balance of payments or currency crises, which had befallen many of them in previous years. The concluding section offers some thoughts on the broader role of EMEs in the global economic system.

2 Rising Prominence of EMEs

The world distribution of GDP has changed quite significantly over the past five decades. To demonstrate this, I first examine the size distribution of countries in 1960–1972 (the Bretton Woods period), 1973–1985 (the period before the recent surge in global integration) and 1986–2007 (the pre-crisis period of globalization). I then look at data for the crisis years, 2008–2010 to evaluate whether the crisis led to an intensification of the patterns detected in the three earlier periods.

Table 1 shows that, during the period 1960–1985, advanced economies on average accounted for about three-quarters of global GDP measured in purchasing power parity (PPP) adjusted current dollars. This share has declined gradually over time — by 1986–2007, it was down to 58 percent,

Table 1. Size Distribution of Groups and Regions, 1960–2010 (In Percent).

Group or region	1960–1972	1973–1985	1986–2007	2008–2010
Advanced economies	80.30	73.21	57.62	47.97
Emerging market economies	16.60	22.86	26.25	35.27
Other developing economies	3.09	3.93	3.17	3.52
United States	32.64	27.08	22.46	19.89
Japan	7.77	9.40	8.02	5.93
G-7	70.19	61.19	48.57	40.27
EU-15	34.41	31.10	22.79	18.60
Major emerging market economies	6.30	9.04	12.68	20.80

Note: Major emerging market economies refer to Brazil, China and India.

a fall of more than 20 percent relative to the 1960s. By contrast, the share of emerging markets has risen steadily, from just about 17 percent in the 1960s to 26 percent during the globalization period, 1986–2007.

This trend intensified sharply during the period of and immediately following the global financial crisis of 2008–2009. Consistent with the trend of a steadily rising share, the last column of Table 1 shows that the share of emerging markets rose to 35 percent by 2008–2010, up 9 percentage points from the average level during the pre-crisis globalization period. This matches a corresponding decline in the share of advanced economies, from 58 percent in 1986–2007 to 48 percent in 2008–2010. The share of other developing economies has remained modest and steady in the range of 3–4 percent of world GDP over the last five decades, highlighting the dramatic difference in growth performance between this group and the more dynamic group of EMEs.

To examine these shifts in more detail, the bottom rows of Table 1 provide data on the relative sizes of some key countries and country groups. The US remains the dominant economy in the world, although its share has declined from 33 percent of the world economy in 1960–1972 to 22 percent in 1986–2007. The share of the core group of EU economies falls more over this period, from 34 percent to 23 percent. The most dramatic shift is for the three major emerging markets — Brazil, China and India — whose share nearly doubles in a relatively short period, from 9 percent in 1973–1985 to 13 percent in 1986–2007. A substantial part of the increase in the share of the EMEs in the world GDP has been due to China and India. For example, China's share of world GDP has increased sharply from 3.2 percent during the Bretton Woods period to 9.8 percent in the globalization period. Similarly, the share of India has risen from 4.4 percent to 5.6 percent across these periods.

These shifts pick up pace during the crisis years. In 2008–2010, the US and EU-15 shares of world GDP continue to decline while that of the major emerging markets increases further. During this period, the main emerging markets account for 21 percent of world GDP, slightly higher than the shares of the EU-15 countries (19 percent) and close to the share of the US (20 percent). Thus, the global financial crisis has only accentuated rather than reversed or slowed down ongoing shifts in the structure of the world economy and the EMEs rising role in it.

To provide a more comprehensive picture of the distribution of global GDP, I now expand the sample of countries in the globalization period to include the emerging markets of Europe, along with a number of other smaller developing countries for which consistent data are available only for the last couple of decades. This provides a more comprehensive picture of shifts in the world GDP distribution, although for a shorter period. Figure 1 shows the output shares of different groups of countries for 1990 and 2010. The top panel of this figure, which shows PPP-adjusted shares of each country or group in world GDP, clearly shows the rising importance of China and India and the relative decline of the US and other advanced economies. Compared to their shares in 1990, the emerging economies of

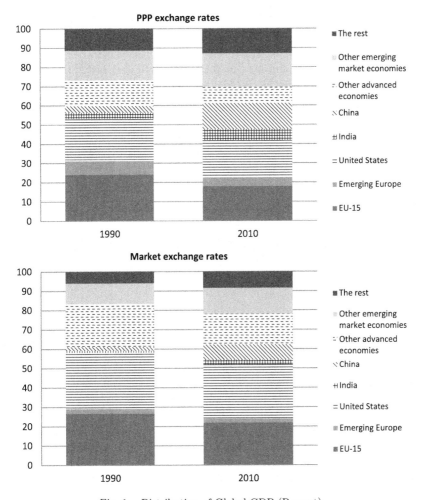

Fig. 1.   Distribution of Global GDP (Percent).

Europe have a smaller share of GDP in 2010. The shares of the EU-15 and other advanced economies also declined during the 2000s.

The lower panel of Figure 1 shows similar calculations as the top panel but based on domestic GDP converted to a common currency (US dollars) at market exchange rates. China and India still account for a larger share of world GDP in 2010 than in 1990, but the increases in their shares, as well as that of other emerging markets, is much smaller when market exchange rates rather than PPP exchange rates are used in the calculations. The broad patterns seen in the top panel are preserved, although it is clear that the choice of exchange rate used in these calculations makes a significant difference because of the large deviations between market and PPP exchange rates, especially in the case of emerging markets.

Other economic indicators provide a broader snapshot of the rising prominence of emerging markets in the world economic order (Figure 2). While their shares of the world population and world labor force have remained relatively stable from 1990 to 2010, the EMEs have now become more important on virtually every other economic dimension. The emerging markets' shares of world GDP, private consumption, investment and trade have nearly doubled in the space of two decades. Thus, this group now has a much larger share of the world economy irrespective of the criterion, although in some respects these shares may still be considered modest. For instance, EMEs still account for only about one-fifth of world private consumption, much lower than their shares of world GDP or world investment. The latter result is of course largely reflective of developments in the Chinese economy, where growth in recent years has been driven largely by fixed investment growth, leading to a rising share of investment and a declining share of private consumption in Chinese GDP.

Despite their economic size, EMEs still account for a smaller share of global financial flows than advanced economies. Kose *et al.* (2009), for instance, note that these economies account for only about one-tenth of the global stocks of gross external assets and liabilities. On one dimension, however, EMEs play a much more important role. The share of world foreign exchange reserves held by emerging markets has nearly tripled over this period, with this group of countries now accounting for a majority of global reserves and continuing to accumulate them, a phenomenon that has implications for future global financial flows and stability and the financing of public debt accumulation in advanced economies.

This section has provided a number of indicators of how EMEs are now playing an increasingly important role in different aspects of the world economy. By virtually any measure, this shift in economic power away from

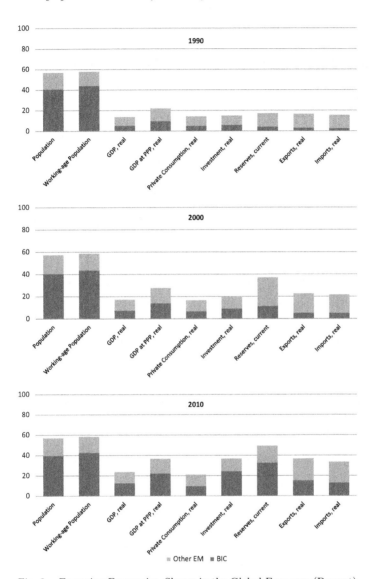

Fig. 2.   Emerging Economies, Shares in the Global Economy (Percent).
Note: BIC refers to Brazil, India and China.

advanced economies to EMEs was accentuated by the global financial crisis and the recession that followed it. The next question is whether EMEs are now driving world growth or if they are still being pulled along by advanced economies.

3   The Distribution of World Growth

The spectacular growth performance of EMEs in recent decades has attracted the most attention. As a group, the EMEs have experienced far greater cumulative growth since 1960 than other developing countries and the advanced economies. Excluding Brazil, China and India — three of the most prominent large, dynamic economies — from the list of emerging markets makes the performance of this group look less spectacular, although it is still much better than that of the group of other developing countries.

I now examine the distribution of world growth, not just in terms of GDP but also in terms of the key components of final demand — private consumption and investment — with all variables measured in PPP terms. This provides an indication of the quantitative contribution of each region or country to world growth. I also look at the contributions of different countries/regions to global export growth.

The top panel of Table 2 shows the growth in world GDP, consumption, investment and exports, averaged over the periods 1960–1972, 1973–1985 and 1986–2007. The final column shows growth in GDP alone for the crisis period 2008–2010 (consistent data on the components for GDP were not available for all of the countries in the sample). The next three panels show the growth contributions to each variable coming from different regions, which add up to overall world growth of the corresponding variable.[2]

World GDP growth averaged 6.2 percent per annum during the period 1986–2007; lower than in the pre-globalization period.[3] Going from the pre-globalization period to the globalization period, one can already see the sharp changes in the relative contributions of different country groups. The contribution of the advanced economies to world GDP growth in 1973–1985 was 7.2 percentage points, almost three-quarters of world

---

[2]The contribution of country i to world GDP growth from time t to t + 1 is given by [GDP(country i, time t + 1) — GDP(country i, time t)]/GDP(world, time t). The sum of the growth contributions of the three regions that constitute the world economy add up to total world GDP growth. Some small discrepancies between the sums of the three regions' contributions and world GDP growth in the latest period are attributable to data availability problems for a handful of countries.

[3]These growth rates are calculated using PPP exchange rates to evaluate the GDP weight of each country in world GDP. World GDP growth based on market exchange rates was lower during 2008–2009 than the number mentioned here, largely because the main emerging markets continued to post relatively strong growth during the global recession and these economies of course have a much higher PPP-based weight in world GDP.

Table 2. Contributions to Global Growth, by Group and Region, 1960–2010 (In Percent).

Group or region	1960–1972	1973–1985	1986–2007	2008–2010
World				
GDP	11.60	10.22	6.18	2.35
Consumption	5.01	3.17	3.03	—
Investment	6.74	2.43	3.77	—
Exports	7.77	5.24	6.61	—
Advanced economies				
GDP	7.18	7.16	3.53	−0.56
Consumption	4.34	2.50	2.32	—
Investment	5.93	1.70	2.46	—
Exports	6.62	4.26	4.11	—
Emerging market economies				
GDP	3.71	2.66	2.43	2.09
Consumption	0.60	0.62	0.81	—
Investment	0.73	0.65	1.34	—
Exports	0.90	0.87	2.37	—
Other developing economies				
GDP	0.70	0.40	0.22	0.16
Consumption	0.07	0.05	0.04	—
Investment	0.07	0.08	0.04	—
Exports	0.25	0.11	0.13	—
United States				
GDP	2.40	2.69	1.48	0.01
Consumption	1.58	1.11	1.16	—
Investment	1.31	0.88	1.03	—
Exports	0.92	0.71	1.01	—
Japan				
GDP	0.99	1.03	0.45	−0.05
Consumption	1.06	0.57	0.34	—
Investment	2.26	0.52	0.44	—
Exports	0.84	0.80	0.38	—
EU-15				
GDP	3.17	2.88	1.32	−0.15
Consumption	1.44	0.68	0.63	—
Investment	2.04	0.17	0.78	—
Exports	3.91	2.32	2.29	—
Major emerging market economies				
GDP	1.48	1.11	1.37	1.66
Consumption	0.16	0.24	0.36	—
Investment	0.27	0.27	0.83	—
Exports	0.18	0.23	0.92	—

growth of 10.2 percent. EMEs contributed 2.7 percentage points to world growth during this period. During the pre-crisis globalization period, these economies contributed about 40 percent of world growth (2.43/6.18) while the share of advanced economies fell to about 57 percent (3.53/6.18).

Interestingly, the contribution of EMEs to global consumption growth is much lower than their contribution to GDP growth. During 1986–2007, this group accounted for less than one-third of global consumption growth (0.81/3.03) and about one-third of global investment growth (1.34/3.77). Thus, advanced economies still appear to be the key contributors to the growth in global domestic demand.

The picture of the growth contributions of different groups of economies shifts dramatically during the crisis years 2008–2010. The last column of Table 2 shows how much these relative contributions shifted. During this period, EMEs accounted for nearly 90 percent of world growth during 2008–2009 (2.09/2.35), while the share of advanced economies was in fact negative as many of them contracted slightly during this period. In other words, the direct contribution of emerging markets to GDP growth has continued to increase over time and was further accentuated during the financial crisis, while the reverse has been true for advanced economies.

The lower panels of Table 2, which show the results for four key sets of advanced economies and also for the three major emerging markets (the group of Brazil, China and India) shows these patterns more clearly. The relative contributions of the US, Japan and the set of EU-15 countries has declined markedly in the globalization period relative to the pre-globalization period and all of them have experienced virtually no growth during the crisis years of 2008–2010. The EU-15 recorded negative growth on average during these three years. By contrast, the group of three major EMEs by themselves account for 71 percent of world growth during the crisis years.

Figure 3 shows similar calculations for world GDP growth for an expanded group of countries including the economies of Emerging Europe but only since 1990. This figure complements the data in Table 2 by showing the contributions of different countries or groups as shares relative to world GDP growth (the table shows absolute contributions rather than shares). To highlight the general trend in the globalization period and distinguish it from the first year of the crisis, I present growth contributions of different countries and regions for 1990, the average for 2000–2007 and separately for 2008–2010.

The top panel of Figure 3 shows growth contributions based on PPP-adjusted GDP data. The growth contributions of China, India and other

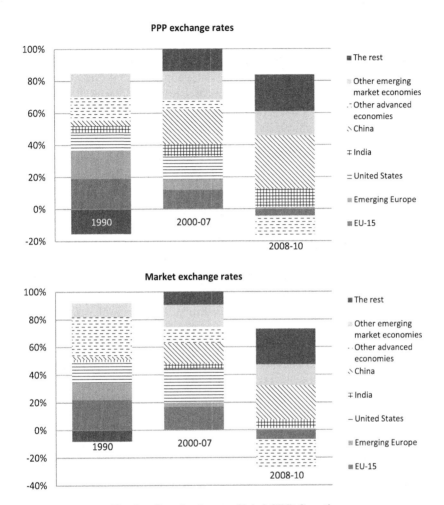

Fig. 3. Contributions to Global GDP Growth.

emerging markets increase from 1990 to 2000–2007, offsetting a decline in the shares of the US and other advanced economies. In 2008–2010, the growth contributions of China, India and other emerging markets continue to rise, but the shares accounted for by the US and other advanced economies fall while the contribution of Emerging Europe remains steady.

The lower panel of Figure 3 shows similar calculations based on GDP converted to a common currency at market exchange rates. As was the case with the GDP levels, the patterns of growth contributions based on market exchange rates are quite similar to those based on PPP exchange rates, but are quantitatively less favorable to EMEs. Interestingly, the growth contributions of Emerging European economies increase in 2008–2010 relative to 2000–2007 when measured on the basis of market exchange rates.

In short, EMEs not only weathered the global financial crisis relatively well but in fact their prominence in terms of driving world growth increased during the period 2008–2010. Nevertheless, it remains an open question whether EMEs have self-sustaining domestic demand that will allow them to remain decoupled from developments in advanced economy business cycles.

4   What Explains the Resilience of Emerging Markets?

Although the EMEs as a group performed well during the global recession, there were sharp differences across emerging economies in different regions.[4] The economies of emerging Asia had the most favorable outcome, experiencing relatively modest declines in growth rates. China and India, which are the two largest economies in Emerging Asia and which maintained strong growth during the crisis, obviously play an important role in the performance of this group. Excluding these two countries (and also Hong Kong SAR) from the Emerging Asia group leaves that group with a less impressive but still solid performance overall.

Emerging Europe had the sharpest fall in total output during 2009, followed by Latin America. By contrast, and somewhat surprisingly, the economies of the Middle East and North Africa (MENA) region as well as those of Sub-Saharan Africa weathered the crisis better, with only small declines in output. For these two latter groups, their relatively modest exposures to trade and financial flows from advanced economies may have limited the extent of spillovers of the global shock. These countries had also improved their macroeconomic policies, giving them more space in responding to the global shock with countercyclical policy tools.

Latin America, by contrast, is more closely integrated with advanced economies, especially the US. Although Latin American EMEs did suffer growth contractions during the crisis, they have bounced back relatively strongly. This is in contrast to previous episodes of global financial turbulence (1982, 1998, 2001), during which Latin American economies proved to

---

[4]See Kose and Prasad (2010). Lane and Milesi-Ferretti (2010) also report that there are substantial differences in the impact of the crisis across regions.

be vulnerable to currency and debt crises.[5] Izquierdo and Talvi (2010) note
the role played by strong macroeconomic fundamentals — low inflation,
twin external and fiscal surpluses, a sound banking system, a large stock of
international reserves and flexible exchange rate regimes — in ensuring the
resilience of Latin American economies during the recent crisis.

Thus, the two sets of emerging markets that present the sharpest contrast in terms of resilience to the global financial crisis are the emerging
markets of Asia and Europe. Prior to the crisis, average per capita GDP
growth was highest in these two groups of emerging markets. In 2009, Asian
emerging markets posted the highest average rate of growth while European
emerging markets had the lowest. Based on the comparative stylized analysis of the experiences of emerging Asian and Eastern European economies
as well as a reading of the rapidly expanding literature on this subject, Kose
and Prasad (2010) identify a few factors that appear to have underpinned
the relative resilience of EMEs as a group during the global financial crisis.
These factors could also help explain differences in resilience across different
groups of EMEs.

1) *Less dependence on foreign finance and a shift away from foreign
   currency-denominated external debt.* As a group, the emerging markets have been net exporters of capital during the last decade. The
   Asian emerging markets, especially China but also others such as Russia
   and some of the Latin American economies, have been running significant current account surpluses in recent years. There are of course certain groups of EMEs, especially those in Emerging Europe, that have
   been running large current account deficits and financing their domestic
   investment using foreign savings. This group indeed proved most vulnerable to the crisis. More generally, Eichengreen (2010) documents that
   countries with large current account deficits and corresponding large
   financing requirements were hit harder by the crisis. The majority of
   emerging markets have become a lot less reliant on foreign finance, particularly external debt.

2) *Large buffers of foreign exchange reserves.* Following the Asian financial
   crisis of 1997–1998, emerging markets around the world have built up
   large buffers of foreign exchange reserves, partly as a result of export-
   oriented growth strategies and partly as a form of self-insurance against

---

[5]See IMF (2009a, 2009b), for economic and financial developments in Latin America
during the crisis.

crises associated with sudden stops or reversals of capital inflows. Frankel and Saravelos (2010) present evidence that foreign exchange reserve levels had a major impact on countries' vulnerability to the global financial crisis.[6]

3) *Greater trade linkages among the EMEs* have increased their resilience as a group. In particular, commodity-exporting countries have been shielded to some extent from the slowdowns in the advanced economies by strong growth in the EMEs. For instance, China's continued rapid growth during the crisis, fueled by a surge in investment, has boosted the demand for commodities from emerging markets such as Brazil and Chile and has also increased the demand for raw materials and intermediate inputs from other Asian emerging markets.

4) *Emerging markets have become more diversified in their production and export patterns,* although this has, to a significant extent, been offset by vertical specialization that has led to rising integration of some emerging markets, particularly those in Asia, through regional supply chains. Such diversification offers limited protection against large global shocks but, so long as the effects of shocks are not perfectly correlated across countries (export markets), it can serve to promote resilience in response to more normal types of shocks. Diversification of production, especially to reduce dependence on exports of commodities and raw materials that have long and volatile price cycles, can also increase resilience.

5) *Broader divergence of EME business cycles from those of the advanced economies.* This has happened on account of the factors noted above, along with greater intra-group trade and financial linkages. There has also been a proliferation of trade and financial flows within the group of emerging markets, both at the regional and inter-regional levels. This phenomenon is partly the natural result of geographical proximity boosting trade flows and of financial flows following trade. There have also been specific policy initiatives in certain regions to promote regional financial integration. Examples of this are the Chiang Mai and Asian

---

[6]Of course, the benefits of large reserves stocks have to be carefully considered relative to the costs of accumulating them, both in terms of the quasi-fiscal costs as well as the more subtle costs in terms of the constraints on domestic policies. Rodrik (2006) estimates the social cost of self-insurance through holding reserves to be about 1 percent of GDP for developing countries as a group. Prasad and Rajan (2006) and Prasad (2009b) discuss how China's currency policy that has resulted in rapid reserve accumulation has constrained domestic macroeconomic policies and hampered financial sector reforms, both of which could have long-term consequences for economic welfare.

Bond Fund initiatives that were set up as ways to encourage regional financial integration and financial market development among the participating Asian countries. However, the scope and scale of these initiatives have remained limited and, even for the Asian region as a whole, financial flows with the rest of the world still dwarf intra-Asian flows. Over the long run, initiatives to develop regional insurance mechanisms by pooling reserves and attempts to increase the use of major currencies such as the Chinese renminbi could serve to insulate the region better from global shocks.

6) *Better macroeconomic policies, including flexible exchange rates in a number of emerging markets.* During the Great Moderation, most emerging markets succeeded in bringing inflation under control, through a combination of more disciplined fiscal policies and more credible monetary policies. Indeed, a large number of emerging markets have now adopted some form of inflation targeting along with flexible exchange rates, which act as shock absorbers for external shocks (Rose, 2007). This has led to moderate and less volatile inflation. In turn, stable macroeconomic policies have facilitated a shift towards more stable forms of financial inflows and also made international investors less concerned about the safety of their investment in emerging markets. Prudent fiscal policies that have resulted in low levels of fiscal deficits and public debt seem to have created room for EMEs to respond aggressively with countercyclical fiscal policies to offset the contradictory effects of the crisis (Ghosh *et al.*, 2009). Economies with high credit growth rates seem to have fared worse, especially if credit expansion was largely financed through foreign capital (as in the case of many countries in Emerging Europe) rather than domestic savings (e.g., China and India).

7) *Rising per capita income levels and a burgeoning middle class* have increased the size and absorptive capacity of domestic markets, making emerging markets potentially less reliant on foreign trade to benefit from scale economies in their production structures and also less susceptible to export collapses (see Kharas, 2010). But, as noted earlier, it is still not clear that EMEs have truly become self-reliant in terms of being able to sustain growth entirely through domestic demand.

5   Global Public Debt and Implications for the Growth Gap

The accumulation of reserves by EMEs has been an important feature of global capital flows and has contributed to the "uphill" flows of capital from poorer to richer countries. As discussed in the previous section, EMEs with large stocks of reserves were less affected by the crisis. In light of ongoing global financial turmoil, these economies are likely to continue accumulating reserves in order to self-insure themselves against future crises and to avoid having to seek financial assistance from the International Monetary Fund. The other side of this coin is related to the trajectories of government debt in advanced economies.[7] To examine the evolution of such assets around the world, I now examine trajectories of net government debt.[8] This has implications for financial flows as well as for global financial stability if these debt burdens become unsustainable and trigger financing problems, as has already happened to some countries in the euro zone.

The global financial crisis triggered a sharp increase in public debt levels, both in absolute terms and relative to GDP. Data from the IMF's June 2011 Fiscal Monitor show that the level of aggregate net government debt in the world rose from $22 trillion in 2007 to an expected $34 trillion in 2011. IMF forecasts indicate the level will reach $48 trillion in 2016. The ratio of world net debt to world GDP rose from 42 percent in 2007 to 57 percent in 2011, and is expected to hit 58 percent in 2016.

Since the onset of the crisis, the bulk of the increase in global public debt is accounted for by advanced economies. Relative to their GDP, debt levels in these economies are expected to continue rising in the next few years. By contrast, debt ratios will shrink for emerging markets. Indeed, advanced economies account for the bulk of the increase in global public debt since 2007, both in absolute terms and relative to GDP.

- Aggregate debt of advanced economies will increase from $18 trillion in 2007 to $30 trillion in 2011, and is expected to rise to $41 trillion in 2016. The corresponding numbers for emerging markets are $4 trillion, $5 trillion and $7 trillion, respectively.[9]

---

[7]Caballero, Farhi and Gourinchas (2008a, 2008b) argue that emerging markets' search for safe assets precipitated global macroeconomic imbalances. Mendoza, Quadrini and Rios-Rull (2010) make a related point that the greater financial depth of advanced economies attracts large inflows.

[8]I focus on central government securities as those are most relevant for reserve accumulation. Net debt is preferable for the purposes of my analysis as the remaining portion of gross debt is typically held domestically.

[9]The reported debt levels of emerging markets should be interpreted with caution. In China, for instance, financial liabilities of provincial governments and contingent liabilities such as nonperforming assets held by the state-owned banking system imply a much higher value of government debt obligations than indicated by official statistics.

Table 3.   Net Debt to GDP (In Percent).

	2007	2011	2016
World	**42.0**	**56.4**	**57.7**
U.S.	42.6	72.4	85.7
Euro Zone	52.4	68.1	69.5
Japan	81.5	127.8	163.9
UK	38.2	75.1	73.5
Other AE	18.5	25.9	22.1
EM	29.2	26.1	21.5

Source: IMF Fiscal Monitor, April 2011 and June 2011
Update; IMF WEO, April 2011 and June 2011 Update.

- The ratio of aggregate debt to aggregate GDP for advanced economies will rise from 46 percent in 2007 to 70 percent in 2011 and further to 80 percent in 2016. The corresponding ratios for emerging markets are 28 percent, 26 percent and 21 percent, respectively.

Table 3 shows net debt to GDP ratios for some of the key countries/ economic groups. In the US, the net debt to GDP ratio has gone from 43 percent in 2007 to 72 percent in 2011, and is expected to rise further to 86 percent by 2016. By 2016, debt in the euro zone and in the United Kingdom will be at about 70 percent of GDP. By contrast, the average ratio of net debt to GDP for the EMEs is expected to decline from 26 percent in 2011 to 22 percent by 2016.

There is also a stark contrast between the two groups of countries in their relative contributions to growth in world debt versus growth in world GDP. Emerging markets contribute far more to growth in global GDP than to the growth in global public debt. Some illustrative statistics follow:

- In 2007, emerging markets accounted for 25 percent of world GDP and 17 percent of world debt. By 2016, they are expected to produce 38 percent of world output and account for just 14 percent of world debt.
- In 2011 (based on IMF estimates at market exchange rates), the four major reserve currency areas together account for 58 percent of global GDP and 81 percent of global debt.

Of course, as the recent crisis has shown, advanced economy governments arguably have similar implicit contingent liabilities if their big banks were to run aground or their public pension systems were to run out of money.

- Emerging markets account for 9 percent of the increase in global debt levels from 2007 to 2011 and are expected to account for 13 percent of the increase from 2011 to 2016. By contrast, their contributions to increases in global GDP over these two periods are 66 percent and 56 percent, respectively.

- The two biggest advanced economies are making a far greater contribution to the rise in global debt than to the rise in global GDP. The US contributes 37 percent of the increase in global debt from 2007 to 2011 and 40 percent from 2011 to 2016. Its contributions to the increases in global GDP over those two periods are 8 percent and 18 percent, respectively. Japan accounts for 20 percent of the increase in debt from 2007 to 2011 and 34 percent from 2011 to 2016 while its contributions to the increase in global GDP are 4 percent and 8 percent, respectively.

High and rising debt levels among advanced economies pose serious risks to global macroeconomic stability that would almost certainly have significant knock-on effects on EMEs. Of course, the implications of rising debt levels and their sustainability depend to a large extent on whether these debts are financed from domestic savings or by foreign investors. In the case of the US, foreign investors — both official and private — hold about half of the outstanding stock of net central government debt. Foreign investors have played an important role in the financing of net US debt. During 2008–2010, when net debt accumulation soared to $1.3 trillion per year, foreign investors accumulated $695 billion per year, accounting for just over half of total US net debt issuance.

This ratio is lower for the UK — about one-third of its net debt is held by foreign investors — and even lower, less than 10 percent, for Japan, which has a very high domestic savings rate. It is harder to obtain a consistent picture for the euro area as available data include within-euro area holdings and do not provide a clear picture of how much euro area sovereign debt is held by investors from outside the euro area.

These figures paint a sobering picture of worsening public debt dynamics and a sharply rising public debt burden in advanced economies, along with a high level of dependence on foreign investors in search of a safe haven, especially in the case of the US. The major reserve currency economies — especially the US and Japan — face daunting trajectories of public debt and weak growth prospects. Indeed, with low levels of population growth, rapidly aging populations and rising costs of health care and other entitlement programs, advanced economies as a group could be in far worse shape beyond the medium-term horizon discussed in this section if they do not bring their public finances under control.[10]

In advanced economies, rising public debt levels imply significant crowding-out effects that will affect productivity growth and could generate a persistent productivity growth gap relative to emerging markets. Balance sheets of households and the financial sector in advanced economies were severely damaged by the financial crisis and are only now beginning to recover, putting a further crimp on these economies' growth prospects. All of this implies that the growth bifurcation between EMEs and advanced economies is likely to persist well into the future. This is likely to be the case even if the major EMEs hit the middle income trap and experience growth slowdowns due to their aging populations and other factors that could constrain long-term growth in these economies (Eichengreen, Park and Shin, 2011).

6   Risks

Given their promising growth prospects, one remaining question is whether emerging markets still face significant risks of crises, which they were vulnerable to in the past. While these economies face a number of difficult policy dilemmas, the discussion in Section 4 suggests that they have in fact become more resilient to external shocks. I now review two aspects of these economies' external balance sheets that imply reduced vulnerability to traditional balance of payments crises, although these countries may still be subject to the effects of capital flow volatility as they become more integrated into international financial markets.

One factor that plays an important role in affecting vulnerability to crises and also the ability to recover quickly from their aftermath is the level of international reserves held by a country (see, e.g., Frankel and Saravelos, 2011). Figure 4 shows the rapid rate of reserve accumulation by emerging markets, which peaked in 2007, declined but remained positive in 2008–2009, and then began to pick up again in 2010. Total foreign exchange reserves of emerging markets now amount to about $6.4 trillion, with China accounting for half of this stock. In short, EMEs have now accumulated a

---

[10]Cecchetti, Mohanty and Zampolli (2010) present sobering projections of advanced economies' long-term debt levels under current policies in those countries.

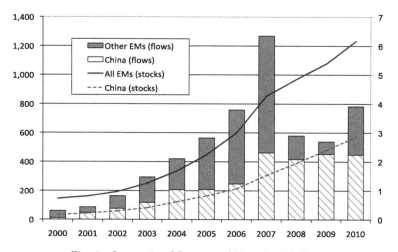

Fig. 4.   International Reserves of Emerging Markets.
Note: Flows refer to annual accumulation of reserves (in billions of dollars, left scale).
Stocks refer to end-of-year stocks of reserves (in trillions of US dollars, right scale).

large stock of reserves that provides a high level of self-insurance against
sudden stops and reversals of capital inflows.

Another important consideration in determining vulnerability to external shocks to the capital account is the structure of EMEs' external
liabilities. These were once dominated by short-term foreign-currency
denominated external debt, making these countries subject to currency risk
as well as the risk of procyclical capital flows (and procyclical access to international financial markets, which reduced the potential risk-sharing benefit
of international financial integration). This pattern has changed markedly,
with foreign direct investment and portfolio equity, far more desirable forms
of capital in terms of their direct and indirect benefits, now accounting for
a majority of their external liabilities. Figure 5 shows that the median
(median across countries) share of debt total external liabilities of EMEs
has fallen from over 80 percent in the mid-1980s to below 40 percent in
2009. By contrast, the share of FDI has climbed to more than 50 percent
and that of portfolio equity is now close to 20 percent.

Moreover, external debt issued by these countries is increasingly denominated in their own currencies. This structure of liabilities helps share risk
across countries, with foreign investors bearing capital as well as currency
risk on such investment. Even taking into account the greater volatility of
portfolio equity flows relative to FDI, this implies more risk sharing with

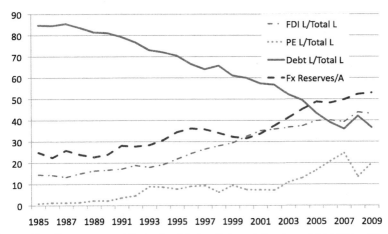

Fig. 5.   Key Components of Emerging Market External Assets and Liabilities (Shares, in Percent).
Notes: Stocks of foreign direct investment (FDI), portfolio equity (PE) and external debt are shown as ratios of total external liabilities (L), with each of these variables summed up across all emerging market economies. The stock of foreign exchange reserves is shown as a ratio to total external assets (A).

international investors. By contrast, portfolio debt and bank loans together still constitute the major share of advanced economies' external liabilities.

In short, changes in the structure of EMEs' external liabilities and the high levels of international reserves have reduced the vulnerability of these economies to balance of payments and currency crises, which had been the bane of these economies in the past.

7   Concluding Remarks

Emerging market economies have become key players in the world economy in terms of their sheer size. This phenomenon has been accentuated during the period of globalization and has further intensified during the global financial crisis as the group of emerging markets continued to expand at a relatively robust rate while advanced economies essentially came to a standstill. It is also clear that EMEs have become increasingly more important in terms of driving global GDP growth, although their contributions to the growth in global domestic demand are lower. This group of economies has essentially been responsible for most of global GDP growth during the latest financial crisis and it is likely that, even if they experience a modest growth slowdown, there will remain a persistent and large growth gap between EMEs and advanced economies.

Along with an increase in their economic heft, EMEs are also becoming more important players in setting the global priorities. The increasing irrelevance of the G-7 and the unofficial anointment of the G-20 as the major body setting the global economic agenda have given EMEs a prominent seat at the table. The same is true in international institutions such as the Financial Stability Board and the IMF, where EMEs have a much larger say than ever before. With this change will come some new responsibilities as emerging markets need to recognize that they need to make a direct contribution to good global governance.

Emerging markets have attained a good level of maturity in terms of their economic size, domestic policy frameworks and influence on the world economy. The global financial crisis presents a unique opportunity for them to mature in another dimension — taking on more responsibility for global economic and financial stability, including strengthening global economic governance.

References

Caballero, R.J., E. Farhi and P.-O. Gourinchas (2008a). Financial crash, commodity prices, and global imbalances. *Brookings Papers on Economic Activity*, Fall, 1–55.

Caballero, R.J., E. Farhi and P.-O. Gourinchas (2008b). An equilibrium model of 'global imbalances' and low interest rates. *American Economic Review*. 98(1), 358–393.

Cecchetti, S. G., M.S. Mohanty and F. Zampolli (2010). The future of public debt: Prospects and implications. BIS Working Paper No. 300.

Eichengreen, B. (2010). Lessons of the crisis for emerging markets. *International Economics and Economic Policy*, 7(1), 49–62.

Eichengreen, B., D. Park and K. Shin (2011). When fast growing economies slow down: International evidence and implications for China. NBER Working Paper No. 16919.

Frankel, J. and G. Saravelos (2011). Can leading indicators assess country vulnerability? Evidence from the 2008–2009 global financial crisis. Unpublisherd manuscript, Kennedy School of Government, Harvard University.

Ghosh, A.R., M. Chamon, C. Crowe, J.I. Kim and J.D. Ostry (2009). Coping with the crisis: Policy options for emerging market countries. *IMF Staff Position Note*, No. 2009/08, International Monetary Fund, Washington DC.

International Monetary Fund (2009a). *Regional Economic Outlook: Asia and Pacific*. International Monetary Fund, Washington DC, April.

International Monetary Fund (2009b). *Regional Economic Outlook: Asia and Pacific*. International Monetary Fund, Washington DC, October.

Izquierdo, A. and E. Talvi (2010). *The Aftermath of the Crisis: Policy Lessons and Challenges Ahead for Latin America and the Caribbean*. Inter-American Development Bank, Washington DC.

Kharas, H. (2010). The emerging middle class in developing countries. OECD Development Centre Working Paper No. 285.

Kose, M.A., E.S. Prasad, K. Rogoff and S.J. Wei (2009). Financial globalization: A reappraisal. *IMF Staff Papers*, 56, 8–62.

Kose, M.A. and E. Prasad (2010). *Emerging Markets: Resilience and Growth Amid Global Turmoil*. Washington DC: Brookings Institution Press.

Lane, P.R. and G.M. Milesi-Ferretti (2010). The cross-country incidence of the global crisis. *IMF Economic Review* (forthcoming).

Mendoza, E.G., V. Quadrini and J.-V. Ríos-Rull (2009). Financial integration, financial development, and global imbalances. *Journal of Political Economy*, 117(3), 371–416.

Prasad, E.S. and R. Rajan (2008). A pragmatic approach to capital account liberalization. *Journal of Economic Perspectives*, 22(3), 149–172.

Prasad, E.S. (2009). Is China's growth miracle built to last? *China Economic Review*, 20, 103–123.

Prasad, E. (2011). Role reversal in global finance. NBER Working Paper No. 17497, forthcoming in *Proceedings of the 2011 Jackson Hole Symposium*, Federal Reserve Bank of Kansas City.

Rodrik, D. (2006). The social cost of foreign exchange reserves. *International Economic Journal*, 20(3), 253–266.

Rose, A. (2007). A stable international monetary system emerges: Inflation targeting is Bretton Woods. *Journal of International Money and Finance*, 26(5), 663–681.

CHAPTER 7

Challenges for Emerging Asia

Bokyeong Park and Jinill Kim

1 Introduction: Asia's Recovery from the Global Financial Crisis

In its most recent *World Economic Outlook* (IMF, 2011), the IMF began its section on Asia with the observation that "Asia's track record during the crisis and the recovery has been enviable." Figure 1 shows the growth of real GDP for developing Asia (China, India and ASEAN-5) and the newly industrialized Asian economies (Hong Kong SAR, Korea, Singapore and Taiwan Province of China) and compares them to that for advanced Asian economies. Evidently, Asian countries — especially developing Asian countries — were not hit as hard by the global financial crisis; Asia's recovery was also faster. In 2010, when the growth rate for world output was 5.1 percent, Asia' real GDP growth rate reached 8.2 percent (IMF, 2011).

Financial turbulence first affected the advanced countries significantly in 2007. Growth in the US and Europe fell sharply. Accordingly, foreign demand for Asian exports fell as well. Figure 2 shows that, after staying relatively stable until the global financial crisis hit, the inflation rate in Asian countries fluctuated considerably. Inflation accelerated as the crisis unfolded; the rise in prices of commodities such as oil was the main factor, although currency depreciation added more pressure once the turmoil waned.

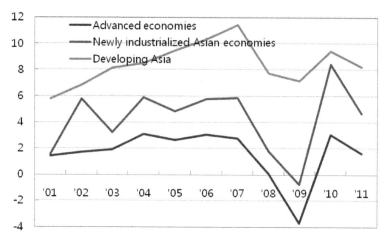

Fig. 1.   Asian Countries' Annual Growth Rate (in Percent).
Source: IMF, World Economic Outlook Database, September 2011.

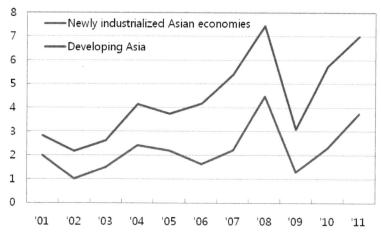

Fig. 2.   Asian Countries' Annual Inflation Rate (in Percent).
Source: IMF, World Economic Outlook Database, September 2011.

As the global financial crisis swept through Asia and growth rates fell,
it became urgent that officials respond with monetary and fiscal policies to
address the problem. Although trade volumes were slow to pick up, these
new measures helped the Asian economies rebound starting in early 2009.
By 2010, Asia became the engine of growth while conditions in Europe

and the US remained lackluster. Despite global financial turbulence, private consumption remained robust in Asia, as labor market conditions improved and consumer confidence remained stable at a high level.

In 2006, the US grew by 3 percent. With the onset of the crisis, growth slowed to 2 percent in 2007, 1 percent in 2008, and negative at -3.5 percent in 2009. Declining house prices and falling residential investment drove the slowdown at the beginning of this period. The private component of aggregate demand — mainly private consumption and business fixed investment — then began falling in late 2007, as consumer sentiment and financial conditions deteriorated. The Federal Open Market Committee responded by cutting the federal funds rate effectively to zero by late 2008. But even this was not enough to avert the most serious recession experienced by the country since the Great Depression.

The euro area was hit as well: growth slowed to 2.6 percent in 2007, 0.6 percent in 2008, and -4 percent in 2009. The property market EU wide contracted for the first time in almost 40 years.

While Asian economies could not sidestep the crisis, several factors softened the blow. Most importantly, Asian banks were not deeply invested in the toxic derivative securities issued in the US. Nonetheless, starting in late 2008 financial turmoil swept through the region as well. Asian economies contracted at rates of more than 10 percent, due mainly to decreased foreign demand from the advanced economies. The drop in global demand was most pronounced in the case of consumer durables like automobiles and electronics. Since such products are central to the input-output structure of many Asian economies, GDP growth was strongly affected.

Governments and central banks around the world responded forcefully to the financial crisis and ensuing downturn. Central banks in the advanced countries cut policy rates and expanded the coverage of financial stability measures like deposit insurance. The Federal Reserve and the European Central Bank adopted unconventional measures — quantitative easing and credit easing — to prevent the flow of credit from becoming frozen. Likewise, governments applied fiscal stimulus to counteract the fall in aggregate demand.

Asian countries responded in a similar manner. Japan, where monetary and fiscal policies had been restrictive, moved quickly to boost aggregate demand. The Bank of Japan cut its policy rate and injected liquidity into financial markets by purchasing Japanese government bonds (JGBs). After the crisis erupted in late 2008, the Japanese government aggressively ramped up public spending.

The goal of Chinese monetary policy prior to 2008 had been to cool off an economy to avoid overheating and to damp down inflationary pressure. But as the global recession deepened, China implemented multiple policy offsets. The People's Bank of China (PBoC) cut its policy rate multiple times following the failure of Lehman Brothers, from 7.47 percent in September to 5.31 percent in December, and raised its credit ceilings on new loans. Fiscal policy measures included investing in a bullet-train system and infrastructure projects in rural areas. The Bank of Korea cut its policy rate five times in 2008 from 5.25 percent to 2.5 percent, and the Korean government boosted public spending by 3 percent of GDP. Southeast Asian countries also adopted expansionary monetary policy measures. Indeed, the policy response was too aggressive in some cases — in Vietnam, for example, where inflation was running in excess of 20 percent in 2009.

Asian countries were able to respond with expansionary fiscal policies because they had been fiscally conservative and their fiscal balances had been healthy. Another reason for fast recovery was Asian banks' strong balance sheets. Recovery, in conjunction with the region's record of financial stability, induced a net inflow of foreign capital in 2010. In some cases this bordered on too much of a good thing; some countries, such as China and Vietnam, began worrying about inflation and bubbles. They responded by tightening monetary policy and winding down fiscal stimulus.

In contrast to the situation in the advanced economies, private demand remained relatively stable during the crisis. Because exports fell, the net effect was progress in rebalancing Asian economies toward domestic demand. Furthermore, many Asian firms reacted to the recession in late 2008 and early 2009 by reducing inventory accumulation. The subsequent recovery of global demand therefore required inventory adjustment, lending additional momentum to the expansion.

On the external side, as financial frictions eased and the global economy emerged from recession, international trade rebounded. This was especially important for Asia insofar as the region depends on exports as an engine for growth, especially exports to advanced economies.

Japan was an exception. Until mid-2009, it remained mired in recession. Although consumption and exports improved, residential investment and business fixed investment continued to slide. Starting in late 2009, personal consumption began to rise in response to government measures, and investment in equipment and structures stabilized as corporate profits improved. It remains to be seen whether deflation will continue to plague the Japanese economy given the deficiency in aggregate demand.

Chinese growth peaked in the second quarter of 2007, at 14 percent, clearly an unsustainable level. That rate has since declined as both private consumption and exports (mainly to the advanced economies) contracted. That said, growth remained in the 8–9 percent range owing to the effect of highly expansionary fiscal and monetary measures. The contribution of urban investment was critical — more than 7 percent in the third quarter of 2009. The growth rate then exceeded 10 percent in the first half of 2010. Although investment demand and net exports came down, consumption expenditure kept increasing; retail sales rose by 15–20 percent in both 2009 and 2010.

Already in this period, the looming danger for China was inflation. In the second half of 2010, CPI inflation rate exceeded 4 percent. The PBoC raised reserve requirements five times in 2010 as well as increasing its policy rate in October, making some headway on the inflation problem, before reversing those measures in response to renewed weakness in the world economy in late 2011. Inflation rates have also been high in Vietnam and India; both countries engaged in some monetary tightening in the effort to bring these down, to mixed effects.

2   Transition from Exports to Domestic Demand

Emerging Asia's rapid economic growth in the last three decades was made possible by exports, whose importance cannot be overstated. But this same dependence on exports has created vulnerability to external shocks. Some economists argue that Asia should now shift from export-led growth to growth driven by domestic demand. They argue that export-led growth in emerging Asia has contributed to the growth of global imbalances and that a fundamental change on the part of Asian countries is needed to correct those imbalances. Asian economies are running large current account surpluses driven by high levels of saving. Global rebalancing therefore requires that they now boost consumption spending.

Shifting from growth led by exports to growth led by domestic demand also promises to enhance economic stability in Asian countries them-selves. Countries highly dependent on exports experienced major declines in growth during the 2008 global financial crisis. These countries recov-ered with the subsequent resurgence of world trade, but the experience nonetheless illustrated the volatility to which they were subject, compared to countries depending less on exports and more on domestic demand. Some

observers find the reason for limited domestic consumption in developing
Asia in strong incentives for precautionary saving motivated, in turn, by
underdeveloped social safety nets. Other factors depressing the growth of
consumption plausibly include low wages, limited urbanization, and income
inequality, inducing a lower propensity for consumption as a whole (Yueh,
2011).

In the wake of the global financial crisis, developing Asia's current
account surplus has declined substantially. Figure 3 shows that the surplus of developing Asia as a whole shrank from 6.6 percent of GDP in 2007
to 3.3 percent in 2010, a level at which it remained in 2011. China's surplus
is expected to fall from 10.1 percent before the crisis to 5.2 percent in 2011.
This is indicative of some progress in narrowing global imbalances. However, the reduction in current account surpluses in Asia is explained mostly
by the reduction in exports due to the slowdown in the world economy, not
by a fall in Asian saving or a rise in consumption. Figure 3 shows that the
saving ratio of developing Asia is still on an upward trend. According to
IMF forecasts, the saving ratio will remain at 45 percent in the medium
term. Thus, reduced global imbalances should be seen not as the result of
structural change but as a temporary effect of the contraction of the global
export market.

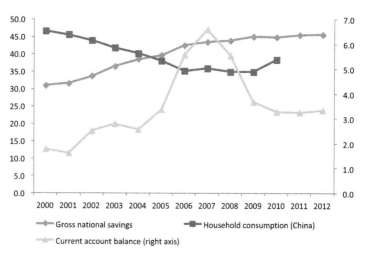

Fig. 3. Saving, Consumption, and Current Account in Developing Asia (in Percentage
of GDP).

Sources: Gross national savings and current account balance from World Economic
Outlook Database, IMF, September 2011; Household consumption in China from World
Development Indicators 2011, World Bank, 2011.

In China, household consumption as share of GDP fell during the crisis before rebounding in 2010. From the point of view of rebalancing, this rebound is a positive sign. It was brought on by China's massive stimulus package. China initiated a RMB 4 trillion recovery program in response to fall in export demand. A large part of the stimulus consisted of measures to improve rural infrastructure and upgrade industry's innovation capacity and energy efficiency. The package also included subsidies for consumption, especially in rural areas. Evidently, the government realized the importance of expanding consumption as a way of better insulating the economy from external shocks. External pressures pointed in the same direction. The US has ratcheted up its pressure on China to reduce its current account surplus since the global financial crisis. International forums like the G20 have also been used to apply pressure for renminbi appreciation. In response, China opted to encourage consumption rather than appreciate its currency. It worried that sharp appreciation would lead to the bankruptcies of many small- and medium-sized enterprises and to unemployment.

The Chinese government's efforts to promote consumption can be seen in the 12th five-year plan announced in 2011. The government made boosting domestic demand the top priority among its ten foremost policies. To accomplish this, the plan proposes to promote urbanization, create job opportunities, improve the distribution of income, and reinforce the social security system. China passed an act in October 2010 increasing the number of its beneficiaries; this act came into effect in July 2011. A stronger social security system is expected to lead to a reduction in precautionary savings. In addition, China is introducing wage increases. Beijing Municipality raised minimum wages by more than 20 percent in both 2010 and 2011, up from 10 percent before the crisis. China's five-year plan targets a minimum wage increase of 13 percent per annum over the next five years. Another example of an indirect increase in wage rates can be found in the Chinese government's changed response to worker protests. Since the crisis, workers in foreign-investment enterprises have often protested for higher wages, but the government chose not to repress the protests. This is a departure from the previous policy of maintaining price competitiveness through low wages; it reflects the priority now attached to controlling income disparities.

It is still too early to tell by how much consumption will grow in emerging Asia. It is hard to know, for example, whether the increase in China's household consumption in 2010 is a temporary result of the stimulus program or a permanent shift. If the shift is permanent, it will have to be accompanied by a rise in the relative price of Chinese goods, to be achieved either through exchange rate appreciation or inflation. Currency appreciation would be the lower-cost alternative, but so far the authorities have been reluctant to proceed down this road.

The reason that Asia's emerging economies are reluctant to appreciate their currencies is, in part, the wish to maintain current account surpluses and accumulate reserves as insurance against currency crises. Asian countries experienced such crises in 1997, and some, including Korea and Indonesia, again were hit by foreign-exchange-market turbulence during the recent global crisis. This encourages their desire to accumulate foreign reserves, feeding fear of appreciation and making it more difficult to expand consumption demand without stoking inflation.

3   Killing the Inflation Dragon

Inflation has become another major concern in emerging Asia. Before the crisis, many developing Asian countries were already suffering from surging inflation. The regional inflation rate of developing Asian economies edged up to 7.4 percent in 2008. The major cause was a sharp increase in international oil and food prices. During the crisis, the sharp fall in trade and production then led to a decline in commodity prices. The IMF's commodity price index fell by 30 percent. Due to this decline, inflation in developing Asian economies fell to 3.1 percent in 2009.

With recovery, concern resurfaced over inflation. The inflation rate of developing Asian economies rose to roughly 7 percent in 2011, up from 5.7 percent in 2010. Commodity prices moved back up to pre-crisis levels. With the increase in demand and political turmoil in the Middle East and North Africa, oil prices rose to more $100 per barrel. The price of food and agricultural products also rose rapidly in response to strong demand and droughts. In addition, since the second half of 2008, expansionary monetary policies and low interest rates encouraged demand and, thereby, inflation. As capital flowed into the region, liquidity increased dramatically, again with inflationary effects.

Since the second half of 2010, China and other Asian countries have tightened monetary policy to rein in inflation. As for China, stabilizing real estate prices, particularly in the eastern coastal area, became a priority. There was much concern that excessive liquidity would spill over into a housing bubble. Although the People's Bank of China raised bank reserve requirement ratios and policy rates several times, inflation accelerated to 6 percent, exceeding the central bank's target of 4 percent.

The European debt crisis and slowdown in global economic growth in the middle of 2011 eased these inflationary pressures somewhat. However, the recovery of the world economy has led to renewed inflationary pressure in the region. In China, India and Vietnam, domestic demand is to blame as well, with actual growth exceeding potential. Moreover, big Asian countries like China and India are, themselves, leading sources of incremental global demand for commodities such as oil, minerals and food. For instance, in 2011, about half of additional global demand for crude oil can be explained by the increase in Chinese demand. The share increases to 70 percent if all of Asia's emerging economies are taken into account. The rise in commodity prices is likely to remain an important source of inflation in Asia so long as its emerging economies continue to grow.

So long as memories of the Asian currency crisis linger, it is hard to imagine that currency appreciation will be actively used to curb inflation. In 2011, Korean inflation was forecast to exceed the central bank's target band, but the government avoided much appreciation of the Korean won. This decision was driven by Korea's wish to run current account surpluses and accumulate yet additional reserves, a strategy further encouraged by financial turmoil and volatility in Europe.

Cost-push inflation due to rising commodity prices is problematic for developing Asian countries, where food and energy account for a large share of the consumption basket. Since the poor are more affected by commodity price increases, higher food and energy prices worsen inequality and poverty problems. According to the Asian Development Bank, a 10 percent increase in domestic food prices leads to an increase of 6.5 million people (or a 7.2 percent percentage-wise increase in population) living in poverty in emerging Asia (ADB, 2011a). The industrial structure of developing Asia is vulnerable to commodity-price shocks because many industries, lacking energy-saving technology, use energy inefficiently. Thus, an energy price increase would badly damage competitiveness. Moreover, some countries subsidize food and energy in order to make exports price competitive and for political reasons. Such price distortions lead to excessive consumption of energy. Also, an increase in commodity prices increases the government's fiscal burden due to more spending on subsidies.

For all these reasons, higher food and energy prices create social tension. Rising soybean prices triggered riots in Indonesia, and soaring rice prices in Bangladesh sparked large protests in 2008. In December 2010, India was hit by riots over high onion prices. Rising food prices were a cause of the political upheavals in Tunisia and Algeria. Similar cases could occur in emerging Asia as well.

Insofar as higher commodity prices affect consumer prices, inflation may trigger wage-price spirals. Workers seek increases in wages, and those wage increases push the inflation rate still higher. Wage-price dynamics in China display all the trademarks of this kind of spiral. Given the country's importance as an exporter, what happens in China may not stay in China. China is the largest source of imports for South Korea and Taiwan, for example. If prices of exports from China rise, this affects consumer prices in these countries. One recent study concludes that the spread of China's inflation to South Korea had a greater impact on South Korea's inflation than an increase in international oil prices (Park *et al.*, 2011).

Controlling the speed of growth in emerging Asia will be crucial for preventing a further increase in inflation. In addition, emerging Asian economies will have to change their energy-intensive industrial structures. Investment in the development and installation of energy-saving and environmentally friendly technologies must increase, and subsidies for food and energy will have to be eliminated. Reining in inflation without damaging price competitiveness of exports is a challenge now facing policy makers in emerging Asia.

4 Risk of the Middle Income Trap

There has been growing concern that Asia's emerging markets will now succumb to the so-called Middle Income Trap. The term describes how, even if a developing country succeeds in completing the transition from a low-income to a middle income economy relatively easily, it may remain stuck in the middle income category without graduating into an advanced economy. Some Southeast Asian countries including Malaysia and Thailand have now joined the ranks of the middle income countries, but during the past 10 years their growth has been lagging. According to the forecasts by the Asian Development Bank, it will be increasingly difficult to sustain Asia's growth momentum going forward (ADB, 2011b). Sustained progress for another 40 years is far from preordained. ADB warns that Asian countries will have to alter their economic structures in order to avoid the Middle Income Trap. According to ADB's outlook, if Asian countries manage to sustain their high growth rates, Asia will account for 51 percent of the world economy in 2050, but in a scenario where they encounter the Middle Income Trap, the figure would only be 32 percent (ADB, 2011b).

There is no agreement on the level of income or stage of economic development that defines a middle income economy. We assume that the relative income per capita of each country compared to the most advanced country determines when a developing country is first exposed to the Middle Income Trap. Figures 5 and 6 show the ratio of income per capita (measured at purchasing-power-parity exchange rates) of several countries relative to that of the US. Figure 5 shows the evolution of relative incomes in three Latin American countries and confirms the presumption that they were caught in the Middle Income Trap. That is, incomes in Brazil, Argentina and Mexico have remained between 20 percent and 40 percent of incomes in the US for more than 30 years starting in the 1970s. Brazil and Mexico had, in fact, been gaining on the US up to the late 1970s, but thereafter their relative incomes have either fallen or stagnated. Similar trends can be seen in Thailand and Malaysia, as shown in Figure 6. Incomes in Thailand reached 20 percent of those of the US in 1995 but have remained at that level ever since. Malaysia's income remained at 20 percent that of the US for more than 20 years and has yet to exceed 30 percent.

These experiences in Latin America and emerging Asia allow us to define the Middle Income Trap as a situation where, after a period of rapid catch-up, a developing economy starts to lose speed and shows growth stagnation, with income per capita hovering at 20 to 40 percent that of the US.

Other recent studies also find that developing countries tend to experience a slowdown after the rapid growth of early industrialization. Morgan Stanley reported that out of 40 countries where per capita income exceeds $7,000 in purchasing power parity terms, 31 experienced growth slowdowns. Their average growth rate over the following 10 years fell on average by 2.8 percent. Eichengreen *et al.* (2011) studied the growth trend of each country and estimated $16,740 per capita income (year 2007 US purchasing power parity dollars) to be the point where growth slowdowns occur. Their study demonstrates that the average growth rate drops from 5.6 percent a year to 2.1 percent after reaching this point. The authors conclude that there is an especially high likelihood of a growth slowdown in countries that focus on labor-intensive activities.

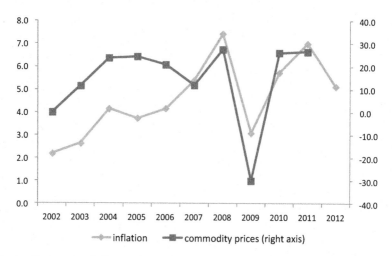

Fig. 4.   International Commodity Prices and Developing Asia's Inflation (in Percent).
Source: IMF, World Economic Outlook Database, September 2011.

Fig. 5.   Income of Latin American and African Countries (as Percentage of the US Income).
Note: Income is the PPP converted GDP per capita at current prices.
Source: Penn World Tables 7.0 (Center for International Comparisons).

Based on these historical experiences, concern is growing over China falling into the Middle Income Trap. Factors leading to the Trap include worsening income inequality, high dependence on exports, weak domestic consumption, an underdeveloped service industry, and an energy-inefficient

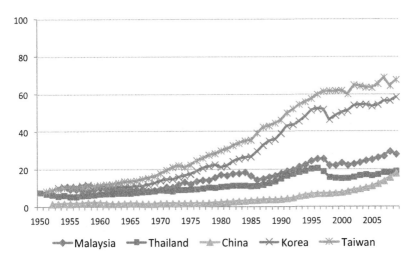

Fig. 6.   Income of Asian Countries (as Percentage of the US Income).
Note: Income is the PPP converted GDP per capita at current prices.
Source: Penn World Table 7.0 (Center for International Comparisons).

industrial structure. As for solutions, most experts suggest that China's current export-based and labor-intensive economy should be transformed into a domestic-based and innovation-based economy (Wheatley, 2010). Such a transformation is the target which China's 12th five-year plan is aiming.

If emerging Asia is vulnerable to falling into the Middle Income Trap, then it is important to detect risk factors that might cause such economic stagnation. Those factors can be identified on the basis of experiences both in the Latin American economies caught in the Trap and in Korea and Taiwan which avoided the Trap.

A first risk is failure to transform industrial structure in response to the transition of the labor market. If a labor market passes the Lewisian turning point, making rising real wages inevitable, production must shift from labor-intensive to labor-saving. When Korea came close to falling into the Middle Income Trap, it reduced the share of labor-intensive industries such as textiles and clothing while promoting capital- and technology-intensive industries like steel, chemicals, motor vehicles and semiconductors (Park, 2011). Malaysia, Thailand, the Philippines, and China are now at a juncture where this kind of transformation is crucial.

Second, input-based growth must be transformed into innovation and productivity-based growth. Rapid growth in China and other emerging

Asian countries has been led by huge investments by foreign enterprises. In its early stages, industrialization depends on the transfer of foreign technology; subsequently, progress requires indigenous innovation. According to Ohno (2010), this transformation is critical for avoiding the Middle Income Trap. In the case of Korea in the 1980s, additional R&D investment by private enterprises played a key role in moving the economy in an innovation-based direction.

Third, it is important to limit government intervention in the economy. When an economy progresses to a middle income status, the costs of government failure are likely to swamp any benefits of the efficient mobilization of productive inputs through the use of directed credit and industrial policy. Such financial controls are conducive to the promotion of specific industries and the supply of money to enterprises at low interest rates. However, they can also have negative side-effects that hinder the development of the banking industry, such as the accumulation of non-performing loans at banks, corruption, and a rise of shadow banking. Recently it has been reported that problems in China's banking system have become an important obstacle to other financial reforms such as greater flexibility of exchange rates and capital account liberalization (Goldstein and Lardy, 2009).

Finally, there is a possibility that some developing Asian countries will face demands for political change. Residents will seek more political freedom once this is no longer viewed as secondary to rapid economic growth. Demands for democracy together with chronic inequality can be an explosive cocktail.

Mexico and Korea are examples of middle-income countries exposed to political changes after the first phase of industrialization. In the 1980s Mexico suffered long-term stagnation because of political unrest combined with economic and regional inequality. Korea was similar in that it also faced massive political protests in the mid-1980s, but this turmoil subsided following democratization, perhaps because inequality was less (Park, 2011).

Currently, the Chinese government appears to regard economic inequality as a threat to both political and economic stability. To reduce the equality, wage increases for blue-collar workers have been promoted in various ways, as mentioned previously. The disparity between eastern coastal and western inland regions is such a grave concern for the Chinese government that it has formulated a Great Western Development Strategy.

5   The Rise of China and the Future of Regional Cooperation

In 2010, for the first time, China's nominal GDP surpassed Japan's. China has become the world's second largest economy after the US (which it will also overtake in a few years). This power shift between China and Japan is not simply a result of the global financial crisis, of course. The Japanese economy has suffered from slow growth and deflation since 1990, while China achieved rapid growth. But even if the contrasting economic performance of the two countries is the fundamental driver of this power shift, the financial crisis has contributed as well. China was affected less by the crisis and grew by 9 percent in 2008, while the Japanese economy shrank by more than 6 percent.

China's rise is not the only challenge for regional cooperation. East Asia is also more heterogeneous than the EU. There are huge differences in economic size, incomes and political structures among countries. Reflecting this heterogeneity, East Asian countries have been pursuing regional cooperation in a gradual manner. Examples of successful incremental initiatives include the Asian Bond Market Initiative (ABMI), designed to develop bond markets at the national and regional levels, and the Chiang Mai Initiative (CMI), intended to provide emergency liquidity to member countries. In 2010, the CMI was further developed into the Chiang Mai Initiative Multilateralization (CMIM), multilateralizing its previously bilateral swap lines.

Here policymakers are essentially following the lead of the markets. One indication is the ratio of intraregional trade to total trade, which rose from 29 percent in 1990 to 38 percent in 2008. This is still behind the EU's ratio of 60 percent but similar to NAFTA's. The share of intraregional investment in foreign direct investment (FDI) has risen as well, from 14.5 percent in 2000 to 27.0 percent in 2006 (See Table 1). Japan and Korea have been increasing their investment in China and ASEAN for the purpose of relocating production, and Chinese intraregional investment has been increasing at the same time. These FDI flows have come to constitute an important driver of growth and integration in Southeast Asia in particular.

Although regional economic integration is necessary for developing regional cooperation, it is not sufficient. Developing institutions for regional cooperation requires political compromise and consensus on the pursuit of common goals. For example, agreement could be reached on the CMIM because of matching interests. ASEAN's experience with the Asian financial

Table 1.   Share of Intraregional Trade in East
Asian Economies (in Percent).

	1990	2000	2008
China	21.3	33.1	26.2
Japan	21.2	30.8	36.8
Korea	29.1	36.6	44.0
Singapore	39.5	46.5	48.7
Indonesia	51.6	50.6	61.3
Malaysia	49.6	49.4	56.7
Thailand	42.6	44.9	48.2
Vietnam	27.8	56.3	52.8

Note: East Asia comprises China, Japan, Korea,
and the 10 member countries of ASEAN.
Source: Calculated from UN Comtrade Database.

crisis required additional crisis prevention measures. On the other hand,
China and Japan were able to expand their influence over Southeast Asian
countries because they could contribute their abundant foreign exchange
reserves. Against this backdrop agreement was reached on establishing the
CMIM, and China and Japan agreed to equal quotas and voting shares.

The rapid rise in China and continued slow growth of Japan make
repeating this success more difficult. While China is looking to expand its
influence, Japan will be putting significant effort toward countering China's
aspirations. Tension between the two countries may then hinder regional
cooperation. East Asia's network of free trade agreements (FTAs) is a case
in point. The region should presumably aim for a single ASEAN+3 FTA.
However, negotiations between China and Japan have been difficult. China
has therefore pursued an FTA with ASEAN, while Korea and Japan have
signed FTAs with the ASEAN member countries separately. In November
2011, Japan announced its interest in joining talks on the Trans-Pacific
Strategic Economic Partnership Agreement (TPP), which is an economic
agreement currently being negotiated among the US and certain Asia-
Pacific countries. The TPP has been recognized as a device for restraining
China's expansion. After Japan's announcement, China expressed strong
dissatisfaction with its exclusion from the TPP. Regional cooperation has
come to grief over less.

China's policy for internationalization of the renminbi is another threat
to regional financial cooperation. China sees the asymmetric role of the
dollar in the international system as a cause of the global financial crisis,

calling for reform of the international monetary system. It has therefore turned its attention to establishing the renminbi as an international currency in its own right. In 2009, the Chinese government established a special task force for renminbi internationalization. Already it has taken three steps toward renminbi internationalization (Ranjan and Prakash, 2010). First, it has been expanding the scope for renminbi settlement of cross-border trade. As a result, the total volume of trade settled in renminbi exceeded RMB 958 billion in the first half of 2011, 13 times that only a year earlier. Second, China is encouraging offshore renminbi transactions. Beginning in 2010, banks were permitted to issue renminbi-denominated bonds in Hong Kong. Renminbi deposits in Hong Kong rose to nearly RMB 300 billion by the end of 2010. Finally, China entered into a currency swap arrangement with Korea, Malaysia and Brazil. According to the arrangement, the RMB will be used in swap transactions.

This program is also creating tensions. Japan would prefer the yen to be the leading international currency in East Asia. Neighboring countries such as Korea may also fear the increasing influence of the RMB in the area. China is likely to expand its quota in intraregional financial arrangements, yet such demands can make agreement more difficult and may alter the regional balance of power (Park and Song, 2011). While the trade and the investment of Asian countries are becoming more integrated, stronger institutional supports are now needed to sustain the momentum. If Asian countries fail to build cooperative institutions of transnational governance, the benefits of integration may be limited or even lost. Tense political relations may threaten economic integration; recall that China has territorial disputes with a number of adjacent countries, not least Japan. Developing a harmonious and durable institutional framework for regional cooperation becomes all the more urgent in that light. The speed of China's rise is a reminder that there is no time to waste.

6 Conclusion

Asian economies were hit hard by the global financial crisis, but they recovered more quickly than other parts of the world. Their rapid rebound reflected the concerted application of expansionary monetary and fiscal policies, which was possible because Asian countries had kept their powder dry. And while Asia's post-crisis economic performance is the envy of other parts of the world, the region now faces significant challenges. These include slowing growth in middle-income countries, the prospect of slowing growth in countries like China poised to cross the middle-income threshold, and high food and energy prices which feed inflation throughout the region. This constellation of problems in turn poses potential threats to political stability. Coping with these challenges requires Asian countries to rebalance and restructure: to transform their input-based and export-driven economies so that rely more heavily on innovation and domestic demand. Completing this transition will be no easy task.

References

Asian Development Bank (2010). *Asian Development Outlook 2010: Macroeconomic Management Beyond the Crisis*. Manila: Asian Development Bank.

———— (2011a). *Asian Development Outlook 2011: South-South Link*. Manila: Asian Development Bank.

———— (2011b). *Asia 2050: Realizing the Asian Century*. Manila: Asian Development Bank.

Bergsten, F. and J.J. Schobott (2011). Submission to the USTR in Support of a Trans-Pacific Partnership Agreement. Washington DC: Peterson Institute for International Economics.

Cai, F. (2010). Demographic transition, demographic dividend, and Lewis turning point in China. *China Economic Journal*, 3(2), 107–119.

———— (2011). The coming demographic impact on China's growth: The age factor in the Middle Income Trap. In *Proceedings of Asian Economic Panel*.

Center for International Comparisons (2011). Penn World Tables 7.0.

Eichengreen, B., D. Park, and K. Shin (2011). When fast growing economies slow down: International evidence and implications for China. NBER, Working Paper 16919.

Goldstein, M. and N.R. Lardy (2009). *Debating China's Exchange Rate Policy*. Washington DC: Peterson Institute for International Economics.

International Monetary Fund. *World Economic Outlook*. Washington DC: International Monetary Fund.

International Monetary Fund (2011). World Economic Outlook Database, September.

Ohno, K. (2010). Avoiding the Middle Income Trap: Renovating industrial policy formulation in Vietnam, mimeo.

Park, B. (2011). The Middle Income Trap and economic transformation: Lessons from Korea's experiences. In *Proceedings of KIEP–AMR Joint Seminar.*

Park, Y.C. and C.Y. Song (2011). Renminbi internationalization: Prospects and implications for economic integration in East Asia. *Asian Economic Papers*, 10(3), 42–72.

Park, Y.J., D. Rhee and E.J. Kang (2011). The prospect and transmission dynamics of China's inflation to Korea. *KIEP World Economy Update*, May. Seoul: Korea Institute for International Economic Policy.

Rajan, R. and A. Prakash (2011). Internationalization of currency: The case of the Indian rupee and Chinese renminbi. RBI Staff Studies, New Delhi: Reserve Bank of India.

United Nations, UN Comtrade Database.

Wheatley, A. (2010). Avoiding the Middle Income Trap. *New York Times.* October 25. Available at http://www.nytimes.com/2010/10/ 26/business/global/26inside.html

World Bank (2011). *World Economic Indicators 2011.* Washington DC: World Bank.

Yueh, L. (2011). Re-balancing China: Linking internal and external reforms. *Asian Economic Papers*, 10(2), 87–111.

CHAPTER 8

Long-Term Challenges for the Advanced Economies: Reducing Government Debt

Joseph Gagnon and Marc Hinterschweiger[1]

1 Introduction

The financial crisis of 2008 brought about the most rapid increase in global government debt since World War II (Abbas *et al.*, 2010). The IMF (2011) estimates that, between 2007 and 2011, net general government debt (as a percent of GDP) will have risen from 52 percent to 69 percent in the euro area, from 43 percent to 73 percent in the US, from 38 percent to 73 percent in the UK, and from 82 percent to 131 percent in Japan.

The deficit spending and financial bailouts that created this debt explosion helped to prevent the global economy from sinking into another Great Depression. More specifically, the newly issued public debt supported aggregate demand while the private sector retreated, defaulting on mortgages and loans in some cases, and also deleveraging and restructuring its balance sheet quickly. Suddenly, public sector debt became more attractive to frightened investors, and interest rates on government debt fell to their lowest levels in decades. Long-term interest rates in the major advanced economies (except Italy) remain near multi-decade lows. Financial markets

---

[1]The opinions expressed are those of the authors and not necessarily those of the Peterson Institute for International Economics.

in these economies appear to be more concerned at present over the weak prospects for economic recovery than they are about rising public sector debt levels. As a result, governments in these economies continue to have scope to support economic activity through fiscal deficits in the near term.

The same is not true for several Euro Area countries, however. Starting last spring, financial market concerns about the ability of these governments to service their debts led to sharp increases in interest rates on government bonds. It seems likely that the Greek, Irish, and Portuguese governments would not have been able to sell bonds at any interest rate in the absence of intervention by their European partners and the IMF, which provided large emergency loans. Significantly, these emergency loans came in conjunction with severe austerity plans for the Greek, Irish, and Portuguese governments. As market concerns spread to Belgium, Italy, and Spain, governments in these countries announced new austerity measures and structural reforms amid tense negotiations within Europe on how to contain market pressures.

Looking further ahead, even after economies recover and temporary stimulus measures are withdrawn, many governments face significant budget deficits. All face trend increases in the costs of public pensions and health care as their populations age. There is widespread agreement on these long-term challenges, but there is disagreement about how rapidly governments should move toward fiscal consolidation. Some observers warn that the experiences of Greece, Ireland, and Portugal could spread elsewhere before long, but others argue that slow growth and high unemployment are the most urgent problems in most of the advanced economies.

This paper explores the fiscal outlook for the advanced economies, with a focus on the US, Japan, and the Euro Area. We project scenarios for future economic growth, interest rates, and government debt under current fiscal plans, including current benefit formulas for public pensions and public health care. The purpose is not to forecast the most likely outcomes. Rather it is to highlight the fact that current policies are not sustainable under some plausible projections for economic variables, and to underscore the importance of actions to put government debt on a sustainable long-run trajectory.

2   Projected Paths of Government Debt

2.1   *General government primary balances*

The starting point for this analysis is a set of projections by the IMF (2011) for general government primary balances in 2016.[2] These projections are based on policies adopted as of mid-2011, and they incorporate the effects of announced government plans for specific spending cuts and revenue increases, even if these plans have not been formally enacted. The projections also assume that economic recovery will boost government revenues. For 2016, we use the cyclically adjusted primary balance.[3] The cyclically adjusted balance is a better starting point for extrapolating debt because GDP should be close to potential on average over the long run. The projections imply substantial declines in primary deficits over the next five years. As with any forecast, there is considerable uncertainty surrounding these projections, and they may well prove too optimistic. Nevertheless, they are a reasonable place to start the analysis. The top row of Table 1 displays the projected primary deficits for 2016.[4]

We assume that the primary deficit would remain constant as a percent of GDP in the years beyond 2016 as long as GDP remains close to trend and there are no special factors, which we will discuss next. In other words, we assume that revenues and expenditures grow in proportion to GDP and therefore result in primary deficits that also remain in the same proportion to GDP.

One special factor that tends to increase the primary deficit over time is the effect of population ageing and rising health-care costs on public pensions and public health care spending.[5] The second and third lines of

---

[2]The primary balance is the difference between non-interest government revenues and spending on government programs. The primary balance excludes net interest payments. Because primary balances are negative in most economies, the discussion below refers to deficits rather than balances in order to avoid a plethora of minus signs.

[3]Cyclical adjustment removes the effect of any shortfall or excess of actual GDP relative to potential GDP on revenues and spending programs that respond directly to GDP. In other words, it provides an estimate of what the balance would be if GDP were at potential.

[4]The advanced-economy aggregate is based on the IMF definition of advanced economies. It includes the US, the Euro Area, and Japan, as well as other economies.

[5]In the US, "public pensions" refers to the Social Security old age and disability insurance programs and "public health care" refers to Medicare and Medicaid.

Table 1.   Fiscal and Economic Assumptions.

	United States	Euro Area	Japan	Advanced Economies
Deficit Components (percent of GDP)				
Baseline Primary Deficit (level in 2016)	1.8	−1.9	4.8	0.4
Public Pensions	*0.04*	*0.07*	*0.07*	*0.11*
Public Health Care (annual increase)	*0.08*	*0.15*	*0.10*	*0.09*
Baseline Primary Deficit (level in 2035)	6.4	1.9	10.5	5.6
Health Care Alternatives				
— Optimistic	*0.04*	*0.05*	*0.06*	*0.05*
— Pessimistic (annual increase)	*0.25*	*0.27*	*0.26*	*0.25*
2017–2035 Real GDP Growth Rate (percent)				
OECD 2016–2026	2.2	1.5	1.4	1.9
Baseline	1.8	1.6	0.9	1.6
Optimistic	2.5	2.3	1.5	2.3
Pessimistic	1.1	1.1	0.2	1.3

Sources: The baseline primary deficits in 2016 are cyclically adjusted primary deficits from IMF (2011). Pension and health care projections are from OECD (2011, Box 4.2). Health care alternatives are from IMF (2010a). Baseline growth rates are described in the text and are based on OECD (2011, Table 4.1) potential growth rates. Optimistic and pessimistic growth rates are described in the text.
Notes: OECD health care projections include publicly funded long-term care. OECD pension and health projections are based on the period 2010–25 and are assumed to grow at the same rate in 2026–2035. IMF health alternative projections are based on the period 2010–2030 and are assumed to grow at the same rate in 2031–35. The advanced-economy aggregate includes the United States, the euro area, Japan, and other countries included in the IMF definition of advanced economies, but growth projections for this group are based on OECD averages. All economies are assumed to have inflation of 2 percent and constant nominal exchange rates.

Table 1 display estimates from the Organization of Economic Cooperation and Development (OECD, 2011) of the annual average increases in these costs over the period 2010 through 2025 under the assumption that current benefits formulas and contribution rates remain unchanged. Note that most of the increased spending is attributed to health care and not public pensions. We assume that these costs continue to rise at the same rates in the years after 2025. These rising costs of social benefits cause expected primary deficits to increase in all economies after 2016.

Another special factor affecting primary deficits is the projected slowing of GDP growth associated with rising public debts, as discussed below. We assume that any reduction of GDP below its previous trend increases the primary deficit by an amount proportional to the share of government revenues in GDP. The fourth line of Table 1 shows the implied levels of primary deficits in 2035 under our baseline scenario after taking into consideration the above special factors.

2.2   *Size of economies (GDP)*

In order to construct aggregate debt measures, we project each economy's GDP in terms of US dollars. From 2005 through 2016, we use IMF data and projections. For 2016–2025, the OECD (2011) projects potential GDP growth rates under the assumption that net government debt ratios gradually stabilize by 2025. We use the OECD growth projections for our baseline estimates for 2017–2020. Beginning in 2021, as net debt in our baseline scenario rises above that in the OECD projection, we reduce the GDP growth rates from those in the OECD projection in proportion to the growth in the ratio of net general government debt to GDP, assuming that each percentage point increase in the net debt ratio permanently reduces GDP by 0.03 percent.[6] This effect occurs either because of rising interest rates or because of heightened uncertainty on the part of businesses and investors about future policies. We do not factor in any effect of the debt ratio on inflation, which is assumed to be 2 percent in all regions. We assume constant exchange rates among all advanced economies.

The bottom half of Table 1 displays the OECD projected real growth rates that are the basis of our projections. For the United States and Japan, the baseline GDP growth rate is lower than the OECD projection on average, reflecting the negative effect of rising debt on GDP. As described below, we also consider scenarios with more optimistic and more pessimistic growth rates, which are shown at the bottom of Table 1.

2.3   *Interest rates*

Interest rates have an important effect on any projection of government debt. For a given path of primary deficits, the future debt level will be higher

---

[6]An effect of this size is incorporated in the OECD's macroeconomic model.

if the government has to pay higher interest on its debt. Averaged over long periods of time, effective government interest rates in most economies have been close to average nominal GDP growth rates.[7] We use the IMF projections of effective government interest rates through 2015, which are generally lower than projected nominal GDP growth rates in 2011–2015. In 2016, we assume that the effective interest rate equals the trend growth rate of nominal GDP.

A major concern about rising government debt is its potential to crowd out productive investment through higher interest rates, especially as debt ratios rise above historical ranges.[8] As discussed in the box titled "Statistical Estimates of the Effect of Government Debt on Interest Rates," recent studies have found surprising agreement as to the size of the effect of rising debt ratios on interest rates. Beginning in 2017, we assume that the effective interest rate equals the growth rate of nominal GDP plus an additional amount related to the growth of a country's ratio of net government debt to GDP. Based on a mid-range estimate from existing studies, the interest rate rises above the nominal growth rate by 3.5 basis points for each percentage point increase in the ratio of net debt to GDP above its 2015 level.[9] This feedback from debt to interest rates exacerbates the cost of serving that debt over time, which in turn makes the reduction of fiscal deficits more difficult.

2.4 *Baseline debt projections*

Table 2 and Figures 1–4 display projections for general government net debt as a percent of GDP through 2035. General government includes all

---

[7]The effective interest rate equals government net interest payments divided by net government debt. It is essentially a weighted average of the interest rates of outstanding bonds. Appendix 1 of IMF (2010b) shows that long-term bond yields in advanced economies generally exceeded growth rates in 1981–2000 and were close to growth rates in 2001–2008. However, the 1981–2000 period was characterized by generalized disinflation that pushed nominal growth rates below nominal bond yields. The opposite phenomenon occurred in the 1960s and 1970s, and growth rates generally were above bond yields in 1960–1980. Moreover, the effective interest rate on government debt tends to be lower than the long-term bond yield because a significant fraction of debt is issued at short maturities.

[8]Higher interest rates may also encourage additional saving, which reduces the crowding-out of productive investment. However, most economists believe the effects of interest rates on investment are greater than the effects on saving.

[9]In light of very low interest rates in Japan despite record debt levels, we reduce this effect by 50 percent for Japan. OECD (2010, Chapter 4) assumes a slightly larger effect (4 basis points versus 3.5) except for Japan, where the effect is 1 basis point.

Table 2.   General Government Net Debt Projections (percent of GDP).

	2006	2011	2016	2025	2035
United States					
Optimistic Growth				105	134
Baseline	42	73	89	114	188
Pessimistic Growth				117	250
Pessimistic Health Cost				128	291
High Interest Rates				116	226
CBO-A (federal debt held by the public)*	36	69	82	119	187
Euro Area					
Optimistic Growth				50	17
Baseline	54	69	69	61	70
Pessimistic Growth				67	105
Pessimistic Health Cost				72	131
High Interest Rates				67	89
Memo:					
Netherlands	25	31	34		
Germany	53	57	55		
France	60	81	82		
Italy	90	100	95		
Belgium	77	80	81		
Spain	31	56	66		
Portugal	59	102	106		
Ireland	12	99	100		
Greece**	106	166	163		
Japan					
Optimistic Growth				217	325
Baseline	84	131	167	225	374
Pessimistic Growth				231	474
Pessimistic Health Cost				233	424
High Interest Rates				233	462
Advanced Economies					
Optimistic Growth				82	92
Baseline	46	69	78	92	144
Pessimistic Growth				93	168
Pessimistic Health Cost				102	210
High Interest Rates				93	158

*Based on CBO (2011) alternative projection.
**Gross debt. Does not include the effect of voluntary debt restructuring negotiated in October 2011.
Sources: Debt ratios through 2016 are from IMF (2011). Debt ratios for 2025 and 2035 are based on calculations described in the text.

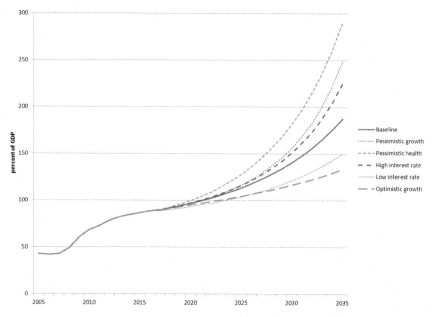

Fig. 1.   General Government Net Debt Projections — United States.

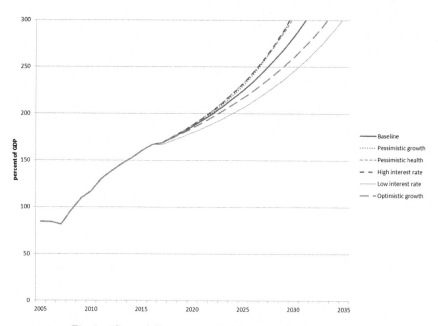

Fig. 2.   General Government Net Debt Projections — Japan.

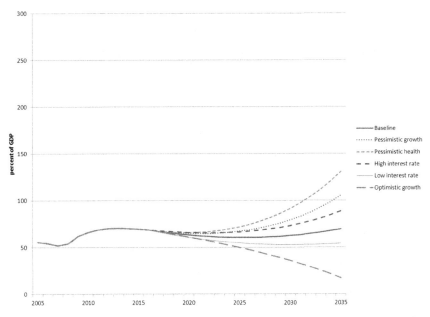

Fig. 3.   General Government Net Debt Projections — Euro Area.

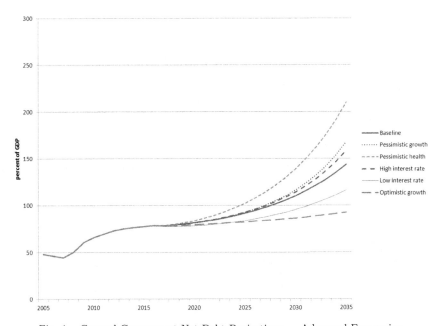

Fig. 4.   General Government Net Debt Projections — Advanced Economies.

levels of government (central, regional, and local) as well as government-run benefits programs. It does not include publicly owned corporations that operate on a market basis without routine subsidies. Net debt is defined as all financial liabilities minus all financial assets of the government sector. Net debt is the appropriate concept for evaluating long-run solvency.[10]

Statistical Estimates of the Effect of Government Debt on Interest Rates

The effect of government debt on interest rates has been an active field of research. Many papers analyze the effect of both budget deficits and debt, but, from a theoretical point of view, the long-run effect on interest rates should be a consequence of the latter. Thus, we focus on the estimated effects of government debt. These papers all examine the effects on real interest rates, either by using measures of the real interest rate as regressands or by including measures of inflation expectations as regressors.

Engen and Hubbard (2005) find that an increase in US federal debt by 1 percentage point (pp) leads to an increase in the long-term real interest rate by roughly 3 to 5 basis points (bps), depending on the time period. Laubach's (2009) estimates are in the same range. Gale and Orszag (2004) find a slightly higher range of 3 to 6 bps. All of these studies use forward long-term interest rates and projected future values of the fiscal variables. Because the business cycle has opposite effects on interest rates and the fiscal position, using current values of these variables would introduce a negative correlation between these variables that biases downward estimates of the long-run relationship.

Focusing on a panel of OECD countries, Chinn and Frankel (2007) obtain a wide range of estimates, both negative and positive, perhaps because of their very short sample. We do not include their results in the table below. Kinoshita (2006) obtains results very similar to those described for the US above. Gruber and Kamin (2010) obtain results at the low end of those described above. Baldacci and Kumar (2010) use panel regressions including both advanced and major developing economies. They, too, find an effect of about 3 to 5 bps.

---

[10]For many countries, gross debt and net debt are nearly equal. In the US, gross debt exceeds net debt by a significant amount because the social security system holds Treasury bonds. Most other countries have a pay-as-you-go public pension system which holds few financial assets. One of the main purposes of extrapolating deficits and debt out for 25 years is to calculate the extent to which public pension systems are underfunded. Thus, to use gross debt for the US would double-count the cost of future social security deficits.

(Continued)

Conway and Orr (2002) and Ardagna *et al.* (2004) find that the relationship between long-term interest rates and public debt is non-linear. They estimate that when government debt is 100 percent of GDP, a 1 pp increase in debt raises long-term interest rates about 1 bp, a value that is lower than the other estimates. However, Ardagna *et al.* find that this effect increases to 3.5 bp when debt is 140 percent of GDP.

Study	Effect of 1 pp debt increase on real long-term interest rate	Countries	Time Period
Conway and Orr (2002)	1 bp (for debt at 100% of GDP	OECD countries	1986–2002
Ardagna *et al.* (2004)	but rising for higher debt levels)		1960–2002
Gale and Orzag (2004)	3–6 bps	US	1976–2004
Engen and Hubbard (2005)	3–5 bps	US	1953/1976–2003
Kinoshita (2006)	2–5 bps	OECD countries	1971–2004
Laubach (2009)	3–5 bps	US	1976–2005
Baldacci and Kumar (2010)	3–5 bps	31 countries	1980–2008
Gruber and Kamin (2010)	2 bps	G7 countries	1988–2007

Under the baseline scenario, general government net debt in the US is projected to rise from 73 percent of GDP in 2011 to 114 percent of GDP in 2025 and 188 percent of GDP in 2035. In Japan, the increase is even more dramatic. Japanese net debt is estimated to be 131 percent of GDP in 2011, and it is projected to rise to 225 percent of GDP in 2025 and 374 percent in 2035. In the euro area, however, net debt is projected to be relatively stable, rising from 69 percent of GDP in 2011 to only 70 percent of GDP by 2035. For the advanced economies in aggregate, net debt is projected to rise from 69 percent of GDP in 2011 to 92 percent of GDP in 2025 and 144 percent in 2035.

For the US, the baseline projection is close to that implied by the Congressional Budget Office's "Alternative" (CBO-A) projection of federal debt held by the public (CBO, 2011).[11] For US Federal debt, it is widely agreed that the CBO-A projection is more realistic than the CBO baseline projection, because it embodies relatively realistic assumptions about future policy actions (at least in the near term) to address the issue.[12]

The large increases in net debt in some of our baseline scenarios should not be viewed as a forecast of likely outcomes. Rather they should be understood to indicate the magnitude of the looming fiscal challenges. For the US and Japan, the challenges in the baseline scenario are so great that a crisis is likely to happen before 2035 if policies are not corrected. We return to the issues of fiscal crises and policy options later.

2.5   The optimistic and pessimistic health care cost scenarios

By far the most important contributor to concerns about mounting government debts and deficits is the exploding cost of health care over the next several decades. As many studies have demonstrated, these costs result from three factors: 1) an ageing population, 2) the increasing cost of medical technologies and technological breakthroughs that become a basic part of what patients expect, and 3) the poorly organized and inefficient incentives that drive up costs in the American health care system, in particular. But there is considerable uncertainty surrounding the future path of public health care expenses, even with the benefit formulas and contribution rates held constant. A recent study by the IMF (2010a) presents both optimistic and pessimistic projections of health care costs, which are shown in the middle lines of Table 1. By the year 2035, the annual increase in health care costs under the pessimistic assumptions leads to a net increase in health costs that exceeds those under the optimistic assumptions by about 4 percent of GDP in each of the advanced economies. The major sources of

---

[11]The main difference between federal debt held by the public and general government net debt is net debt of state and local governments.

[12]The CBO baseline debt projection assumes that all the 2001 tax cuts are allowed to expire, that coverage of the Alternative Minimum Tax is expanded considerably, that Medicare payments to doctors will not be increased, and that other types of spending will decline as a share of GDP. The CBO-A debt projection assumes that all of the 2001 tax cuts will be extended, that the Alternative Minimum Tax will not be allowed to expand, that Medicare payments will be increased, and that other spending will grow in line with GDP.

this uncertainty are health care technology and the scope for improvements in the efficiency of health care delivery.

For each of the advanced economies, the projected future debt ratios under the optimistic health care scenario are only modestly lower than those of the baseline scenario. To save space, they are not displayed in Table 2 or Figures 1–4. The future debt ratios under the pessimistic health care scenario are displayed in Table 2 and Figures 1–4. These are significantly higher than those under the baseline scenario for all regions.

2.6 *Two interest rate scenarios*

Because there is considerable uncertainty about the future path of interest rates, this chapter projects deficits and debts under two alternative interest rate scenarios, one optimistic and the other more dire.

The "low interest rates" scenario is based on the implied prediction of low future interest rates built into current long-term bond yields. For example, the 10-year interest rate in the US is around 2 percent and the 30-year rate is around 3 percent. These rates appear to indicate that markets expect short-term interest rates to remain low for decades. It is unlikely, however, that interest rates would remain low over the next 20 to 30 years if government debt were to rise as projected in the baseline scenario for the US and Japan. To the extent that rates are low, it is probably because financial market participants expect that governments will take steps, however unknown or undefined, to prevent such alarming increases in debt over the long run.

Despite the hope of many that deficits will come under control over time, we believe that most US and Japanese market participants do not expect faster fiscal cuts in the next few years than are built into our baseline scenario.[13] Thus, it may be reasonable to assume that long-term interest rates will remain low even if debt ratios rise as projected in the baseline scenario over the next few years. Current 5-year forward interest rates, at 2-year and 5-year maturities, are a good measure of market expectations of government borrowing costs in 2016. For the US, these rates are around

---

[13]See, for example, Lupton and Hensley (2010:13), who forecast changes in primary balances between 2010 and 2013 for the euro area, Japan, and the US that are close to those in our baseline scenario.

2 to 4 percent, below the projected growth rate of nominal GDP. In Japan, they are even lower.

Effective interest rates tend to adjust slowly to any change in market interest rates. This is because effective interest rates include the rates paid on long-term bonds issued many years previous. For example, the effective interest rates estimated by the IMF for each of these economies in 2010 are higher than the average yields on newly issued government debt. Accordingly, even if market interest rates were to rise in line with the implied prediction of current yield curves, the effective rates might continue to decline for a few years. The low interest rates scenario thus assumes that effective rates are about 1 percentage point below the nominal GDP growth rate in 2016 and then rise smoothly in proportion to the growing debt ratio using the same relationship as in the baseline scenario.

To save space the low interest rate scenario is not included in Table 2 but it is displayed in Figures 1–4. In all regions, the future debt ratios under the low interest rates scenario are lower than those under the baseline scenario.

The "high interest rates" scenario uses a larger coefficient (5.5) for the effect of the debt ratio on the interest rate (compared to 3.5 in the baseline scenario).[14] This estimate is near the high end of the range discussed in the box titled "Statistical Estimates of the Effect of Government Debt on Interest Rates." For the euro area, which does not have a rising debt ratio, we assumed an effective interest rate that is 1 percentage point higher than the nominal GDP growth rate, which may be viewed as a scenario in which many countries in the euro area continue to struggle with high interest rate spreads indefinitely. Under the high interest rate scenarios, fiscal deficits grow rapidly and debt ratios rise above baseline.

2.7   *The optimistic growth scenario*

The baseline growth projections for the advanced economies are somewhat lower than their average growth rates before the global financial crisis, and there is little rebound from the recession of 2008–2009. As shown in the bottom of Table 1, the "optimistic growth" scenario assumes higher growth than the baseline GDP growth projections for advanced economies.[15] One

---

[14] As in the other scenarios, the interest rate effect in Japan is assumed to be only half as large as in the other economies.

[15] Trend GDP growth in each advanced region is 0.5 percentage points higher than in the baseline after 2016. A small additional positive effect on growth occurs because of the reduced accumulation of public debt.

factor that would support the optimistic growth scenario is the potential for a global rebalancing of demand toward the advanced economies. Although China and some other emerging economies have been slow to move in this direction, they are likely to come under increasing pressure to do so in the future. In such a rebalancing, emerging economies with large current account surpluses would allow their exchange rates to appreciate, reducing the rate at which they accumulate foreign exchange reserves, and purchasing more exports from the advanced economies.

The increase in GDP lowers primary deficits in advanced economies by an amount proportional to the share of general government gross revenues in GDP as projected by the IMF (2011) for 2016.[16] Table 2 and Figures 1–4 show that relatively moderate but persistent increases in economic growth do significantly reduce projected debt ratios in the advanced economies. Sustained growth is thus, as always, an excellent remedy for deficits, however unsustainable they may be. But the higher growth rates projected in this scenario are not sufficient to prevent debt ratios from rising in the US and Japan.

2.8 *The pessimistic growth scenario*

The "pessimistic growth" scenario results from the fulfillment of fears that rising debts will choke off investment and threaten a potential crisis. In this sense, the scenario may be viewed as a crisis scenario, though the nature of an actual crisis, not to mention its effects, is extremely hard to predict. The pessimistic growth scenario deepens the negative drag on GDP that would result from rising debt ratios, reflecting the effects of "crowding out" of productive investment when governments run large deficits after economic activity has fully recovered from recession. Beginning in 2017, the levels of real and nominal GDP are reduced by 0.06 percent for each percent increase in the ratio of net government debt to GDP, double the effect in the baseline scenario. In addition, the effect of debt on interest rates is assumed to be the same as that assumed in the "high interest rates" scenario. These changes would tend to increase GDP growth initially in the euro area because its debt ratio is falling, so in this scenario we exogenously reduce GDP growth in the euro area by 0.5 percent per year. As shown in the bottom lines

---

[16]For example, when the revenue share is 50 percent, a 1 percent increase in GDP lowers the primary deficit 0.5 percentage points.

of Table 1, this scenario implies large reductions in the US and Japanese growth rates. The pessimistic growth scenario may exaggerate the negative effect of government debt on GDP, but it does help to flesh out the range of possible outcomes.[17] The feedback from higher debt to both higher interest rates and lower GDP creates larger increases in debt ratios over time.

2.9 *Implications of net debt projections*

None of the optimistic scenarios discussed above leads to a decline in net debt ratios for the US and Japan. Under more pessimistic assumptions about future economic growth, health care costs, or interest rates, the implied increases in net debt ratios by 2035 in all of the advanced economies are considerable. Indeed, the large increases in debt under some of the pessimistic scenarios almost certainly are not feasible, and even the baseline path for debt is probably not feasible for the US and Japan. These scenarios likely would lead to a fiscal crisis in which governments would be forced to choose some combination of higher taxes, reduced spending, default on debt, or monetization of debt before 2035. The limits of debt are the topic of the next section.

3   The Burden of Debt and Fiscal Limits

How much debt is "sustainable"? Ultimately, the level of sustainable debt depends not on some abstract formula, but on the willingness of society and government to pay the interest on the debt and to accept the reduction

---

[17]Reinhart and Rogoff (2010) suggest that the effect of debt on GDP growth may be highly nonlinear, with relatively little effect when debt is less than 90 percent of GDP and a large effect when debt is greater than 90 percent of GDP. They do not estimate a specific functional relationship between debt and growth. Caner *et al.* (2010) and Checherita and Rother (2010) find significant nonlinear relationships between government debt and GDP growth for developing economies and euro-area economies, respectively, with inflection points around 70 to 100 percent of GDP. Kumar and Woo (2010) also find a negative effect of debt on GDP for a broad panel of advanced and developing economies. Irons and Bivens (2010) point out that the Reinhart-Rogoff result is heavily influenced by the experiences of developing economies with poor institutions and by major wars in advanced economies. They also suggest that the causality seems to run from low growth to high debt rather than the reverse. We note that the results of Caner *et al.*, Checherita and Rother, and Kumar and Woo are obtained in samples dominated by government borrowing in currencies not under the control of the sovereign, for which interest rate effects and debt intolerance appear to be greater.

in GDP caused by the higher interest rates and higher tax rates associated with such a burden. There is no automatic way to calculate that effect but some obvious economic and financial norms do apply. The following analysis seeks to apply the lessons of history for understanding likely future developments. We note that our analysis does not make any strong assumptions about rationality or foresight of either the public or the private sector. However, there is no guarantee that markets or governments will behave the same in the future as they did in the past.

3.1   *Effect of debt on interest rates and interest payments*

Figures 5–8 display effective interest rates on government debt, both past and projected. Since 2006, interest rates have fallen in the US and the euro area, in part because of the economic downturn which led investors to buy government securities in dollars and euros as a safe haven, and in part because of the trend increase in reserve accumulation by many governments in developing economies. At the same time, rates have risen in Japan because of the end of the quantitative easing policy. In the baseline scenario, interest rates are projected to equal the trend growth rate

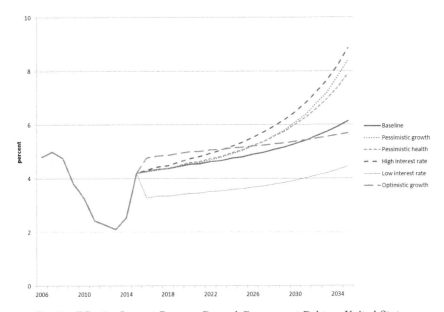

Fig. 5.   Effective Interest Rate on General Government Debt — United States.

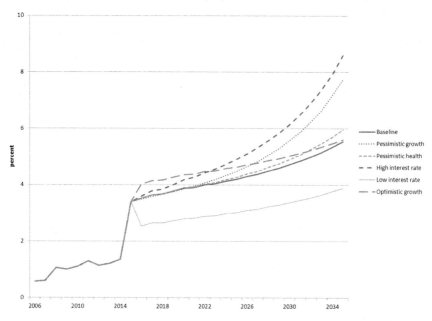

Fig. 6.   Effective Interest Rate on General Government Debt — Japan.

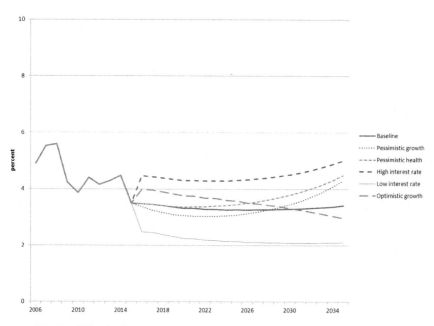

Fig. 7.   Effective Interest Rate on General Government Debt — Euro Area.

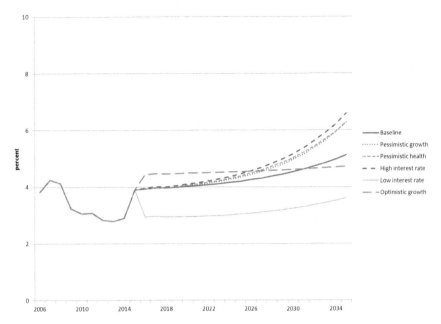

Fig. 8.   Effective Interest Rate on General Government Debt — Advanced Economies.

of nominal GDP in all economies in 2016, roughly consistent with historical average behavior and the assumption that output will be near its long-run potential. This projection implicitly assumes that developing economies will halt their rapid purchases of bonds in the advanced economies.

What is significant is that beyond 2016, interest rates gradually rise in line with net debt ratios, especially in the US and Japan. The projected levels of interest rates in 2035 may seem rather modest given the large increases in government debt in some scenarios. Three factors explain this muted rise in interest rates.

First, and perhaps most important, our estimates of the effect of government debt on interest rates essentially assume that there is no risk of default. This assumption is appropriate for governments that borrow in currencies they control because they can print money to pay their debts in extremity. The US, the Euro Area as a whole, Japan, and other advanced economies borrow in currencies they control. But individual euro-area governments borrow in currencies they do not control; in such cases, default becomes a serious risk when debt levels rise. A number of studies have found large effects of debt on interest rates for governments that borrow in currencies they do not control.[18] Our baseline projection is based on the assumption that euro-area governments will be able to contain spreads in interest rates across member countries to the values experienced in 2010 on average, which represents a noticeable reduction from 2011 spreads for some countries.

Second, all of our scenarios assume constant low inflation and stable inflation expectations. There is no way of predicting how future fiscal developments would affect inflation and prices, but the behavior of central banks over the past 20 years suggests that there is a reasonable chance that inflation may remain low even with large increases in debt. At some point, however, increases in the cost of servicing debt are bound to force governments to resort to inflationary money creation. If inflation were to increase significantly, interest rates would surely be even higher than projected here. But the real rate of interest (i.e., the nominal interest rate minus the expected inflation rate) would not necessarily move by more than we have assumed. Higher real rates of interest are the primary channel through which government budget deficits crowd out productive investment and ultimately reduce the growth rate of the economy.

The third, and probably least important, factor is that in our scenarios the increase in government debt restrains the growth of GDP, which holds down interest rates. This factor becomes significant only in the final few years of the more extreme scenarios.

3.2   *The limits of debt*

A sovereign default in a major advanced country is obviously unthinkable for policymakers. Nevertheless, markets can react to the possibility of such an occurrence in the long-term future. It is extremely difficult to lay down a hard and fast rule on the limits of borrowing, and the prospect for default, for economies in the modern era. Reinhart, Rogoff and Savastano

---

[18]See, for example, Baldacci *et al.* (2008) and Bayoumi *et al.* (1995). Prior to 2008, bond yields in the euro area were not sensitive to debt ratios, probably reflecting market expectations that fiscal transfers would prevent any defaults. Despite the partial confirmation of these beliefs with the loan packages for Greece, Ireland, and Portugal, markets appear to have substantially revised upward their views concerning the possibility of future defaults or restructurings. See Caceres *et al.* (2010a), Haugh *et al.* (2009), Schuknecht *et al.* (2009), and Sgherri and Zoli (2009). Note that European governments have negotiated an agreement with many international banks for a "voluntary" restructuring of Greek debt that implies a large write-down in its value.

(2003) — in their study of the history of borrowing and default around the world, with a particular focus on emerging economies — have shown that economies differ sharply in the levels of debt that governments have tolerated without default. These differences in "debt intolerance" reflect the quality of institutions and the political dynamics in each economy. Reinhart, Rogoff, and Savastano argue that changes in debt intolerance happen only slowly; they point to Brazil and Chile as examples of economies with rising abilities to bear debt. Of particular interest in light of recent fiscal stresses in Europe, they find that Greece has the lowest debt tolerance of the advanced economies covered by their study.

Ostry *et al.* (2010) seek to find the limits to the "tolerance" of debt in a sample of advanced economies. For each country, the estimated limit is based on the responsiveness of its fiscal policy to past changes in the level of debt. Not surprisingly, countries with a record of addressing their past problems of deficits and debts are able to run up large amounts of debt without a financial crisis. The results differ moderately across economies, but Ostry *et al.* find that debt ratios of around 200 percent of GDP are at the extreme limit of what advanced economies can experience without becoming destabilized.[19] Their model, however, assumes that financial markets tolerate this level of debt primarily because they expect governments to take actions to reduce this burden in the future. Thus, the maximum *sustainable* level of debt is considerably lower than 200 percent of GDP.

A simple test of the plausibility of these estimated debt limits is to compare them to the historical intervals when maximum temporary and sustained debt ratios were incurred but without the expectation of default or high inflation.[20] One obvious case of such tolerance is a time of war. According to CBO (2010), US federal net debt peaked at just over 100 percent of GDP in 1945, at the close of World War II, and then declined steeply. According to Mares (2010), UK public sector net debt peaked at roughly 250 percent of GDP at the ends of the Napoleonic Wars and World War II and declined steeply after each episode. According to Reinhart (2010) the Netherlands after the Napoleonic Wars and France

---

[19]Ostry *et al.* (2010) use gross debt ratios, which range from only slightly larger than net debt ratios in some countries to considerably larger in other countries. The estimated debt ceilings for individual countries range from 150 to 260 percent of GDP.

[20]We believe that the high inflation episodes of the 1970s and 1980s were caused by errors in monetary policy rather than fiscal pressures.

after World War I each had a peak government debt of around 250 percent of GDP which subsequently declined steeply. Special factors such as rationing and appeals to patriotism may allow governments to run up higher debts during wars than otherwise. But there are limits even to these circumstances. We are not aware of any episodes of net government debt ratios above 250 percent of GDP that did not lead to default or high inflation. Indeed, in many cases — particularly among emerging markets — debt ratios much lower than 250 percent of GDP led to default or high inflation.

Overall, 200 percent of GDP is a reasonable — perhaps even conservative — estimate of the maximum temporary net debt ratio during peacetime, at least for advanced economies. We judge the maximum sustainable level of debt to be at least 100 percent of GDP, because Belgium and Italy each have experienced periods lasting more than 10 years with net debt ratios around or above 100 percent of GDP.

An alternative way of measuring the limits of debt is based on the level of net interest payments that governments can sustain indefinitely. A minimum requirement for a sustainable level of debt is that a government must raise sufficient tax revenues to pay the interest on the debt in addition to its operating expenses. In other words, a debt is sustainable in the long run only when the primary fiscal balance is not negative.[21] A higher level of debt thus increases the burden of taxes or reduces government services. According to OECD data for the advanced economies since 1980, the highest sustained share of government revenues in GDP is around 60 percent. The lowest sustained share of government spending in GDP is around 30 percent. In principle, a government could raise revenues equal to 60 percent of GDP and have spending equal to 30 percent of GDP, leaving 30 percent of GDP for net interest payments. However, such a large burden of interest payments is not likely to be sustainable because the social characteristics of countries with high government revenues are different from those with low government spending. It is not likely to be politically feasible for a low-spending country to raise its revenues to 60 percent of GDP and it is similarly unlikely for a high-taxing country to lower its spending to 30 percent of GDP. Based on available data, no advanced economy has had net debt interest payments above 12 percent of GDP in any year. Belgium and

---

[21] This statement is correct when the interest rate on debt equals the nominal growth rate of the economy, which roughly characterizes historical data. At high levels of government debt, the interest rate is likely to exceed the growth rate of the economy and the primary balance must be positive.

Italy each experienced more than 10 consecutive years with net debt interest payments above 9 percent of GDP. Thus, one estimate of the maximum sustainable net debt interest payments in advanced economies is roughly 10 percent of GDP.

Future projections suggest that if trends continue, the US and Japan will surpass the existing records set by OECD countries. Table 3 shows that net debt interest payments are projected to exceed 10 percent of GDP under all scenarios for Japan and all but the most optimistic scenarios for the US. Note that the relationship between net debt interest payments and net debt ratios depends on the effective interest rate. When the effective interest rate is 10 percent, net debt interest payments of 10 percent of GDP occur with a net debt ratio of 100 percent of GDP. When the effective interest rate is 5 percent, net debt interest payments of 10 percent of GDP occur with a

Table 3. Net Interest Payments on Government Debt (percent of GDP).

	2006	2011	2016	2025	2035
United States					
Optimistic Growth				5.1	7.1
Baseline	1.9	1.6	3.1	5.1	10.5
Pessimistic Growth				5.4	18.5
Pessimistic Health Cost				5.9	20.3
High Interest Rates				5.7	17.7
Euro Area					
Optimistic Growth				1.8	0.6
Baseline	2.6	2.6	3.2	1.9	2.2
Pessimistic Growth				2.0	4.1
Pessimistic Health Cost				2.3	5.3
High Interest Rates				2.7	4.1
Japan					
Optimistic Growth				9.4	16.9
Baseline	0.5	1.4	2.5	8.8	19.1
Pessimistic Growth				9.6	33.0
Pessimistic Health Cost				9.2	23.1
High Interest Rates				10.6	35.7
Advanced Economies					
Optimistic Growth				3.6	4.1
Baseline	1.7	1.9	2.6	3.6	6.7
Pessimistic Growth				3.7	9.4
Pessimistic Health Cost				4.1	11.8
High Interest Rates				3.8	9.4

net debt ratio of 200 percent of GDP. Because 5 percent is a relatively low interest rate in historical terms, and because interest rates tend to increase with the debt ratio, it is extremely unlikely that a net debt ratio of 200 percent of GDP could be maintained indefinitely.

3.3   *Fiscal crises*

Have Greece, Ireland, and Portugal provided a cautionary tale for the rest of the world? The sharp increase in fiscal deficits after the global financial crisis posed enormous challenges, not only for these countries, but for some other countries in the euro area as well. Table 2 shows that Portugal, Ireland, and Greece had much larger increases in debt than the euro-area average between 2006 and 2011. They also had among the highest levels of debt in 2011. Among other countries that have experienced rising interest rate spreads, Belgium and Italy have high but relatively stable levels of debt, whereas Spain has a low but rapidly rising level. Note that France, which has faced only moderate pressures to date, has both a slightly higher level and experienced a slightly greater rise in its debt ratio than the euro-area average.

In late 2009, interest rates began to rise on government debt of Greece. In early 2010, the European Council set up an emergency mechanism, the European Financial Stability Facility (EFSF), to lend to members of the EU. Greece received an initial €30 billion from the EFSF with participation by the IMF. The loan was later increased to €110 billion for three years. In return, Greece committed to an ambitious plan to cut its deficit to 8 percent of GDP in 2010 and less than 3 percent by 2014, as well as to undertake comprehensive structural reforms to boost long-run economic growth and efficiency in the public sector. In 2011, it became clear that Greece was not going to achieve its fiscal targets and its program was renegotiated in July and October. Heads of European governments pressured a group of international banks into agreeing to a voluntary reduction in the value of Greek bonds by 50 percent.

In the fall of 2010, Ireland became the focus of financial market concern, after the Irish government revealed that the cost of fixing Irish banks would raise the national debt by 21 percent of GDP. Yield spreads on Irish government debt rose further after the release of a fiscal plan that markets appeared to view as overly optimistic about future Irish economic growth and tax revenues. In November 2010, Ireland arranged an emergency loan from the EFSF and the IMF in conjunction with a 4-year fiscal austerity program. In May 2011, Portugal also negotiated an emergency loan package in return for a fiscal austerity program.

During the summer of 2011, interest rates in Italy, Spain, and Belgium rose further, signaling a new and dangerous stage of the crisis. European leaders agreed in October 2011 to leverage the EFSF to enable it to deal with these additional troubled countries, but it remains to be seen whether the latest measures will be sufficient. In addition to the EFSF, the European Central Bank (ECB) in 2010 established a limited program to purchase government bonds of troubled countries and it affirmed in October 2011 that it would continue this program. The ECB has not used its bond purchase program aggressively to hold down interest rate spreads, perhaps because it wants to create the hope of more purchases in the future as an incentive for affected governments to undertake politically difficult structural reform measures to boost economic growth and reduce long-term fiscal deficits.[22]

Belgium, Ireland and Italy were not identified by Reinhart, Rogoff and Savastano (2003) as relatively debt intolerant countries. The recent experiences with these countries raise an urgent question. Could the core advanced economies experience a similar crisis, with sharply higher interest rates and the possibility of suddenly being unable to borrow in financial markets?

As discussed above, the US, Japan, and Germany are not close to the maximum temporary debt ratio of around 200 percent of GDP and only Japan has debt in excess of 100 percent of GDP.[23] The smooth paths of interest rates shown in Figures 5–8 should not be taken as a prediction of the smoothness with which actual interest rates will evolve on current policies. These figures are based on average historical behavior, and by necessity are smooth. In reality, markets are more likely to swing quickly from under-reaction to over-reaction. As discussed above, financial markets

---

[22]A leaked letter from the ECB to then Prime Minister Berlusconi of Italy demands specific fiscal and structural reforms as the apparent price for more ECB purchases of Italian bonds. See Guy Dinmore and Ralph Atkins, "ECB Letter Shows Pressure on Berlusconi," *Financial Times*, September 29, 2011.

[23]It is possible that circumstances unique to Japan, namely a high private saving rate and a strong preference of domestic savers for domestic assets, mean that the limits to government debt are higher for Japan than for other advanced economies. However, these unique advantages are threatened by the rapid ageing of Japan's population.

currently appear to expect that governments will take actions over the medium term to prevent a debt explosion. Thus, long-term interest rates currently are lower than they would be if markets expected debt ratios to rise as projected in many of the scenarios shown in Figures 1–4. Should financial markets come to doubt that governments will correct the problem in an orderly way, interest rates would surely rise rapidly and the prices of most financial assets would likely decline or at least become more volatile. Thus, the response of financial markets to a growing fiscal problem is likely to be discontinuous, rather than smooth. On the other hand, the extreme speed and severity with which the crises occurred in Greece, Ireland, and Portugal reflects circumstances that are not present in the core advanced economies.

Crises are inherently unpredictable, but one thing we do know is that the most extreme and sudden debt crises occur when a government cannot sell more bonds despite raising the interest rate it offers. In these extreme cases, creditors come to see higher interest rates as self-defeating because they make it harder for the government to service its debt. At this point investors refuse to buy the bonds at any interest rate. In such crisis situations, the government must suddenly choose one of three options: 1) default on its debt; 2) immediately reduce spending or increase revenues enough to service its debt; or 3) arrange a loan from other governments or international financial institutions.[24]

This sudden disruption in the ability to sell bonds does not occur when governments borrow in their own currency and when they have not committed to maintaining that currency's value in terms of other currencies. Under those conditions — which characterize each of the core advanced economies — governments can print enough money to pay off bonds at any interest rate.[25] For these economies, there may never be a single defining moment of crisis, but rather a drift into ever-higher inflation and interest rates, ever-lower growth or deeper recession, and eventually hyperinflation

---

[24]If the government is running a primary deficit at the time of the crisis, option (1) is not sufficient by itself and the primary deficit must be brought into balance.

[25]Note that Greece, Ireland, and Portugal cannot print euros to pay their debts. Indeed, no individual member of the euro area has control over the creation of euros, but the area as a whole does have such control. Thus, it is the Euro Area countries with fiscal prospects that are worse than the Euro Area average that are susceptible to this pressure. Germany has better than average fiscal prospects within the euro area and we assume that Germany will retain this privileged position. As can be seen in Table 2, the big uncertainty now concerns the position of France.

along with rapid currency depreciation. Most economists would view such a prospect as a progressive strangulation of a nation's wellbeing. Although a sudden Greek-style crisis is not a significant risk for the US, Japan, or Germany, the implications of a fiscal crisis are still serious.

In the summer of 2011, the debate over lifting the US federal debt ceiling raised the specter that the US Treasury might choose to default on Treasury securities rather than prioritize their servicing ahead of government operating expenses and benefit payments. That would be a catastrophic self-inflicted wound, and markets appear to have a high degree of confidence that the Treasury will not make such a decision in the future. Although political polarization and divided government make it harder for the US to adopt long-run fiscal reforms and more likely that there will be a temporary government shutdown, they do not directly threaten the ability of the US government to service its debt. As can be seen in Table 3, debt interest is a small share of GDP (considerably smaller than federal revenues) and will remain small under all scenarios at least through 2025.

Is it possible to have a *moderate* fiscal crisis? The answer appears to be "yes." For the major advanced economies, the most relevant examples of moderate fiscal crises are those that affected Australia and Canada in the early 1990s. Governments in these economies did not borrow in foreign currencies to a significant extent and they were not committed to maintaining fixed values of their currencies. In these episodes, real interest rates rose and economic growth stagnated over a period of months and years. Governments eventually responded by cutting primary deficits significantly and debt ratios were put on a sustainable track, thus avoiding a drift into more severe crisis.

For the core advanced economies, the most relevant examples of severe fiscal crises are the episodes that led to hyperinflation, including in Austria, Germany, Hungary, and Poland in the 1920s, and in Argentina and Brazil in the 1980s. Even in these extreme episodes, governments did not face a specific day on which wrenching change was forced upon them. Instead, their economic decline was relatively continuous, albeit accelerating. According to Sargent (1982), in the hyperinflations of the 1920s, accelerating inflation continuously eroded the real resources that governments could command via taxes and money creation, and economies slid deeper into recession, until eventually it became clear that a deliberate move to a new monetary and fiscal regime was the only way to avoid anarchy.

4 Paths to Safety

This section examines the size and timing of fiscal actions needed to restore each region to the net debt ratio it had in 2005 by 2035. The choice to target debt ratios in 2005 is somewhat arbitrary, but it reflects a judgment that government debt in 2005 was comfortably below the long-run limits of debt and thus allows considerable room for governments to respond to future economic downturns.[26] Many observers believe that the net debt ratios in 2005 were higher than optimal in most advanced economies, but the issue of the optimal long-run level of government debt is beyond the scope of this paper. Figures 9–12 redisplay the baseline net debt paths. For each economy (except the Euro Area), two alternative paths are shown that get the ratio of net debt to GDP in 2035 back to its value in 2005. It is not

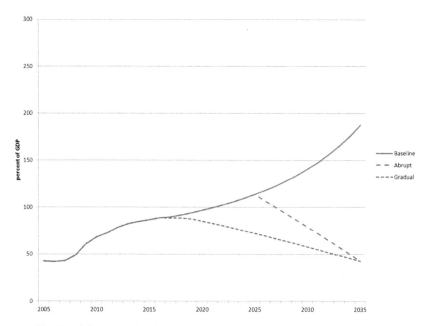

Fig. 9.   Adjustment Paths for General Government Debt — United States.

---

[26]The 2005 debt ratios are similar across economic regions except for Japan, where the ratio is higher. As discussed above, the limits of debt may be higher in Japan than in the other economies. For the US, the 2005 debt ratio is very close to that targeted by the National Commission on Fiscal Responsibility and Reform (2010).

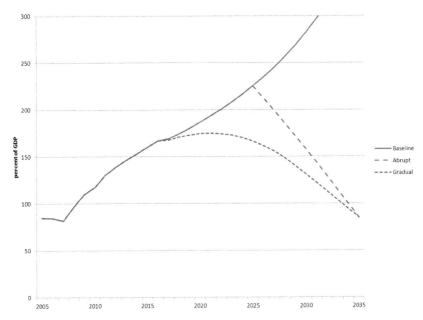

Fig. 10.   Adjustment Paths for General Government Debt — Japan.

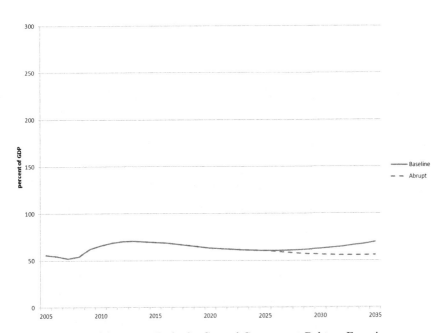

Fig. 11.   Adjustment Paths for General Government Debt — Euro Area.

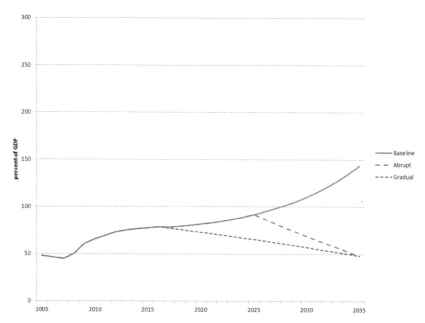

Fig. 12.   Adjustment Paths for General Government Debt — Advanced Economies.

the purpose of this paper to outline specific courses of action on revenues or spending, and we will focus only on changes to the primary deficit.

4.1   *Gradual (early) adjustment*

The first set of paths, labeled "Gradual," consists of a sequence of cumulative reductions in the primary deficit by 1 percent a year beginning in 2017 coupled with an elimination of the trend increases in pension and health care deficits in the years 2017–2035.[27] The reductions do not start before 2017 because primary deficits are already projected to be declining significantly through 2016 as fiscal stimulus measures run off, governments implement current plans for fiscal cuts, and economic recovery boosts

---

[27]The trend increases could be reduced, for example, by linking the retirement age to average longevity and linking health-care program revenues to health-care costs. Abbas *et al.* (2010) show that raising the retirement age 1½ years would be sufficient to stabilize public pension expenditure in EU countries over the next 20 years. National Commission on Fiscal Responsibility and Reform (2010) discusses other options to stabilize these costs.

revenues.[28] Additional budget cuts in the next two or three years would threaten the durability of the recovery. However, in the case of Japan, the IMF projects relatively little reduction in primary deficits between 2013 and 2016, and thus additional cuts might usefully be implemented in 2014 through 2016. We did not insert additional earlier cuts in these adjustment scenarios for Japan in order to keep the treatment comparable across countries and because the long-run effects of slightly earlier cuts are not large. The magnitude of the annual cuts (1 percent of GDP) is designed to allow for a relatively smooth transition, but making cuts of this magnitude nevertheless requires difficult choices for a society and its leaders.

The sequence of discrete budget cuts is assumed to last as long as needed to achieve the target debt ratio in 2035.[29] For the US, the primary deficit must be cut 1 percentage point per year for 4.3 years, for a total cut of 4.3 percent of GDP. For Japan, it lasts 13.4 years. For the advanced economies in aggregate, it lasts 1.8 years.

Because the euro area already has a declining path of debt in the baseline scenario through 2025, no early adjustment is needed to achieve the 2005 target debt ratio. All that is needed is a modest cut in 2026, which is identical to the "abrupt" path described in the next section.

4.2   Abrupt (delayed) adjustment

The second set of paths, labeled "Abrupt," assumes that no action is taken until 2026, at which time there is a large permanent cut in the primary deficit. This scenario might arise as the result of a fiscal crisis. Of course, even in a crisis it might not be necessary or even feasible to make the budget cuts all in one year, so this scenario should not be taken too literally. The point is that delaying adjustment is likely to require future cuts that are both larger and more abrupt. For the US, the delayed cut is 11 percent of GDP. For the euro area, it is 1 percent of GDP. For Japan, it is a whopping 22 percent of GDP. For the advanced economies in aggregate, it is 7 percent of GDP.

---

[28]As discussed previously, achieving the IMF projected primary deficits in 2016 requires that governments follow through on current plans to cut deficits, many of which have not yet been enacted into law.

[29]For computational reasons, this scenario does not include a positive feedback from faster GDP growth to lower primary deficits, so these magnitudes of adjustment are conservative.

For the US and Japan, these abrupt budget cuts would be enormously disruptive. In the US, for example, a budget cut of 11 percent of GDP in 2026 could be achieved by eliminating almost all federal spending on Social Security, Medicare, Medicaid, and other health programs or by increasing all federal taxes by 50 percent.

4.3   *Benefits of early and gradual adjustment*

Both the gradual and the abrupt adjustment are associated with lower interest rates after 2026 than in the baseline scenario. In part because of these reductions in interest rates, GDP growth picks up in both adjustment scenarios.[30] But these benefits kick in much earlier under the gradual adjustment scenario and they result in a level of US GDP that is 5 percent higher by 2035 than in the abrupt adjustment scenario and 13 percent higher than in the baseline. For Japan, gradual adjustment raises 2035 GDP by 12 percent relative to baseline. The benefits of adjustment in the euro area are very small, reflecting the small increase in the debt ratio in the baseline scenario.

Other benefits of the gradual adjustment scenario for the United States and Japan are harder to measure, but perhaps even more important. First, gradual adjustment minimizes the risk of crisis because it prevents the build-up of debt that occurs under the "Abrupt" scenario. Second, gradual adjustment announced well in advance allows citizens time to plan and adjust smoothly. For example, in the 1983 reforms to the US social security pension system, tax increases were phased in over 7 years and future increases in the retirement age did not affect any worker within 20 years of retiring under the existing system.[31] Giving citizens time to plan is a powerful motivation for enacting the necessary long-run fiscal adjustment now, even though implementation would not begin for several years.

5   Conclusion

The run-up in government debt in response to the global financial crisis is unprecedented for peacetime. This massive increase in public debt has

---

[30]Neither scenario includes any negative short-run effect of fiscal cuts on GDP. This assumption is plausible for pre-announced gradual cuts but is surely too optimistic for the abrupt adjustment scenario.

[31]See the Social Security Administration website at http://www.ssa.gov/history/1983amend.html.

provided a counterweight that very likely averted a Great Depression while households and businesses deleveraged and restructured their balance sheets quickly. However, the current trajectory of fiscal policy in the US and Japan is not sustainable.

The US, and perhaps Japan, are not likely to face serious debt-related problems in the next 5 to 10 years, but both face very difficult policy choices within the next 25 years. Although there is time to make these choices, policymakers do not have time on their side. The benefits of early planning and phased adjustment are considerable. Failure to tackle these fiscal problems in a timely manner will lead to rising interest rates and an eventual slowdown in the rate of economic growth. Failure to act probably will result in a fiscal crisis of some form in these two countries over the next 25 years. Uncertainty about the timing or nature of a potential crisis is not an excuse to do nothing. The current weak state of the US and Japanese economies argues against implementing budget cuts in the next couple of years, but now is the moment to adopt concrete plans to return public finances to sound conditions over the medium term. The longer decisions are delayed, the more costly will be the ultimate adjustment and the greater the risk of a damaging economic crisis.

The situation in the euro area is very different from that of the US and Japan. Taken as a whole, the euro area does not have a pressing long-term fiscal problem, although one might develop if health care costs rise faster than expected or economic growth is slower than expected. The current crisis in the euro area has arisen because individual member countries have different fiscal prospects and yet they share a common monetary policy. Attempts by the more indebted euro-area countries to cut their fiscal deficits lead to a vicious circle in which austerity reduces growth and therefore worsens the fiscal outlook. In countries with independent monetary policy, fiscal austerity can be offset by easier monetary policy, but individual euro-area countries do not have that option. The best solution is a combination of credible measures that reduce the long-term deficit without reducing the near-term deficit (such as phased-in increases in the retirement age), structural reforms to boost economic growth, and temporary loans from the rest of Europe and the IMF.

References

Abbas, S.M.A., O. Basdevant, S. Eble, G. Everaert, J. Gottschalk, F. Hasanov, J. Park, C. Sancak, R. Velloso, and M. Villafuerte (2010).

Strategies for Fiscal Consolidation in the Post-Crisis World. International Monetary Fund Fiscal Affairs Department.

Ardagna, S., F. Caselli, and T. Lane (2004). Fiscal discipline and the cost of public debt service: Some estimates for OECD countries. European Central Bank Working Paper Series (411).

Baldacci, E., and M.S. Kumar (2010). Fiscal deficits, public debt, and sovereign bond yields. IMF Working Paper WP/10/184. International Monetary Fund.

Baldacci, E., S. Gupta, and A. Mati (2008). Political and fiscal risk determinants of sovereign spreads in emerging markets. IMF Working Paper WP/08/259. International Monetary Fund.

Bayoumi, T., M. Goldstein, and G. Woglom (1995). Do credit markets discipline sovereign borrowers? Evidence from the US. *Journal of Money, Credit and Banking*, 27(4), 1046–1059.

Caceres, C., V. Guzzo, and M. Segoviano (2010). Sovereign spreads: Global risk aversion, contagion or fundamentals? IMF Working Paper WP/10/120. International Monetary Fund.

Caner, M., T. Grennes, and F. Koehler-Geib (2010). Finding the tipping point — When sovereign debt turns bad. World Bank Policy Research Working Paper WPS5391.

CBO (2010). *Federal Debt and the Risk of a Fiscal Crisis*. Congressional Budget Office, July.

CBO (2011). *The Long-Term Budget Outlook*, Congressional Budget Office, June.

Checherita, C. and P. Rother (2010). The impact of high and growing government debt on economic growth: An empirical investigation for the Euro Area. ECB Working Paper No. 1237.

Chinn, M. and J. Frankel (2007). Debt and interest rates: The US and the Euro Area. Economics Discussion Papers 2007–2011.

Conway, P. and A. Orr (2002). The GIRM: A global interest rate model. Westpac Institutional Bank Occasional Paper, Wellington, New Zealand, September.

Engen, E.M. and R.G. Hubbard (2005). Federal government debt and interest rates. *NBER Macroeconomics Annual 2004*, 19, 83–138.

Gale, W.G. and P.R. Orzag (2004). Budget deficits, national saving, and interest rates. Brookings Papers on Economic Activity (2).

Gruber, J. and S. Kamin (2010). Fiscal positions and government bond yields in OECD countries. International Finance Discussion Papers No. 1012. Board of Governors of the Federal Reserve System.

Haugh, D., P. Ollivaud, and D. Turner (2009). What drives sovereign risk premiums? An analysis of recent evidence from the Euro Area. OECD Economics Department Working Papers No. 718.

IMF (2010a). From stimulus to consolidation: Revenue and expenditure policies in advanced and emerging economies. International Monetary Fund, Fiscal Affairs Department, April 30.

IMF (2010b). Fiscal exit: From strategy to implementation. *Fiscal Monitor.* International Monetary Fund, November.

IMF (2011). Addressing fiscal challenges to reduce economic risks. *Fiscal Monitor.* International Monetary Fund, September.

Irons, J. and J. Bivens (2010). Government debt and economic growth: Overreaching claims of debt "threshold" suffer from theoretical and empirical flaws. EPI Briefing Paper 271. Economic Policy Institute.

Kinoshita, N. (2006). Government debt and long-term interest rate. IMF Working Paper WP/06/63. International Monetary Fund.

Kumar, M.S., and J. Woo (2010). Public debt and growth. IMF Working Paper WP/10/174. International Monetary Fund.

Laubach, T. (2009). New evidence on the interest rate effects of budget deficits and debt. *Journal of the European Economic Association,* 7(4), 858–885.

Lupton, J., and D. Hensley (2010). Government debt sustainability in the age of fiscal activism. JPMorgan Chase Bank Economic Research, June 11.

Mares, A. (2010). Ask not whether governments will default, but How. *Sovereign Subjects.* Morgan Stanley Research, August 25.

National Commission on Fiscal Responsibility and Reform (2010). *The Moment of Truth.* December. Available at www.fiscalcommission.gov.

OECD (2010) *Economic Outlook,* vol. 2010/2. Organization for Economic Cooperation and Development.

OECD (2011) *Economic Outlook,* vol. 2011/2. Organization for Economic Cooperation and Development.

Ostry, J.D., A.R. Ghosh, J.I. Kim, and M.S. Qureshi (2010). Fiscal Space. IMF Staff Position Note SPN/10/11. International Monetary Fund.

Reinhart, C.M. (2010). This time is different chartbook: Country histories on debt, default, and financial crises. NBER Working Paper 15815.

Reinhart, C.M. and K.S. Rogoff (2010). Growth in a time of debt. NBER Working Paper 15639.

Reinhart, C.M., K.S. Rogoff, and M.A. Savastano (2003). Debt intolerance. *Brookings Papers on Economic Activity*, 1, 1–62.

Sargent, T.J. (1982). "The ends of four big inflations." In R.E. Hall (ed.) *Inflation: Causes and Effects*. Chicago: University of Chicago Press.

Schuknecht, L., J. von Hagen, and G. Wolswijk (2009). Government risk premiums in the bond market: EMU and Canada. *European Journal of Political Economy*, 25.

Sgherri, S. and E. Zoli (2009). Euro Area sovereign risk during the crisis. IMF Working Paper WP/09/222. International Monetary Fund.

Index